The People's Democratic Republic of Yemen

Marxist Regimes Series

Series editor: Bogdan Szajkowski,
Department of Sociology, University College,
Cardiff

Further Titles

The People's Democratic Republic of
YEMEN

Politics, Economics and Society

The Politics of Socialist Transformation

Tareq Y. Ismael
and
Jacqueline S. Ismael

Frances Pinter (Publishers), London
Lynne Rienner Publishers, Inc., Boulder

© Tareq Y. Ismael and Jacqueline S. Ismael, 1986

First published in Great Britain in 1986 by
Frances Pinter (Publishers) Limited
25 Floral Street, London WC2E 9DS

First published in the United States of America by
Lynne Rienner Publishers, Inc.
948 North Street
Boulder, Colorado 80302

Printed in Great Britain

British Library Cataloguing in Publication Data
Ismael, Tareq Y.
  The People's Democratic Republic of Yemen: politics,
  economics and society: the politics of socialist
  transformation.—(Marxist regime series)
  1. Yemen (People's Democratic Republic)
  I. Title   II. Ismael, Jacqueline S.   III. Series
953'.35053   DS247.A2
ISBN 0-86187-450-1
ISBN 0-86187-451-X Pbk

Library of Congress Cataloging in Publication Data
Ismael, Tareq Y.
  The People's Democratic Republic of Yemen.
  (Marxist regimes series)
  Bibliography: p.
  Includes index.
  1. Yemen (People's Democratic Republic)—
Politics and government.   2. Yemen (People's Democratic
Republic)—Economic conditions.   3. Yemen (People's
Democratic Republic)—Social conditions.   I. Ismael,
Jacqueline S.   II. Title.   III. Series.
JQ1825.Y5I85   1986   953'.32   86-15442
ISBN 0-931477-96-4 (lib. bdg.: L. Rienner)

Typeset by Joshua Associates Limited, Oxford
Printed by SRP Ltd, Exeter

Editor's Preface

South Yemen, the only Marxist regime in the Arab world and located in one of the most strategically important areas of the globe, occupies a unique place among the panoply of contemporary left-wing experiments. This, the first full study of politics, economics and society in the People's Democratic Republic of Yemen, comes out at a time of renewed interest in that country following a short but bloody civil war in January 1986 between two Marxist factions in the South Yemeni party and government leadership. The confrontation resulted in the accession to power of a new group of politically expedient young technocrats. This book provides an indispensable background to the understanding of the future course of events and the political evolution of one of the most socially and politically complex and unstable Marxist polities in existence today.

This work also makes an important and timely contribution to the overall appraisal of contemporary Marxist regimes. The study of Marxist regimes has for many years been equated with the study of communist political systems. There were several historical and methodological reasons for this.

For many years it was not difficult to distinguish the eight regimes in Eastern Europe and four in Asia which resoundingly claimed adherence to the tenets of Marxism and more particularly to their Soviet interpretation—Marxism–Leninism. These regimes, variously called 'People's Republic', 'People's Democratic Republic', or 'Democratic Republic', claimed to have derived their inspiration from the Soviet Union to which, indeed, in the overwhelming number of cases they owed their establishment.

To many scholars and analysts these regimes represented a multiplication of and geographical extension of the 'Soviet model' and consequently of the Soviet sphere of influence. Although there were clearly substantial similarities between the Soviet Union and the people's democracies, especially in the initial phases of their development, these were often overstressed at the expense of noticing the differences between these political systems.

It took a few years for scholars to realize that generalizing the particular, i.e. applying the Soviet experience to other states ruled by elites which claimed to be guided by 'scientific socialism', was not good enough. The relative simplicity of the assumption of a cohesive communist bloc was questioned after the expulsion of Yugoslavia from the Communist Information Bureau in 1948 and in particular after the workers' riots in Poznań in

1956 and the Hungarian revolution of the same year. By the mid-1960s, the totalitarian model of communist politics, which until then had been very much in force, began to crumble. As some of these regimes articulated demands for a distinctive path of socialist development, many specialists studying these systems began to notice that the cohesiveness of the communist bloc was less apparent than had been claimed before.

Also by the mid-1960s, in the newly independent African states 'democratic' multi-party states were turning into one-party states or military dictatorships, thus questioning the inherent superiority of liberal democracy, capitalism and the values that went with it. Scholars now began to ponder on the simple contrast between multi-party democracy and a one-party totalitarian rule that had satisfied an earlier generation.

More importantly, however, by the beginning of that decade Cuba had a revolution without Soviet help, a revolution which subsequently became to many political elites in the Third World not only an inspiration but a clear military, political and ideological example to follow. Apart from its romantic appeal, to many nationalist movements the Cuban revolution also demonstrated a novel way of conducting and winning a nationalist, anti-imperialist war and accepting Marxism as the state ideology without a vanguard communist party. The Cuban precedent was subsequently followed in one respect or another by scores of regimes in the Third World who used the adoption of 'scientific socialism' tied to the tradition of Marxist thought as a form of mobilization, legitimation or association with the prestigious symbols and powerful high-status regimes such as the Soviet Union, China, Cuba and Vietnam.

Despite all these changes the study of Marxist regimes remains in its infancy and continues to be hampered by constant and not always pertinent comparison with the Soviet Union, thus somewhat blurring the important underlying common theme—the 'scientific theory' of the laws of development of human society and human history. This doctrine is claimed by the leadership of these regimes to consist of the discovery of objective causal relationships; it is used to analyse the contradictions which arise between goals and actuality in the pursuit of a common destiny. Thus the political elites of these countries have been and continue to be influenced in both their ideology and their political practice by Marxism more than any other current of social thought and political practice.

The growth in the number and global significance, as well as the ideological political and economic impact, of Marxist regimes has presented scholars and students with an increasing challenge. In meeting this challenge, social scientists on both sides of the political divide have put forward a dazzling profusion of terms, models, programmes and varieties of interpretation. It is against the background of this profusion that the present comprehensive series on Marxist regimes is offered.

This collection of monographs is envisaged as a series of multi-disciplinary textbooks on the governments, politics, economics and society of these countries. Each of the monographs was prepared by a specialist on the country concerned. Thus, over fifty scholars from all over the world have contributed monographs which were based on first-hand knowledge. The geographical diversity of the authors, combined with the fact that as a group they represent many disciplines of social science, gives their individual analyses and the series as a whole an additional dimension.

Each of the scholars who contributed to this series was asked to analyse such topics as the political culture, the governmental structure, the ruling party, other mass organizations, party-state relations, the policy process, the economy, domestic and foreign relations together with any features peculiar to the country under discussion.

This series does not aim at assigning authenticity or authority to any single one of the political systems included in it. It shows that depending on a variety of historical, cultural, ethnic and political factors, the pursuit of goals derived from the tenets of Marxism has produced different political forms at different times and in different places. It also illustrates the rich diversity among these societies, where attempts to achieve a synthesis between goals derived from Marxism on the one hand, and national realities on the other, have often meant distinctive approaches and solutions to the problems of social, political and economic development.

University College
Cardiff

Bogdan Szajkowski

To our brothers
Khalid
Sa'd
Salah
Salam
Gregory

Contents

List of Illustrations and Tables

Maps

Figures

Tables

Preface

As will be noted in Chapter 1, the People's Democratic Republic of Yemen (PDRY) is a land of geographic, historical, economic, political and social paradoxes. To these might be added one further, academic, paradox: despite (or perhaps because of) its multifaceted uniqueness as a Marxist state in the Arab World, there have been few attempts by scholars to understand the country and its revolution. Arab and East European scholars, both of whom might be expected (for very different reasons) to show interest in the country, rarely turn their attention to it—a fact attested to by the small number of articles on the PDRY in such leading journals as *Dirisat 'Ara-biyya* (Arab Studies) and *World Marxist Review*. Western analyses are even scarcer. Moreover, what Western analyses do exist are—with some notable exceptions—so coloured by the lenses of East-West confrontation and the PDRY's 'strategic significance' that they distort the complexity and internal dynamics of South Yemeni society and politics beyond recognition. Indeed, a few, with their cold-war myopia and ethnocentrism, would be grounds for considerable amusement were it not for the rather sobering thought that they provide one of the bases upon which Western policy towards the country is constructed.

This book—like the Marxist Regime Series as a whole—represents a modest attempt to cut through the mythmaking to the reality of the PDRY as it is. It follows a format similar to other volumes in the series, with minor modifications to accommodate the particular environment of the PDRY. Considerable attention has been given to the dynamics of the regime itself, a regime which (as Chapters 2 and 3 show) has demonstrated both stability and turmoil since the 'Corrective Step' of 22 June 1969. Whole chapters are also devoted to social (Chapter 5), and to foreign (Chapter 6) policy, reflecting the importance of these two areas in fostering the internal and external conditions under which the leaders of the PDRY can pursue their goals of socialist transformation.

One difficulty encountered by any analyst undertaking research on South Yemen is, as suggested above, scarcity of reliable information. Government and party documents, supplemented by secondary Arabic sources (news-papers, books, journals) constitute the main sources used here. Information from international agencies provided another major source. Secondary analysis—in Arabic, English, French and Russian—was used very cautiously, and checked for reliability before use.

The system of transliteration from Arabic that has been adopted is based on the Library of Congress system, modified to stress phonetic rather than linguistic conventions. To facilitate identification of sources, the English translation of titles have been provided in the Bibliography.

We wish to acknowledge the research assistance of Rex Brynen in the preparation of this manuscript. Not only did he co-author Chapter 6, but he also provided indispensable assistance, personal commitment, and many, many hours of work on research and the final preparation of this volume. Without his efforts, this volume would not have met the printing press. We would also like to acknowledge the valuable assistance of Alex Brynen in the preparation of Chapter 5. Finally, we would like to thank Judi Powell, Mary Gray and Ella Wensel. Their patience, good humour and hard work in the typing and retyping of the manuscript was, as always, much appreciated.

Tareq Y. Ismael and Jacqueline S. Ismael
The University of Calgary
21 April 1986

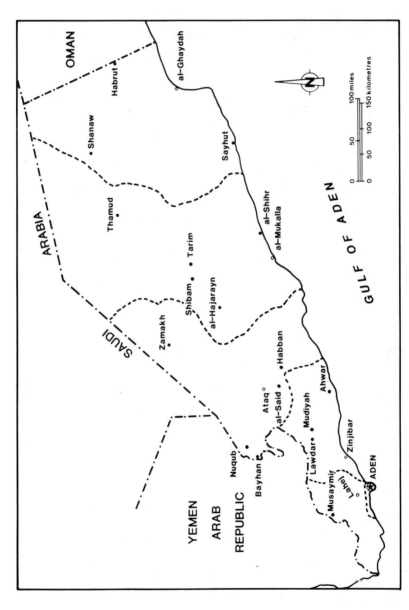

Map 1.1 Governates and major towns, PDRY

Basic Data

Official name	People's Democratic Republic of Yemen
Population	2.12 million (1985 est.)
	1.59 million (1973 census)
Population density	6.3 persons per sq. km.
Population growth (% p.a.)	2.7 (1985 est.)
Urban Population (%)	37% (1983) urban population, growing at 3.5% p.a.
Total labour force	567,000 (1983), of which 45% in agriculture; 15% industry; 40% services. Approximately 85,000 employed abroad, primarily in the Gulf.
Life expectancy	46.5 (1985 est.)
Infant death rate (per 1,000)	137 (1983)
Child death rate (per 1,000)	27 (1983)
Ethnic groups	Over 95% Arab; some East Indian, Somali, other African minorities
Capital	Aden (350,000)
Land area	336,869 sq. km., of which 0.6% arable; 27.2% pasture; 7.3% woodland and forests (remainder waste, primarily desert and mountains)
Official language	Arabic
Other main languages	Related Semitic language spoken by al-Mahrah and on Socotra
Administrative division	6 governates, subdivided into directorates and districts
Membership of international organizations	Arab League (1967); UN (1967); Islamic Conference Organization (1971); CMEA observer (1979); Arab Common Market (1982)
Foreign relations	Diplomatic and consular relations with 57 states. 26 states (1985) in four major categories have resident missions in Aden: Algeria, Iraq, Kuwait, Libya, Saudi Arabia,

Somalia, Sudan (Arab countries); Bulgaria, China, Cuba, Czechoslovakia, East Germany, Ethiopia, Hungary, North Korea, Romania, Soviet Union, Vietnam (socialist countries); France, West Germany, Italy, Japan, United Kingdom (Western countries); India, Iran, Pakistan (non-aligned)

Political structure
    Constitution   1970, amended in 1978
    Highest legislative body   Supreme People's Council
    Highest executive bodies   Presidium
                                 Council of Ministers
    Prime Minister   Yaseen Said Numan (February 1986)
    President   Haidar Abu-Bakr al-Attas (February 1986)
    Ruling party   Yemeni Socialist Party
    Secretary-General of YSP   'Ali Salem al-Bidh (February 1986)
    Party membership   Uncertain, around 26–30,000

Growth indicators (% p.a.)

	1970–81
National income	8.7
Industry	12.1
Agriculture	2.1
Food production per capita	80 (1985), (1974–6 = 100)

Trade and balance of payments
    Exports $30.7 million (1984), excluding petroleum. Private transfers (workers' remittances) from abroad brought in a further $479.5 million, representing nearly a half of GNP
    Imports $824.6 million (1984), excluding petroleum
    Exports as % of GNP   3.7
    Main exports (%)   Fresh fish 37; petroleum (mainly refined) 37; cotton lint and seed 8; coffee 8; also salt and hides (1977). Figures do not

	include the operations of foreign-owned companies.
Main imports (%)	Machinery and transport 35; food and live animals 23; petroleum (mainly crude) 18; basic manufactures (1977)
Main trading partners	Exports: France 31%; UAE 27%; India 8%; UK 7%; Italy 4%. Imports: UAE 25%; Kuwait 12%; Japan 8%; UK 6%; China 4% (1982). The volume of non-oil trade with African, Asian and socialist countries has increased steadily, with the latter of these now accounting for 24.5% of the total (1983)
Foreign debt	$1,268 million (1984), with debt-servicing accounting for approximately 4% of GNP (1982)
Foreign aid	$165.6 million (1984)
Main natural resources	Salt and cement. Indications of oil, copper, lead, zinc, gold, manganese, potassium, bauxite, iron ore, lignite and molybdenum.
Food self-sufficiency	About two-thirds of food requirements are imported; 205,000 metric tons of cereals imported in 1983, of which 9,000 metric tons food aid. Average per capita calorie intake of 97% of requirements (1983)
Armed forces	27,500 (18,000 conscripts): Army 24,000; Navy 1,000; Air Force 2,500. Reserves 45,000; Militia 15,000.

Education and Health

School system	Eight years compulsory education—ages 7-14; compulsory literacy classes for adults. All state fees for education abolished in 1974.
Primary school enrolment (%)	64 (1983)
Secondary school enrolment (%)	28 (1981)
Higher education	2% of ages 20-24 (1983)

Adult literacy (%)	40 (1980)
Population per hospital bed	645 (1980)
Population per physician	7,120 (1981); 830 per nursing person
Economy	
GNP	$1,020 million (1983)
GNP per capita	$520 (1983)
GDP by %	13% agriculture and fisheries; 10% industry; 16 % construction; 17% trade, hotels, restaurants; 13% transport and communications; 5% financial, business and personal services; 26% government services (1981)
State budget (expenditure)	$924.8 million (1982). $1,471.3 million to be spent on development under 1981–5 Five Year Plan
Defence expenditure as % of state budget	18.4 (1982)
Monetary unit	(South) Yemeni Dinar (1 YD – US$2.8952)
Main crops	Millet, wheat, cotton, coffee, tobacco, maize, dates, barley, sesame; livestock, fisheries
Land tenure	Land redistributed under 1970 Land Reform Law into maximum holdings of 25 *feddans* (irrigated) or 40 *feddans* (un-irrigated). Agriculture now organized into state farms (10%), first-, second-, and third-stage co-operatives (70%), and peasant freeholdings (20%)
Main religions	Islam, primarily Shafi (Sunni), with small Zaydi (Shiʾa) minority in Aden
Transport	
Rail network	none
Road network	Approximately 11,000 km., of which 1,781 km. paved.

Population Forecasting

The following data are projections produced by Poptran, University College
Cardiff Population Centre, from United Nations Assessment Data published
in 1980, and are reproduced here to provide some basis of comparison with
other countries covered by the *Marxist Regimes* Series.

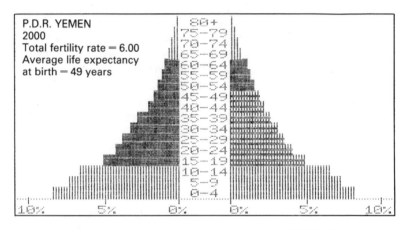

MALES   FEMALES

Projected Data for P.D.R. Yemen 2000

Total population ('000)	3,150
Males ('000)	1,567
Females ('000)	1,583
Total fertility rate	6.00
Life expectancy (male)	47.0 years
Life expectancy (female)	51.0 years
Crude birth rate	41.9
Crude death rate	16.6
Annual growth rate	2.53%
Under 15s	44.63%
Over 65s	3.37%
Woman aged 15–49	22.29%
Doubling time	28 years
Population density	9 per sq. km.
Urban population	42.0%

List of Abbreviations

ANM	Arab Nationalists' Movement
ATUC	Aden Trade Union Congress
bpd	barrels per day
CMEA	Council for Mutual Economic Assistance ('Comecon')
DFLP	Democratic Front for the Liberation of Palestine
FAO	Food and Agriculture Organization
ECWA	(UN) Economic Commission for West Africa
FLOSY	Front for the Liberation of South Yemen
GCC	Gulf Co-operation Council
GUYW	General Union of Yemeni Women
IDA	International Development Agency
IISS	International Institute for Strategic Studies
IMF	International Monetary Fund
KFAED	Kuwait Fund for Arab Economic Development
NDF	National Democratic Front
NF	National Front (for the Liberation of Occupied South Yemen)
NGPF	National Grouping of Patriotic Forces in South Yemen
OLOS	Organization for the Liberation of the Occupied South
OPEC	Organization of Petroleum Exporting Countries
PDRY	People's Democratic Republic of Yemen
PDU	Popular Democratic Union
PFLO	Popular Front for the Liberation of Oman
PFLOAG	Popular Front for the Liberation of the Occupied Arab Gulf
PFLP	Popular Front for the Liberation of Palestine
PLO	Palestine Liberation Organization
PORF	Popular Organization of Revolution Forces
PROSY	People's Republic of South Yemen
PSC	People's Supreme Council
PSP	People's Socialist Party
PUP	Popular Unity Party
PVP	Popular Vanguard Party
SAF	South Arabian Federation
SAL	South Arabian League
UAE	United Arab Emirates

UK	United Kingdom
UN	United Nations
UNF	United National Front
UNFPA	United Nations Fund for Population Assistance
UPONF	Unified Political Organization of the National Front
US	United States of America
USSR	Union of Soviet Socialist Republics
YAR	Yemen Arab Republic
YD	(South) Yemeni Dinar
YSP	Yemeni Socialist Party
YTC	Yemen Telecommunications Company

1 *feddan* = 1.04 acres = 0.42 hectares.

1 The Geographic, Social and Historical Setting

South Yemen is a land of many paradoxes. Geographically, it is isolated from the rest of the Arabian Peninsula by rugged mountains and parched deserts, yet it is situated at the intersection of important Middle Eastern and African trade routes which date back to antiquity. Historically, the area has experienced a unique combination of isolation and interaction, of peripheralism and strategic centrality. South Yemen's major city—the port of Aden— occupies an important commercial and strategic position and, as a result, has suffered foreign occupation for much of the past four centuries, first by the Ottoman Turks (1538–1839) and then by the British (1839–1967). Yet during most of this period the Yemeni hinterland remained largely undisturbed.

On 30 November 1967 these geographic and historical paradoxes were inherited by the newly independent People's Republic of South Yemen (PROSY), renamed the People's Democratic Republic of Yemen (PDRY) in 1970. Economically, the modern PDRY is a poor state endowed with few natural resources. Socially and politically, it is the only state in the Arab world to genuinely embrace 'scientific socialism'. It is a state in which the traditional tribal-based social structure has undergone significant transformation in two decades of independence.

Physical Geography and Climate

The People's Democratic Republic of Yemen occupies some 336,869 sq. km. (figures vary) on the southern edge of the Arabian peninsula. Its mainland extends for nearly 1,200 km. along the Gulf of Aden and the Arabian Sea from approximately 19° N, latitude to 13° N., and from approximately 43° E. longtitude to 53° E. In addition, the country includes a number of offshore islands. The most important of these are Perim (13 sq. km., located in the middle of the Straits of Bab el-Mandeb at the southern end of the Red Sea); Kamaran (57 sq. km., located 320 km. north of Perim, off the coast of the Yemen Arab Republic); and the Socotra group (3,625 sq. km., located in the Arabian Sea east of the Horn of Africa). The PDRY shares ill-defined and often disputed borders with three other Arabian peninsula states: the Yemen Arab Republic, commonly known as North Yemen or Yemen (San'a), to the north-west; Saudi Arabia to the north; and Oman to the east. It faces Somalia, Djibouti and Ethiopia across the Gulf of Aden and the Red Sea.

Southern Yemen has some of the most rugged and inhospitable terrain in the region, a fact that has had considerable influence on its social, economic and political development. Composed of ancient African granites covered in many places by younger sedimentary deposits, the South Arabian plateau has here undergone significant decline to the east and elevation to the west. As a result, mountains of over 2,500 m. tower up above the Red Sea in the west, gradually giving way to plateau, which merges with the Empty Quarter (*Rub al-Khali*) in the north-east. Fracturing of the plateau in the south and west has created the South Yemeni seacoast, and in places extinct volcanic craters (such as the one which serves as Aden port) provides evidence of the magma flow once associated with these fractures. A coastal belt, varying in width from 6 to 64 km., extends for some 1,180 km. along the shoreline, separated from the interior plateau by a coastal mountain range of varying height.

Further inland, the interior plateau is broken up into blocks by numerous valleys and *wadis* (riverbeds). The most important of these is the Wadi Hadhramawt, an immense valley running parallel to the coast 150–200 km. inland for most of its length. The Hadhramawt is occupied by a seasonal torrent (perennial in places), which allows the alluvial soil of its upper reaches to be cultivated.

To date, salt and limestone (cement) are the only mineral resources actively exploited in the PDRY. There have, however, been indications of discoveries of oil deposits along the North Yemeni frontier, offshore, and elsewhere in the country, raising hopes of possible future oil production. In the same way, lignite, iron ore, copper, manganese, lead, zinc, molybdenum, gold, potassium and bauxite have been indicated, although no deposits large enough to warrant exploitation have yet been found. Most of the Republic remains unprospected.

Rainfall in South Yemen varies—being more abundant in the highlands and the south-west—but nowhere is it plentiful. The coastal mountains play a crucial role in the east-west distribution of moisture carried by the westerly winds of the Red Sea. Aden has approximately 125mm. of precipitation per year, entirely in the winter (December to March), while up to 900mm. per year—mainly in the summer—falls in the mountains and foothills above the city, tapering off to approximately 500mm. per year in the eastern highlands. Rainfall decreases steadily as one moves inland to the fringes of the Arabian desert, where no rain may fall for ten years or more. Temperatures are high along the coastal plain: Aden has a January mean of 24°C, a June mean of 27°C, and commonly reaches a maximum in the 40–50°C range. Humidity is also very high in the summer. Inland it is somewhat cooler in the summer, and can be very cold in winter. Because of the limited and erratic rainfall, all drainage is seasonal and intermittent. Drought is frequent. At the other end of the scale, flash-flooding can also occur. In 1982 this flooding was particularly severe: 448 people died, 64,000 were made homeless, and an estimated $1 billion of damage was done to the PDRY's dams, irrigation and communication networks, and standing crops.

Apart from shrubs and dwarf trees in the highlands and irrigated tracts on the coastal plain and in the Hadhramawt, the Republic's terrain is largely barren. Natural cultivation is confined to terraces alongside riverbeds or deltas, on the sides and bottom of the Wadi Hadhramawt, or in oases. Irrigation from wells or cisterns has been practised for centuries, particularly at Lahej (near Aden), al-Mukalla, and sections of the Hadhramawt. Under current usage, approximately 0.6 per cent of the Republic's land is arable, 27 per cent pasture, and 7 per cent woodland. The remainder is wasteland—primarily mountains and desert (FAO, 1984a). The offshore waters of the PDRY are relatively abundant in fish.

Population and Society

Because of the rugged and hostile nature of its terrain, South Yemen has only a small population—of approximately 2.1 million. Administratively, the country is divided into a number of governates (six since March 1980). The size and population of these, based on the most recent census for which full

Table 1.1 Size and Population of Governates, PDRY

Governate	Capital	Area sq. km.	Population†	Density‡
First (Aden)	Aden	6,980 (2%)	291,000 (18%)	41.7
Second (Lahej)	Hawatah	12,766 (4%)	273,000 (17%)	21.4
Third (Abyan)	Zinjibar	21,489 (6%)	311,000 (20%)	14.5
Fourth (Shibwah)	Ataq	73,908 (22%)	162,000 (10%)	2.2
Fifth (Hadhramawt)*	Mukalla	155,376 (46%)	492,000 (31%)	3.2
Sixth (al-Mahra)	Ghaydah	66,350 (20%)	61,000 (4%)	0.9

* Formed by a merger of Thamud and Hadhramawt governates in March 1980.
† 1973 census.
‡ Persons per sq. km.
Source: PDRY, 1980c; Fisher & Unwin, 1986.

figures are available (1973), are given in Table 1.1. The largest single population centre is the port of Aden, capital of the Republic, with some 350,000 inhabitants; the only other sizeable city is al-Mukalla (population 80,000), located on the coast 500 km. north-east of Aden. Smaller towns are dotted along the coast or situated in the Hadhramawt or other major *wadis*. Roughly 40 per cent of the PDRY's population live in urban areas, primarily Aden. Most of the remainder are engaged in settled or semi-settled agriculture or fishery; only a small minority (approximately 10 per cent) are true nomadic bedouin.

Ethically, the population of the Republic is now quite homogeneous, consisting mainly (90 per cent) of Arabic speakers of the Mediterranean racial type. A minority of non-Mediterranean Vedoids (Australoids), speaking a semitic language related to but different from Arabic, are found in increasing numbers as one moves eastwards in the hinterland, finally comprising a majority in the tribes of al-Mahrah. A similar ethnic group, intermixed with more recent African, Arab and East Indian arrivals, can be found on the island of Socotra. Small African communities descended from former slaves or invaders are also found in the interior.

Aden (and to some extent other coastal towns) has retained a more cosmopolitan composition, as befits a city which has served as a major trading port for centuries. Before independence there existed in the city a small European population (4,500 in the 1955 census, consisting primarily of colonial administrators, military personnel, managers and missionaries); some 16,000 East Indians (primarily merchants, traders, civil servants, and professionals); and well over 10,000 Somalis as unskilled labourers (Gavin, 1975, p. 445). Independence in 1967 led to the departure of the British administrative and military staff and their dependants as well as much of the trading community. Some 80,000 people departed at that time, leaving behind predominantly native Yemenis in the PDRY with a much-reduced Somali and East Indian minority in Aden.

Most of the indigenous population of South Yemen are Sunni Muslims, adhering to the Shafi school of jurisprudence. There are also, however, a large number of Zaydi Shi'ites in Aden, primarily immigrants from the north. Very small Christian, Hindu and Zoroastrian minorities are found in Aden and other coastal towns, reminders of a cosmopolitan colonial and mercantile past. South Yemen also has a small, two-thousand-year-old Jewish community. This is only the remnant of the community, however, most of which emigrated to the newly-founded state of Israel in 1948—some 7,000 leaving Aden alone.

Traditionally, large numbers of Yemenis have left the area to work abroad.

Before independence, East Africa and South Asia were common destinations for South Yemeni emigrants and traders; today, many are employed in the oil-rich Gulf states. As of the early 1980s, approximately 85,000 people (or 15 per cent of the PDRY's active labour force) were employed abroad (Arif, 1983, p. 120). South Yemeni expatriates usually retain strong social ties with their families and native towns and villages, and expatriate remittances and investments have been an important source of income for the country since independence.

Social Structure

It is difficult to describe the complex structure of society found in the PDRY. Geographical factors account for much of this complexity: South Yemen's geographical position has both attracted outside influences and helped it to resist them, while the rugged nature of the terrain and the isolation of inland population centres has allowed for considerable local variation.

South Yemen did not share the historical experience of much of the rest of the Middle East. Consequently it remained significantly different in many aspects of social life. Unlike many other countries in the region, outside political control was often too tenuous to have any social effect. Sheltered from the rest of the Arabian peninsula (and hence from much of the influence of Islamic armies and migrating bedouin tribes) during the rise of Islam, Islam modified but failed to transform the pattern of status ascription, land ownership and land usage that lay at the root of the existing social order. Thus, within the tribes of modern South Yemen, secular tribal law (*'urf*), which owes much to pre-Islamic practice, is dominant, rather than the *shari'ah* (Islamic law). Later, Ottoman Turkish rule was too weak to bring about significant social changes apart from in the city of Aden, and hence South Yemen was not subject to the homogenizing effect of Ottoman administration (particularly the Ottoman land reforms of the mid-nineteenth century) that so affected much of the rest of the Middle East. The result was the existence in many areas of the south of semi-feudal or slave/retainer-based social structures that differed markedly from those found in other Arab countries (Omar, 1970, pp. 1–41). In the nineteenth and twentieth centuries the hinterland continued largely undisturbed under the British as a matter of deliberate colonial practice. In coastal areas, centuries of maritime commerce served to further increase local variation in the nature of Yemeni society. Finally, the multiple factors of modernity, nationalist struggle and domestic social revolution have all had a fundamental and differential impact on the country in recent decades. The effect of social reforms and programmes implemented by the revolutionary government will be explored in detail in Chapters 4 and 5; here it is sufficient to sketch the traditional social structure which those actions have sought to transform.

If there has been a common demoninator running through the complex social history of South Yemen it is to be found in the network of kinship, clan ties and social identity known as tribalism. In contrast to its relatively homogeneous ethnic and religious make-up, South Yemen boasts an almost infinitely complex tribal composition: it has been estimated that in the Hadhramawt alone some 1,300 to 1,400 tribal units can be found. The most important tribal units include the Subayhi, ʾAbdali, ʾAqrabi, Hawshabi, ʾAmiri, ʾAlawi and Fadhali near Aden; the Yafiʾi tribes in the north; the ʾAulaqi, Audhali, Dathina and Bayhan in the mid-west; the Wahidi, Shenafir, Saybani, Quʾayti, Kathiri and Hamuni confederacies in and around Wadi Hadhramawt in the east; and the Mahrah of the far east (FAS, 1971, pp. 71-3). In turn, these tribal units are characterized by an extended segmented structure, with each tribe divided into sub-tribes by lineage, and these further divided and subdivided until the basic building block of tribal society, the clan or family group, is reached. Such family groups may be territorial as well as kinship groups, representing perhaps a single village or portion thereof. Although geneology provides a common tribal ideology—with all tribe members tracing descent from a single historical figure (who may have lived hundreds of years ago)—this tribal ideology is neither inflexible nor transcendent. This is evident in the fact that political manipulation of geneaological 'histories' and serious conflict among segments of the same tribe have both been commonplace in South Yemeni society (FAS, 1977, pp. 78-9).

Within the tribes, power generally rests in the hands of secular tribal sheikhs, to whom all members of the tribe look as mediators and judges in intra-tribal affairs. In many cases, tribal sheikhs are selected by formal election, although in practice most owe their position to their member ship of a traditional ruling family and the political machinations of their forerunners and forebears. In most tribes certain rights and privileges regarding land use and distribution accrue to these tribal sheikhs. This serves to reinforce their social and political power, and the power of their clan.

A significantly different system of social organization is found in the larger villages and towns of South Yemen. Here, social status is a function not only of descent, but also of religious status and occupation (Bujra, 1971). At the top of the traditional town hierarchy are the *sayyids*, claiming descent from the Prophet Muhammad and from the Adnani (or nothern) Arabs. Although the

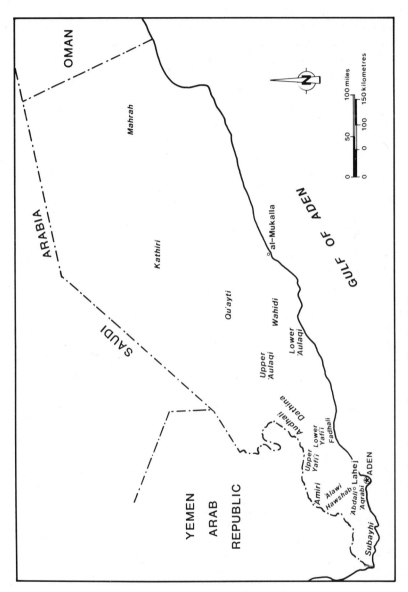

Map 1.2 Geographic distribution of major tribes, South Yemen

sayyids are town-based notables, their prestige extends into tribal areas, allowing them to act as mediators in inter-tribal conflicts.

A second stratum is occupied by the religious sheikhs and town-dwelling tribesmen. Both trace their descent to the Qahtan (southern, or 'pure') Arabs; the former, however, also trace their descent to well-known holy men and scholars from the past and hence have a slightly higher social status.

The third stratum (the *masakin* (poor) or *dhu'fa* (weak)) consists of those who can trace their descent neither to religious figures nor the Qahtan. This group in turn is subdivided into those artisans and labourers who traditionally pursue 'respectable' occupations (such as agriculture), and the *akhdam* who traditionally engaged in despised trades (butchers, barbers, bloodletters, bath attendants, tanners; in some areas also clayworkers, sweepers and fishermen). At the very bottom of the hierarchy lies the *subayan* (servant) group. The lowest groups (*akhdam* and *subayan*) are commonly descended from former slaves, and have remained outside the mainstream of traditional Yemeni life (Omar, 1970, pp. 1–41; Stookey, 1982, pp. 4–9).

Although these distinctions were based on social status rather than economic activity, social divisions did overlap with wealth and occupational divisions to the extent that the above strata also constituted a fairly clear socio-economic class system. The *sayyids* tended to own more land (and other means of production), to be wealthier, and to derive further wealth from their land by renting it to those at the bottom end of the scale. In towns certain occupations were traditionally carried out by members of a given social group, and this was reinforced by the existence of occupational guilds.

Finally, it is important to note that the structure of social life in pre-revolutionary South Yemen was maintained and perpetuated by customs and rules governing social interaction of almost caste-like severity. Status was almost invariably ascribed as a function of descent. Marriages were arranged by families, with women forbidden to marry into a group of lower social status. In urban areas neighbourhoods were commonly segregated by clan and status group. Such restrictions meant that upward social mobility, even inter-generational social mobility, was severely limited. Only in the large city of Aden did pre-revolutionary South Yemen's social structure show any major signs of flexibility or change. Here, however, geneological stratification was replaced by an ethnic one, with European administrators heading a hierarchy comprised (in descending order) of East Indian merchants and civil servants, Arab artisans and workers, and unskilled Somali labourers.

Political Traditions

Despite their substantially different economic and social bases (and the reproduction of the usual rural–urban tensions between them), the towns and tribal areas of the South Yemeni hinterland have traditionally shared many economic, political and social ties. Since antiquity, the towns have formed trading points and neutral meeting places amid the hostile tribal areas. Tribal settlement permeates Yemeni towns. Both tribal areas and hinterland towns were often ruled by a common sultan, to whom tribal units pledged (often only nominal) political allegiance and under whom towns were ruled directly or enjoyed semi-autonomy guaranteed by custom or treaty. Traditionally, the sheikhs of several tribal units came together to select the sultan, usually from a traditional ruling family (or families). The sultan then acted as a mediator and co-ordinator between the tribal leaders and their nominal leader, and as local head of state. The power of the sultan was thus contingent upon support given him by the tribes and townspeople. Although this was supplemented by other means (notably by the sultan's private wealth, the wealth and power of any areas ruled directly, and whatever private army the sultan could finance independent of tribal levies), the dependence of the sultan's position on tribal support introduced a significant degree of responsibility into the traditional political system.

The net result, therefore, was a series of parallel structures of social and political power in uneasy relation with one another (illustrated in Figure 1.1). British colonial policy merely reinforced this structure by adding a single authority at its head and policing relationships among its constituent elements. In doing so, however, the British inadvertently caused the structure

Figure 1.1 The pre-colonial power structure in South Yemen

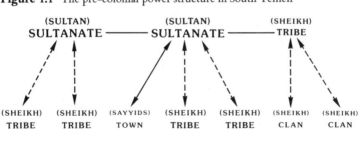

to become considerably more rigid and inflexible than had previously been the case.

Before the colonial intrusion sultans and sheikhs had been subject to some degree of scrutiny by those who had selected them, and it had been not uncommon for incompetent or brutal leaders to be removed by those to whom they owed their position. Furthermore, relations among different tribal groups had been characterized by a constantly changing balance of power, as each group vied for a better position and greater power *vis-à-vis* its neighbours.

As shown in Figure 1.2, British colonial policy changed all this. Under the protectorate treaty system, a sultan's position and the existing intra- and inter-tribal status quo were guaranteed by the overwhelming power of the British—in exchange for which the sultan and the existing elite pledged their support for British interests. Moreover, the British usually provided direct financial support for a sultan, hence reducing his reliance on those under him. Increased political rigidity was accompanied by decreased responsibility, and the sultans of South Yemen grew more powerful and less accountable at the same time. This happened at a time when considerable pressures in any event, were being brought to bear on the traditional social system by modernization and political and social development in the broader Arab world. The system was unable to contain the social and political changes it experienced in the twentieth century. Discontent with the status quo was

Figure 1.2 The colonial power structure in South Yemen

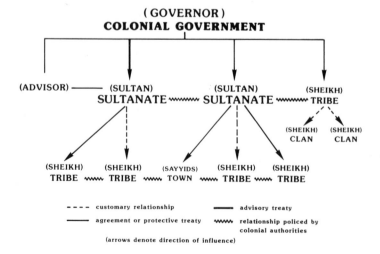

thus channelled into an anti-colonialism that ultimately drove the British from South Yemen and toppled the power of the traditional elite.

Historical Evolution

Just as geography has shaped the social structure in South Yemen, so geography and tribal social patterns have exerted a fundamental influence on the historical evolution of the area. In ancient times South Arabia was particularly noted for two things: its location astride the maritime trade routes linking the Middle East, East Africa and South Asia and its role as an entrepôt for Arabian peninsula caravan routes; and for the production of frankincense and myrrh (for historical references to the region see Doe, 1971, pp. 30–59). These two factors brought the area considerable wealth until the sixth century AD, when Christian-Jewish religious conflict, the reduction of South Arabia's share of maritime and inland trade, and invasion first by Abyssinia and then by Persia weakened the power and prestige of the area. The rise of Islam hastened this decline still further by moving the centre of political power northwards. The Persian satrapy of South Arabia, established in the late sixth century, was converted to Islam in 628, and by the time of the Prophet Muhammad's death in 632 South Arabia had become a peripheral part of the Islamic world.

Despite the decline in power of South Arabia, the area retained significant commercial and strategic importance. Successive Islamic caliphates laid claim to portions of South Yemen; in practice they exerted only nominal control over Aden and a few other South Yemeni ports while the interior of the country continued undisturbed under tribal rule. By the time Portuguese navigators entered the Indian Ocean at the turn of the sixteenth century, Aden had become a major port of call not only for local trade but for ships *en route* to the Red Sea, East Africa, the Arabian Gulf and India.

With the decline of the Arab caliphates, it was the Ottoman Turks who warded off the Portugese and other European intruders and captured Aden from its Sultan in 1538. Thus began the first of three centuries of precarious Ottoman rule. The Turks successfully quelled two serious and sustained Yemeni revolts in 1547–51 and in 1566–70. The decay of the empire during the next 150 years, however, gradually reduced Ottoman suzerainty to a mere façade, and effective control over Aden and its districts passed first to the Imams of San'a (approximately 1630–1730), and later to local sultans and tribal sheikhs (notably the Sultan of Lahej after 1735). At the same time, energetic European exploitation of eastern trade and increasing use of the Cape route to India led to a deterioration in Aden's commercial importance.

The Arrival of the British

It was Napoleon's military campaign in Egypt (1798) that rekindled European interest in Aden and its strategic position. British forces briefly occupied Perim Island (controlling what was then the only entrance to the Red Sea) in 1799, until lack of water and food there forced them to decamp to the mainland under the watchful eye of the Sultan of Lahej. By 1802 the British government had consolidated its influence on the mainland through the conclusion of a friendship treaty with the Sultan (see Aitchison, 1933, XI, pp, 53–6 for text). The next three decades saw British officials in London and Bombay cast increasingly covetous eyes on South Arabia until, in 1839, the plunder of a British shipwreck in the area provided the pretext for the exercise of British gunboat diplomacy. After a short but sharp fight, a force of seven hundred British and Indian soldiers supported by Royal Navy and East India Company ships under Captain S. B. Haines of the Indian Navy conquered Aden. In a subsequent peace treaty (Aitchison, 1933, XI, pp. 56–60) the city was incorporated into the British Empire under the administration of the Indian government.

The growth of steam navigation in the nineteenth century and the opening of the Suez Canal in 1869 revitalized Aden. The port became a major coaling and fuelling station for the Royal Navy, and for freight and passenger liners negotiating the Suez Canal and Indian Ocean. From Aden, the British began to consolidate their position in the interior of South Yemen. Here the existing social order assumed paramount importance in British policy, for the British were aided in the extension of their influence by the chaotic political conditions prevailing among the local rulers—internecine tribal feuds, the absence of a strong central government, and the general backwardness and poverty of the inhabitants of the region. Britain offered protection to tribal rulers and to their heirs, in return for which the rulers gave up their right to enter into any relations whatsoever with any foreign power; promised not to sell or cede any territory except to Britain; and undertook to inform the British Resident in Aden if any power tried to interfere in any way in tribal territory. Advisory treaties (thirteen in all) further stipulated that the local ruler would accept a British Resident adviser who fulfilled the dual function of adviser to the local ruler and main executor of British policy. He was also responsible for security and for relations between princedoms and tribes.

In practice, of course, British protection, advice and support fostered dependence. The sheikhs and sultans of the South Yemeni hinterland became increasingly tied to Britain, and increasingly unable to resist British demands. (For their part, the British came to rely on the maintenance of a semi-feudal social structure which ultimately proved unequal to its role in British policy.) By fostering the division of the area along tribal and sub-tribal lines, the British inhibited the development of either a national consciousness or a national opposition to colonial rule. Finally, this elaborate yet simple system of dominance was extremely inexpensive for the British. They paid a mere £5,435 per year in subsidies for the loyalty of twenty-five sultans. In addition, the British saved themselves the trouble and expense of administering the fiercely independent tribesmen (Hassan 1974, pp. 13-15). Thus, through a system of agreements and alliances signed between 1839 and 1914, the British extended their control over the whole of South Yemen.

To the north, the limits of Britain's expanding control in South Arabia were governed by her relations with the Imams of North Yemen and their Ottoman Turkish overlords. Relations with the latter were, until the outbreak of the First World War, relatively cordial, and it was the Turks who proposed the demaraction lines that after 1904 formed the legal boundary between North and South Yemen. After the Turkish evacuation of the North in 1918, however, Britain encountered increasing difficulties with the independent Yemeni regime of Imam Yahya. The Imam claimed South Yemen was an integral part of the Yemeni kingdom, and cross-border fighting and intrigues became commonplace.

As a result of local and international developments during the First World War and the 1920s, the British reviewed their policies in South Yemen in an effort to consolidate their position. This new urgency for entrenchment appears to have been induced by several factors. First, Aden was assuming growing significance in the commercial routes that linked Asia with the rest of the Empire, particularly the European metropole. Secondly, newly-discovered oil in Iraq and Iran, coupled with heavy financial investments there and the rising threat of American oil companies' explorations in Saudi Arabia, further added to the significance of Aden. Third, political unrest and turmoil in India and Indian demands for independence increased British uncertainty. If future contingencies were to be met, it seemed prudent to strengthen the British position in Aden. Finally, the rise of fascism in Italy and Mussolini's subsequent military conquest and colonization of the Horn of Africa lent a new importance to Aden's strategic position.

This increased significance of Aden meant that a different political and administrative infrastructure was required to carry the weight of British interests in the Middle East and Indian Ocean. Aden was therefore declared a Crown Colony in 1937, bringing the city under direct British colonial rule. For nearly a century Aden had remained under the jurisdiction of the Indian government; now, with this new step, Aden came under the closer supervision, control and administration of the Colonial Office in London. Soon after, those territories in the South Yemeni hinterland whose petty rulers had entered into treaty relations with the British government were organized into two large protectorates. The Western Protectorate comprised a conglomerate of eighteen sultanates, sheikdoms and tribal confederacies administered by the British governor in Aden. The Eastern Protectorate, comprised of five sultanates and two sheikdoms (including Hadhramawt, al-Mahrah and the island of Socotra), was administered by a British political agent appointed by the Governor of Aden.

The Road to Independence

The constitutional route to South Yemeni independence envisaged by the British government—a route which could leave intact the power of the largely pro-British traditional elite—went much futher away in South Yemen than in many other British colonies. In large part this was attributable to Britain's policy of governing through the sheikhs and sultans of the hinterland, a policy which resulted in an indelible association between British colonialism and the hated, repressive, semi-feudal social and political structure of the interior in the minds of many Yemenis. Similarly, British involvement in the creation of Israel in 1948 and the failure of the Anglo–French–Israeli intervention at Suez in 1956 did much to discredit the colonial power.

The most important factor, however, was an ideological one. There had always been some degree of opposition to British colonial rule, primarily from the hinterland tribes. In lower 'Aulaqi the tribes had rebelled in 1936, 1937 and 1946; in Radfan in 1918, 1938 and 1948 and 1957; in al-Subayhi in 1942; in Hadhramawt and Mahrah in 1944, 1951, 1952, 1955 and 1961; in Bayhan in 1942, 1943, 1948 and 1957; in Shuaib, Halmin and Dhawali' in 1947, 1948 and 1957; in the Yaf'i in 1958-9; in the Wahidi in 1941; in the Fadhali in 1945, 1956 and 1957; in the 'Awathil in 1946 and 1947; in the Dathina in 1958; in Hawshabi in 1950; and, most importantly, a revolt by the Kathiri Emir Ubay Bin Salih Bin Abdat in the Hadhramawt during the Second World War (National Front, 1969, p. 21). All these revolts, however, had been crushed by the British, often with the support of other tribal groups. What had been lacking was the necessary ideology to bind the South Yemeni anti-colonial struggle and to organize into a viable force.

Early attempts during the inter-war period to use Islam (and in particular the ideas of such Islamic anti-imperialists as al-Afghani and Abdu) as the basis for resistance were unsuccessful. The *Jami'yat al-Irshad* (Society of Guidance), founded in 1913, was typical of these. The Society opposed the social dominance of the Yemeni *sayyids*, arguing that it was a flagrant violation of the basic Islamic tenet of equality. Although the Society did have some impact on South Yemen (particularly in the Hadhramawt where its ideas played a part in the Second World War revolt of Emir Abdat), it had the greatest impact outside the country, where the attempts of expatriate members of *sayyid* families to dominate local Yemeni immigrant communities in the East Indies and elsewhere were much resented. Later, in the 1940s, nascent efforts as political organization were manifest in the formation of a number of small social and political clubs. In Aden, the Arab Literary Club (*Nadi al-ʾArabi*), the Reform Club (*Nadi al-Isbah*), the Adeni Club (*al-Nadi al-Adeni*), the Islamic Association (*al-Jamiyah al-Islamiyah*), and the Yemeni Union (*al-Itihad al-Yamani*) were quasi-political groups with nationalist inclinations dedicated to various reform programmes. The existence outside Aden of the People's Club (*Nadi al-Shaab*) in Lahej, the Nationalist Party (*al-Hizb al-Watani*) in the Quʾayti sultanate, the Committee for the Unification of the Hadhramawt (*Laianat al-ʾAmal li Wahdat Hadhramawt*) and the Charity Association (*Jamiyat al-Ihsan*) in the Khathiri sultanate reflected how widespread, if fragmented, these efforts were (Mashahdi, 1963, p. 107; al-Habashi, 1968, pp. 88–9).

It was not until after the Second World War that an ideology arose that was capable of binding together and organizing South Yemeni opposition to colonial rule: Arab nationalism. Following the 1952 Egyptian Revolution, President Nasser of Egypt articulated this new ideology in powerful and popular terms, and lent strong verbal, diplomatic and material support to the nationalist cause in South Yemen. Further impetus came in 1962, when a Nasserite republican coup in Sanʾa toppled the Imam and brought Egyptian troops and advisers to the neighbouring North. Small Arab nationalist groups and newspapers appeared on the scene; pan-Arab parties such as the Arab Nationalists' Movement (ANM) and the Baʾath began to organize cells in the South. Through the transistor radio, North Yemeni and Egyptian broadcasts brought these developments into the smallest South Yemeni towns and villages, raising aspirations and popularizing the nationalist struggle (Bujra, 1971, pp. 169–71).

All this looked very threatening to London, which had already come to see Arab nationalism (and its leading exponent, President Gamal ʾAbd al-Nasser of Egypt) as the major threat to British interests in the Middle East. In an attempt to resist growing Arab nationalist pressures in the region, the British undertook a series of discussions, beginning in 1954, with sheikhs and sultans interested in the formation of a Federation of Arab Emirates of the South. This autonomous entity would be tied to Britain by treaty and protected by the British Army. It was hoped that such a Federation would provide a somewhat more cohesive and coherent unit with which to resist regional pressures, going beyond the thirty-one major protectorate treaties and ninety conventions that by this time defined Britain's status and power in the hinterland. The nucleus of the Federation was formed by six Western Protectorate territories in 1959; eleven more hinterland states (and Aden) joined the Federation over the next few years, and in 1962 it was formally renamed the Federation of South Arabia. In 1961, as part of this process, Britain assigned formal command of its Arab levies in South Yemen to the Federation to serve as its army.

Meanwhile, in Aden, British attempts to make colonial rule more stable and attractive took the form of a series of administrative reforms introduced soon aftter the First World War. A Legislative Council was established in January 1947 to advise the British Governor. Its members were chosen by the Governor (half from the colonial administration itself) and lacked any real power. In 1955 a small elected element was added. These reforms were, of course, intended to foster the growth of the pro-British Adeni elite and to involve it in the governing process. The most important political manifestation of this elite was the Aden Association (*al-Jami'yah al-'Adeniyah*), a moderate reformist group formed in 1949–50 by members of Aden's merchant class. The Association adopted the slogan 'Aden for the Adenese', and sought government autonomy—separate from the hinterland sultanates—within the British Commonwealth. Members of the Association took part—and were elected—in the limited Legislative Council elections of 1955.

The first acid test of British policy came in 1959, when full elections to the Legislative Council were held. These took place under a series of highly restrictive conditions: most Adenis were disenfranchised by strict property and residency requirements, and many popular candidates were denied permission to run for office altogether. As a result, the Arab population boycotted the polls, with a mere 5,600 votes cast by a total of 21,554 registered voters, who in turn represented only a small minority of Aden's population of 180,000. The Aden Association again won most of the available seats—although given the scope of the boycott this indicated the limit rather than the extent of their support in the city. In any event their victory proved to be a swan-song. After 1958 severe divisions appeared within the organization, and by the 1960s the internal disputes, coupled with political pressure from growing nationalist aspirations, had caused the organization to fragment. Neither it nor its successors and offshoots (the National Union Party, the Independence Party and the Organization of the People's

Constitutional Conference) were ever able to play more than a marginal role in Adeni politics in the years which followed. Aden's merchant elite had proved unable to organize their interests and resist the growing nationalist tide.

The failure of the 1959 legislative council elections (and later elections in 1964) to create a viable local client administration in Aden soon led the colonial authorities to attempt the consolidation of pro-British influence over the city by linking it to the traditional pro-British tribes and principalities of the hinterland. Thus, in 1962, the British government oversaw constitutional talks concerning the incorporation of Aden into an enlarged South Arabia Federation, and in January of the following year, this took place in the face of intense popular opposition from Adenis unwilling to be tied to the sheikhs and sultans of the hinterland. In 1964 Federal leaders and British officials meeting in London agreed that the Federation would receive its independence by 1968.

Despite British efforts, nationalist demands for immediate independence grew ever louder and more organized during this period. In the late 1950s strikes and nationalist protests, often led by the Aden Trade Union Congress (ATUC), became commonplace. Nationalist demands also won international support from the United Nations which in 1963 and again in 1965 called for the decolonization of South Yemen.

On 14 October 1963 opposition to colonial rule finally entered the military phase, when the nascent National Front for the Liberation of Occupied South Yemen (NF) launched its first armed actions against the British in the mountainous Radfan district north of Aden, where the death of a tribal leader (Bin Rajeh Bin Ghaleb) at the hands of the British had helped the NF to create a strong support base. The insurrection soon spread to al-Dhali', al-Fudhala, Duthaina and al-Awathel (Ahmad, 1968, pp. 122–31). In December an unsuccessful assassination attempt was made on the life of the British Governor in Aden. The colonial authorities responded by announcing a state of emergency and detaining many political activists.

Because of the scale of nationalist resistance encountered in South Yemen, the British adopted a somewhat different approach when the next constitutional conference was held in London in the summer of 1965. This time, in an effort to co-opt the more accommodationist forces within the nationalist movement, representatives of groups such as the South Arabian League (SAL) and the People's Socialist Party (PSP) were encouraged to participate alongside federal and tribal leaders. Also, in recognition of the disdain felt for the backward hinterland by many Adenis, the conference discussed different constitutional arrangements that would grant greater power to Aden.

Table 1.2 Chronology

1538	Ottoman Turks occupy Aden.
1799	Britain occupies Perim Island.
1839	Britain occupies Aden. Over the next century British power is gradually extended into the hinterland through treaties and agreements with sultans and tribal leaders.
1869	Suez Canal opens.
1937	Aden becomes Crown Colony.
1951	South Arabian League formed.
1955	First (partial) Legislative Council elections in Aden.
1956	Aden Trade Union Congress formed.
1959	Federation of Arab Emirates of the South (later South Arabian Federation) formed. Boycott of Legislative Council elections.
1962	People's Socialist Party formed. London constitutional conference.
1963	National Front for the Liberation of Occupied South Yemen formed. Aden joins federation.
1964	National Front launches Radfan revolt.
1965	Constitutional conference. Britain suspends Adeni constitution. PSP and SAL form Organization for the Liberation of the Occupied South.
1966	British White Paper on Defence. OLOS and NF form FLOSY; NF leaves.
1967	Civil war between NF and FLOSY as British depart; NF triumphs. *South Yemen becomes independent*.
1969	President Qahtan al-Sha'abi overthrown by NF radicals in June 22 'Corrective Step'. Nationalization laws.
1970	Second Agrarian Reform Law. Country renamed People's Democratic Republic of Yemen under new Constitution.
1971	First Three Year Plan begins.
1972	Border war with Yemen Arab Republic.
1974	First Five Year Plan begins.
1975	NF superseded by United Political Organization of the National Front.
1978	President Rubayi Ali executed after implicated in assassination of the President of the YAR. UPONF replaced by Yemeni Socialist Party.
1979	Second Five Year Plan begins. Border war with YAR ends in unity agreement. Treaty of Friendship and Co-operation signed with Soviet Union.
1980	Ismail removed from positions; Muhammed becomes President.
1981	Revised Second Five Year Plan begins. PDRY-Libya-Ethiopia alliance concluded.
1982	PDRY reaches agreement with Oman on normalization of relations. Floods cause serious economic and human damage.
1986	Ousting of President Muhammed after days of heavy fighting.

However, there was little consensus among participants on these issues, and the conference finally broke up in August without agreement. Following its failure, the deteriorating security situation in Aden by 25 September 1965 led the British High Commissioner to suspend the Constitution; to dismiss 'Abd al-Qawi Makkawi, the increasingly nationalist Adeni Chief Minister; and to re-establish direct British rule over the colony. This only served to accentuate the crisis, however, driving many hitherto moderate nationalists (including Makkawi) to accept the necessity for armed struggle.

Up to this point, the British government had continued to pin its hopes on the consolidation of a South Arabian Federation tied to Britain by treaty—a policy which now seemed quite unworkable given the failure of the London conferences and the collapse of traditional authority in the hinterland. In the Defence White Paper of 22 February 1966 Britain's Labour government announced the death-knell of this approach when it declared that British forces would withdraw from Aden by 31 December 1968—the absence of a constitutional structure or defence treaty notwithstanding (Great Britain, 1966). In May 1967 Aden's new High Commissioner, Sir Humphrey Trevelyan, announced that Britain would grant South Yemen independence on 9 January 1968. This date was later brought forward to 30 November by the Foreign Office in the face of mounting nationalist pressure. Last-ditch efforts by the British to patch together a friendly caretaker regime for the country met with little success.

With independence now in sight, all that remained was for the two major nationalist movements—the NF and the Front for the Liberation of South Yemen (FLOSY)—to struggle for supremacy in the country. In the ensuing civil war it was the NF that triumphed, and on 21 November it entered into final negotiations with the departing British in Geneva. On 30 November 1967 the independent People's Republic of South Yemen was born. Four centuries of foreign domination had finally come to an end.

2 The Political System I: The Ruling Party

The starting-point for any analysis of the politics of the contemporary PDRY must necessarily begin with its ruling party, a party whose ideology, objectives and internal conflicts have played a fundamental part in the post-independence evolution of South Yemen. There can be little doubt that the National Front and its successors—the Unified Political Organization of the National Front (UPONF, 1975–78) and the Yemeni Socialist Party (YSP, 1978–present)—have retained tight control over the apparatus of power in the country as they seek to foster revolutionary socialism in the South. In fact, only two organized political forces (both with ideologies consonant with those of the NF) have been tolerated: the Popular Vanguard Party (al-Tali'ah al-Shabiyah, a Ba'athist party) and the Popular Democratic Union (Itihad al-Sha'ab al-Demuqrati, a communist party). Both these have been co-opted within the ruling structure, joining the NF-dominated Unified Political Organization in October 1975. They retained secondary place when the UPONF became the YSP three years later.

Because of the party's leading role in the political (and hence socio-economic) life of the country, it is important to gain an accurate under-standing of its ideological and organizational foundations. Such an understanding necessarily begins with a detailed examination of the nationalist struggle in the 1950s and 1960s—a complex era in South Yemen's political development which was only briefly sketched in Chapter 1. It was at this time, under the pressures of a war of national liberation and amidst one of the most ideologically tumultuous periods in modern Arab politics, that the ideology of the nascent National Front crystallized. It was also at this time that the seeds of intra-party conflict—conflict that was to play a prominent part in shaping South Yemen's path after independence—were first sown.

The Ruling Party

The Formative Period: Nationalist Struggle

At the time of the National Front's initiation of armed resistance to the British in October 1963, the nationalist movement in South Yemen was already characterized by a multiplicity of groups and splinter groups. This factionalism continued throughout the years preceding independence, a pattern graphically illustrated in Figure 2.1. At the risk of oversimplifying an extremely complex political situation, three main nationalist tendencies lay beneath this complex array of parties and forces. Each grouping reflected a somewhat different social base and leadership. As a result, each was represented by a different organization (or organizations), and approached the struggle with different tactics, ideology and internal and external supporters.

The oldest major nationalist political group in South Yemen was the *Rabitat Abna al-Junub al-Arabi* (League of the Sons of the Arab South), better known as the *South Arabian League* (*Rabitat al-Janub al-'Arabi*, or SAL). Founded in 1950 under the chairmanship of Muhammed al-Jifri with Sheikhan al-Habshi as Secretary-General, the League sought to unite the divided, British-dominated principalities of the South into an independent South Arabia. Despite growing somewhat more militant during the years following its creation under the twin stimuli of political competition inside South Yemen and political developments outside it, the League tended to political conservatism (al-Mashadi, 1963, p. 9). In terms of strategy, the League (although making attempts to mobilize the rural and urban masses in support of the nationalist cause) tended to rely on the traditional pattern of

Figure 2.1 The nationalist movement

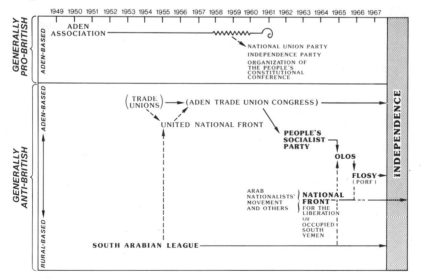

Yemeni politics—coalition-building among rural Yemeni notables—to further its political goals. In the late 1950s, for example, the League forged close ties with the Sultan of Lahej, Ali 'Abd al-Karim. The Sultan saw South Yemeni independence as a vehicle for the reassertion of the traditional primacy of the Lahej Sultanate; the League hoped to make Lahej a centre of nationalist activity. Co-operation continued until 1958, when the British deposed the Sultan and forced him to join South Arabian League leaders Muhammed 'Ali Jifri and Sheikhan Abdullah al-Habshi in exile in Cairo (Little, 1968, pp. 44–58, 70). For most of its history the League also rejected the notion of anti-colonial armed struggle and was willing to compromise with the British; it took part in the 1955 Legislative Council elections and the 1962 London Constitutional Conference. Most of the League's financial and material support came from conservative sources, notably Saudi Arabia after 1962 which saw SAL as a counterweight to Egyptian-sponsored groups within the nationalist movement.

An important role in Aden's political organization during this period was played by the small but active *al-Jabhah al-Wataniyah al-Mutahidah* (United National Front, UNF) which called for independence from Britain and, after the republican coup there, for unity with the North. Originally formed as a coalition of SAL, trade union activists and other nationalist groups in 1955, it soon came to be dominated by dissident SAL members who had split from that organization in protest over its ties with the sultans, the nepotism within its ranks, and the League's decision to participate in Legislative Council elections. Indeed, this latter move cost SAL dearly in terms of its influence in Aden while simultaneously strengthening the hand of the UNF, and the League was gradually frozen out of the Adeni trade union movement, to be replaced by other organizations (al-Habashi, 1968, pp. 97–9; National Front, 1969, p. 24).

The UNF, which found its support in Aden among the Yemeni *petit bourgeoisie* and the rapidly-growing Adeni trade union movement, stood in sharp contrast to the primarily hinterland- and elite-based politics of its parent organization, the South Arabian League. It reflected a new tendency within the nationalist movement, one rooted in a growing Aden labour movement. Under the stimulus of changing economic conditions and returning Yemeni expatriate workers with trade union experience, the 1950s and 1960s saw trade-union membership in Aden rapidly expand. From a mere handful of unionized workers in 1953 (when the first three trade unions were registered), the movement grew to number some twenty-two thousand people (or more than one-third of all Adeni workers, excluding servants) ten years later (Gavin, 1975, p. 327).

As the 1950s progressed, the various Adeni trade unions gradually coalesced into this second major nationalist grouping. On 20 March 1956, twenty-five of these unions came together to form the umbrella *al-Mu'atamar al-'Umali* (commonly known as the Aden Trade Union Congress or ATUC). The Congress soon proved to be a major social and political force in Aden under the leadership of Abdullah al-Asnaj. It led opposition to both the legislative council elections of 1959 and the merger of Aden within the South Arabian Federation in 1963. It also led some eighty-five work stoppages against Adeni companies until new labour regulations introduced in 1960 severely limited the right to strike.

In 1962, amid the debate over merger, the Trade Union Congress formally established its own political wing, the *Hizb al-Sh'ab al-Ishtiraki* (People's Socialist Party, PSP). Led by former ATUC Secretary-General Abdullah al-Asnaj, the PSP superseded both the United National Front and the Trade Union Congress as the nationalist political voice of many Adeni workers. It called for South Yemeni independence from Britain, the withdrawal of British forces, and unity with the North. For many years, however, its commitment to anti-colonialism did not include a commitment to armed struggle as a way of achieving such goals; rather, it relied on political and diplomatic means (such as participation in the second London constitutional conference). Sympathetic to the British Labour Party, the People's Socialist Party and ATUC hoped that negotiation—and the establishment of a Labour government in Britain (such as happened in October 1964)—would ease the road to independence.

As the power of the rival National Front (discussed below), grew, however, the PSP was forced to adopt different approaches. First it aligned itself with other nationalist groups, especially those representing the Aden or hinterland elite. In the summer of 1965 the PSP initiated a series of meetings with other nationalist groups and leaders, including 'Abd al-Qawi al-Makkawi (president of a company and Chief Minister of Aden under the British between 1955 and 1966); Ahmad Abdullah al-Fadhli (a sultan and large landowner); and Hassan Ismail Khadah Bakhish (a landlord and Deputy Prime Minister under Makkawi), as well as the South Arabian League. In May 1965 these meetings progressed a stage further with the formation of the Organization for the Liberation of the Occupied South (*Munadhamat Tahrir al-Janub al-Muhtal*, or OLOS), a coalition embracing both the PSP and the League. Soon after, a second change in PSP strategy became evident when OLOS announced its willingness to resort to military action in pursuit of its anti-colonial objectives. SAL, jealous of its independence and seeing the PSP as a recent upstart in the nationalist movement, soon drifted away from OLOS, which consequently became dominated by al-Asnaj and Makkawi.

The third major grouping within the South Yemeni nationalist movement was represented by the party which eventually acceded to power at independence, the *National Front for the Liberation of Occupied South Yemen (al-Jabhah al-Qawmiyah li Tahrir al-Janub al-Yaman al-Muhtal*, hereafter referred to as the National Front or NF).

The rising tide of Arab nationalism and the rising star and charisma of President Nasser in Egypt had given a new impetus to the national movement in South Yemen, particularly after the 1956 Suez crisis. The younger generation of South Yemenis began to see armed struggle as a viable route to the achievement of independence. Moreover, the dependence of British control over South Yemen on a virtual condominium between the interests of the colonial power and those of the traditional hinterland ruling classes suggested that such a struggle should be internally as well as externally directed—that is, aimed at reordering society as well as removing the colonial presence. The revolutionary overthrow of the Imamate in North Yemen in September 1962 (and the establishment there of a regime with close ties with Nasser's Egypt) only served to confirm the value of military action and to buoy up the spirits of potential revolutionaries. A short while later, the arrival of Egyptian forces into North Yemen to support and bolster the nascent revolution gave South Yemeni revolutionaries a base from which to organize.

Clandestine meetings were held in the North Yemeni city of Ta'iz to discuss strategies for action among the chief political groupings in South Yemen, notably the Yemeni branch of the Arab Nationalists' Movement, the Ba'ath Party and the PSP. The latter rejected the notion of armed struggle and withdrew from further discussions. The others did not, and in February 1963 the representatives of these groups (numbering some thousand people in total) met in San'a to establish a preparatory committee which would oversee the formation of a revolutionary nationalist movement in South Yemen. A few months later, in June 1963, another conference was held in San'a. It was here that the National Front was born, a coalition of seven groups committed to bringing to an end British colonial rule through military action. These initial founding members were: the Arab Nationalists' Movement (*Harakat al-Qawmiyyun al-Arab*), the Tribe's Formation (*Tashkil al-Qabaiel*), the Nasserite Front (*al-Jabhah al-Nasriyyah*), the Clandestine Organization of Free Officers and Soldiers (*al-Tandhim al-Siri lil Dhubat wa al-Junud al-Ahrar*), the Yafi'i Reform Front (*Jabhat al-Islah al-Yafi'yah*), the Patriotic Front (*al-Jabhah al-Watanniyah*) and the Revolutionary Organization of the Free People of Occupied South Yemen (*al-Munadhmah al-Thawr'yah Li Ahrar*

Junub al-Yaman al-Muhtal). Three more organizations joined at a later date: the Organization of the Revolutionary Vanguard in Aden (*Munadhamat al-Tali᾿al-Thawriyah fi Aden*), the Organization of Mahrah Youth (*Munadhamat Shabab al-Mahrah*), and the Youth Organization of Occupied South Yemen (*al-Munadhamah al-Thawriyah li Shabab Janub al-Yaman al-Muhtal*) (National Front, 1969, pp. 27–9, 198–200; al-Fattah, 1974, pp. 52–4; Lackner, 1984, p. 49).

The National Front drew upon a broad base of support in South Yemen, both from urban workers and from the rural and tribal populations. It was, however, the latter which represented the most powerful reserve of NF fighters and, following its initiation of armed struggle against the British on 14 October 1963, the Front rapidly gained strength in the countryside—threatening not only British influence, but also that of the traditional rural and tribal elites. Later, in the summer of 1964, the NF carried its armed attacks against the colonial authorities into the centre of Aden itself. Because of its military activism against the British in what represented the very heart of the colonial administration, the NF increasingly displaced the PSP as the leading nationalist organization among Adeni workers. This growing power of the NF even extended into ATUC where, by 1965, NF supporters had managed to prevent al-Asnaj's re-election as Secretary-General of the labour organization.

The ideology and objectives of the young National Front were first comprehensively set forth in the National Charter adopted by the Front at its First Congress, held in Ta᾿iz (North Yemen) on 22–25 June 1965. On the Yemeni question, the Charter called for the complete liberation of all South Yemen and the dismantling of British bases in South Yemen; for the overthrow of the sultanate system of government; and for the unity of South and North. On the economic level, the National Charter set forth a series of measures whereby the principles of independence and social justice would be embedded in the South Yemeni economic system. These included an enlarged public sector, the construction of a much-needed economic infrastructure, free education, the emancipation of women, economic planning and land reform and reclamation. On foreign policy issues the National Front declared its support for Arab unity, the liberation of Palestine, positive neutralism, and the struggle against imperialism and colonialism (National Charter, in National Front 1969, pp. 212–33).

It was at this Congress that divisions in the National Front—divisions that were to feature prominently in the evolution of the party and government after independence—were first manifested. Two wings emerged. The first, led by NF Secretary-General Qahtan al-Sha᾿abi (formerly of SAL), primarily consisted of those based outside South Yemen. This group was heavily influenced by Nasserism, and upheld social-democratic, Arab nationalist ideals. Initially it dominated the National Front's governing General Command.

The second wing within the party consisted primarily of NF cadres fighting inside the country, cadres whose ideological outlook had been radicalized by the experience of armed struggle and who had grown ever more distant from the formal leadership of the Front. Some had been influenced by contact with Aden's small Popular Democratic Union (communist party, founded in October 1961), or through links with the emerging Marxist faction within the Arab Nationalists' Movement; others experienced Marxism while working in East Asia. For most, however, their radicalization was less coherent—a dismay, perhaps, at the limited vision of the official leadership, or frustration with what ʿAbd al-Fattah Ismail (the Adeni guerrilla chief who led this wing) later described as the 'Arab chauvinism and petit-bourgeois reformism' of Nasserism (Le Monde, 29 May 1971, p. 5). In its place they turned to more radical variants of Arab socialism or Marxism—presaging, in many ways, the emergence of an Arab New Left throughout the region (Kazziha, 1975; Ismael, 1976).

At the first congress, the dispute between the General Command and the 'secondary' or 'internal' leadership of the party (so-called because of their exclusion from power and active involvement in the struggle inside South Yemen) surfaced in the debate over the National Charter. The latter pressed for a commitment to radical social transformation at independence; the former resisted any such commitment. In the end the General Command's agenda generally prevailed, despite the success of the internal leadership in getting a reference to revolutionary socialism formally included in the manifesto.

After the Congress tensions within the party declined somewhat, until they were brought to crisis level by another issue altogether: that of the National Front's relations with other nationalist organizations. As armed struggle had grown more powerful and popular in South Yemen, other groups had begun to see its use as essential to their own political survival—particularly in the wake of the collapse of British-sponsored constitutional talks and the announcement of a 1968 target date for independence. At the same time, Egypt (and particularly the Egyptian intelligence apparatus) lent its weight to the idea of unity among South Yemeni nationalist forces, partly because it thought such a move would increase the effectiveness of nationalist resistance, partly because it hoped that it would thereby consolidate its influence over the movement as a whole. The support which the National

Front enjoyed and the close ties it had with the Egyptians all became contingent on the National Front joining such a unified organization. In November, amid Egyptian threats to stop financial and military support for the Front, the NF held unification talks (under Egyptian auspices) in North Yemen. These culminated on 13 January 1966 when ʾAli al-Salami of the NF General Command announced that the National Front and the OLOS would merge to form a new organization, the *Jabhat Tahrir Janub al-Yaman al-Muhtal* or Front for the Liberation of Occupied South Yemen (FLOSY) (Hawatmeh, 1968, pp. 33–45).

It is no exaggeration to argue that the Egyptian-imposed unity exposed the deep divisions which existed within the ranks of the National Front and brought the organization to the point of rupture. Many of the Nasserites in the NF General Command supported the merger. Others in the external leadership saw the move as precipitate and potentially dangerous, and National Front Secretary-General Qahtan al-Shaʾabi almost immediately issued a statement condemning FLOSY and questioning al-Salami's authority. Because of this, he and Faysal ʾAbd al-Latif al-Shaʾabi (his cousin and close supporter within the NF leadership) were detained by the Egyptians in Cairo for a year and a half (National Front, 1969, pp. 64–5).

Among the internal leadership of the Front there was virtually unanimous opposition to unity with SAL and the PSP, and it soon became apparent that most of the military leadership of the National Front in the field and its underground cells had not been consulted seriously about the move. There was a strong ideological opposition to the programme and composition of FLOSY, and particularly to the participation in it of sultans, princes, sheikhs and members of the Adeni elite. Capitalizing on their opponents' dissaray, the leftist wing of the party convened a Second Congress of the National Front in January 1966. Here they denounced FLOSY and accused certain members of the Front's leadership (Salem Zayn, ʾAli al-Salami, Taha Ahmad Muqbel) of being co-opted by Egyptian Intelligence; Qahtan al-Shaʾabi was criticized for insufficient opposition to their activities. The leadership role of the General Command was suspended, and the party memberships of Qahtan al-Shaʾabi, Jaʾafar ʾAli Awadh, Salem Zayn, Taha Muqbel, ʾAli al-Salami, Saif al-Dhaliʾi, Faysal al-Shaʾabi and ʾAli al-Shaʾabi were frozen pending investigation by a special party committee (Hawatmeh, 1968, p. 45).

Subsequent events seemed to confirm the left's distrust of FLOSY. The appointment of Makkawi as FLOSY Secretary-General and al-Asnaj as head of its political bureau underscored the isolation of the National Front (and particularly its active cadres) within the new organization. As NF resistance to integration grew, Egyptian intelligence and FLOSY responded with mounting pressure. The Arab Nationalists' Movement and others close to the National Front were used in an effort to convince recalcitrant NF cadres of the value of the united organization (Habash, 1985, pp. 77–8, 97–100). When this failed FLOSY tried stronger methods, including the withholding of funds, the disarming of National Front members, bribing cadres, and assassination attempts against some underground NF activists (National Front, 1969, pp. 65–76). As a result of this combination of blandishments and threats the National Front leadership signed the 'Alexandria Agreement' of August 1966 upholding the FLOSY–NF merger.

Agreements signed in Egypt meant little if they could not be enforced among the National Front's fighting members, however. On 14 October 1966, the third anniversary of the Radfan Revolt, the underground National Front in South Yemen announced its withdrawal from FLOSY. The Third Congress of the National Front (held in Homr on 29 November 1966) upheld the withdrawal decision and called for the formation of a new party leadership. Some members of the previous leadership resigned from the party or had their membership frozen. They were replaced by representatives of the leftist wing: ʾAbd al-Fattah Ismail (leader of the guerrilla forces in Aden at the time); Mahmoud Ashish, Ahmad al-Shaʾer, ʾAli Salih ʿAyyad, ʾAli Salem al-Bidh, Faysal al-Attas (all trade-union activists); Muhammed Ahmad al-Bishi, Salem Rubayi ʾAli, and ʾAli Antar (Liberation Army) (Hawatmeh, 1968, pp. 45–6; for the text of the communiqué explaining the withdrawal see Murshed 1981, pp. 196–7).

The struggle between the National Front and FLOSY continued until independence in the form of a bloody civil war, the intensity of which grew with the imminence of the British withdrawal. Attempts to reach agreement between the two failed as NF cadres, scenting victory, ignored ceasefire calls issued by al-Shaʾabi. A number of factors contributed to the National Front's success over its rival. The National Front drew members from all over South Yemen. It could credibly claim to be an authentic South Yemeni movement, untainted by intrigues with Egypt, Saudi Arabia, or Britain. It had greater internal discipline. The NF Liberation Army had extensive combat experience; FLOSY had little, despite Egyptian attempts to create (and control) and elite military wing (the Popular Organization of Revolutionary Forces) within its ranks. Egypt's withdrawal from Yemen in the aftermath of the June 1967 Arab–Israeli war cut FLOSY off from its main source of supply during a critical period. Finally, the wavering Federal Army (whose recruits were drawn from NF powerbases in the hinterland) committed itself to the National Front at a decisive stage in the fighting in October 1967 (al-Habashi, 1968, pp. 587–94; Hawatmeh, 1968, pp. 58–61). Because of the evident control it exerted over most of South Yemen, it was with the National Front that Britain negotiated the final transfer of power at Geneva. On 30 November 1967 the People's Republic of South Yemen was formally created, with Qahtan al-Sha'abi serving as its first president and prime minister.

Post-Independence Developments

With the military defeat of the forces of FLOSY, the National Front established itself as the sole governing power in South Yemen. The General Command of the NF was then composed of twenty-one members who appointed Qahtan al-Sha'abi as President for two years. The General Command was the authority which outlined the main programme of the new state; it co-ordinated relations between the Front and the Army, and acted as the legislative authority at that time (Ahmad, 1968, p. 129).

The assumption of power did not mean, however, that a harmonious organization with a unified political programme had installed itself in power. We have already seen how the question of unity with FLOSY had brought major divisions within the National Front to the fore, and how the Third Congress at Homr in 1966 had served to formalize this split. At the Third Congress the leftist wing had demonstrated its superior support within party ranks. With independence, a new battle between the 'external' and 'internal' factions of the party emerged, this time over control of the formal apparatus of state (as opposed to party) power. The former group held the initial advantage, with Qahtan al-Sha'abi in post as President of the Republic. It was the latter group, however, which ultimately triumphed. After many months of conflict, al-Sha'abi (and his wing of the party) was forced from power on 22 June 1967—an event which has become known, in the argot of the Yemeni revolution, as the June 22 'Corrective Step'.

The question of how best to respond to the many pressing economic, social and political issues facing the nascent People's Republic of South Yemen provided the immediate battleground for the ideological dispute within party ranks. The moderates and conservatives led by al-Sha'abi and other prominent Yemenis stressed the importance of restoring the ailing economy to pre-independence levels through gradualist reforms. They opposed radical measures, and supported only limited land reform. The al-Sha'abi faction sought to acquire foreign aid from any and all sources, including the West; a conciliatory attitude towards even the reactionary Arab states (such as Saudi Arabia) was not too high a price to pay for much-needed development assistance. Because of this, the moderates were unwilling to support the Popular Front for the Liberation of Oman (PFLO), a National Front-like group which was fighting to overthrow the repressive government of Sultan Said bin Taimur in neighbouring Oman.

The leftists, led by party ideologist 'Abd al-Fatah Ismail and Salem Rubayi 'Ali ('Salimayn') of the Liberation Army (together with Sultan al-Omar, 'Ali Salih Abbad 'Muqbel', Abdullah al-Khamri and 'Ali Salem al-Bidh) subordinated all issues to the cause of social and political revolution in South Yemen. The service-orientated economy had to become independent and geared towards agricultural and industrial production. In the hinterland this required radical measures to break up the large landholdings of the sultans, to redistribute land among the peasants, and to establish collectives. In industry state-led planning and investment, and the nationalization of the foreign enterprises, was seen as crucial. In the foreign sphere the radicals favoured close association with the socialist bloc ('Abd al-Fattah Ismail favoured the Soviet camp, while Salem Rubayi 'Ali preferred the Chinese model). The radicals strongly supported the PFLO. On only a few practical and theoretical issues—the need to repress SAL and FLOSY, the importance of the public sector, the desirability of Yemeni unity, solidarity with the Arab revolution, and support for the Palestinian cause—could the left and right agree.

As the National Front's Fourth Congress (and its first since independence) approached, the two sides began jockeying for position. The leftists, because of their greater support among active party cadres, secured a majority on the Congress Preparatory Committee. In consequence, some of their opponents began to work towards convening the Congress independent of the Preparatory Committee, a move to which the Committee responded by publishing articles openly critical of the moderates in the party newspaper al-Thawri. This provoked the General Command to suspend the party membership of the Preparatory Committee until after the Congress (Hawatmeh, 1968, pp. 87–9; National Front, 1969, pp. 134–45).

When the Fourth Congress finally convened in Zinjibar on 2 March, the leftists platform was contained in a series of Preparatory Committee reports which later became known as the Barnmii Istikmal Marhalat al-Tahrur al-Watanniya al-Demuqrati (Programme for Completing the Stage of National Democratic Liberation, reproduced in National Front, 1969, pp. 245–93). The Programme recognized the presence of both a theoretical (or ideological) crisis and an organizational crisis within the National Front. These crises were manifest in a 'lack of centralist thinking', a lack of accountability among members and the expression of confusing and often contradictory ideological viewpoints within the various information organs of the party (14 Uktubar, al-Thawri, and al-Sharara). The Programme criticized rampant opportunism, individualism and tribalism within the NF. Finally, the Programme condemned the dual authority which prevailed within South Yemen—that of the State and the NF—and called for closer supervision of the former by the latter in accordance with a clearly developed ideology and programme. This, together with 'collective leadership' and 'effective participation of the productive social forces' were seen as vital necessities in the aftermath of liberation.

The opposition presented its critique of the left in a statement by 'Abd al-Malek Ismail of Qahtan al-Sha'abi's faction. The statement was entitled *Wiihat Nadhir Hawl al-Qadhiya fi Jadwal a'amal al-Mutamar* (A Viewpoint Concerning the Issues Submitted on the Agenda of the Congress). The document attacked the vagueness of the leftists' espousal of a 'non-capitalist' path of development. It condemned its opponents' insufficient consideration of the objective conditions in Yemen, conditions which made Yemen unready for socialism without a transitional stage of state capitalism. The document emphasized the absence of a proletariat class in Yemen which made it necessary to adopt gradualism in political action, to refrain from antagonizing the middle class, and to adopt a policy of 'positive neutralism'. The moderates defended the regular army (a successor to the pre-independence Federal Army) against the leftists, who labelled it a reactionary body. They also stressed that the State should be accepted by all as the state of the National Front (Hawatmeh, 1968, pp. 228–38).

Despite the moderates' critique—and a threat by al-Sha'abi to resign rather than accept the principle of collective leadership—the resolutions adopted by the Fourth Congress reflected a victory by 'Abd al-Fattah Ismail and the radical wing of the party. The Zinjibar resolutions (reproduced in National Front, 1969, pp. 237–41 and Hawatmeh, 1968, pp. 250–3) called for:

(1) developing the National Front into a political party based on the ideology of 'scientific socialism';
(2) opening the NF to other national democratic forces;
(3) reorganizing the NF;
(4) liberating the economy of South Yemen from the control and hegemony of foreign capital;
(5) purging the State structure and the army of all undesirable and reactionary elements;
(6) the election of a new forty-one member General Command to be the supreme authority in South Yemen, and to act as the legislative authority until a Supreme People's Council was established;
(7) land reform whereby the land belonging to sultans and ex-ministers under the British would be confiscated without compensation.

At this point, in the wake of the Fourth Congress, the army began to assume a pivotal role in South Yemeni politics. Even before the Congress, the leftists had entrenched themselves in Hadhramawt and had begun to initiate a programme of radical changes, including land confiscations, purges in the army, and the formation of a local supreme people's council. The protests of legal, Aden-appointed officials in the Eastern Governates about the leftists' activities were ignored, and in their weekly theoretical journal *al-Sharara* the radicals declared that 'making the socialist revolution means transforming existing social relations and installing revolutionary social relations, in other words destroying the old state apparatus and building an entirely new one in its place' (quoted in al-Ashtal, 1976, p. 276).

These measures prompted top army officers (notably Muhammed Ahmad Bali'id, Muhammed al-Sayyari and Ahmad 'Ali Zanjabila) to initiate a political campaign against the leftist group in the party. The officers singled out for attack as communists 'Abd al-Fattah Ismail (Minister of Culture at the time), 'Ali Salem al-Bidh (Minister of Defence), Sultan al-Omar, 'Ali Salih Abbad, Abdullah al-Khamri (chief of the State Security Court), and Hussein al-Jabri. The army officers called for the disbanding of the Liberation Army (the guerrilla forces during the war of national liberation), and the People's Guard (a popular revolutionary militia). On 27 January 1968, the officers submitted a memo to the General Command announcing their intention to assume sole responsibility for the army and its political organization. On 30 January a meeting of the General Command was held which resolved to purge the army. The resolution was never implemented, however, largely because of the objections of al-Sha'abi who saw in the regular army a potential power base from which to oppose the leftists (Hawatmeh, 1968, pp. 83–6).

Under these circumstances of mistrust, ideological differences and political posturing, a violent turn of events could not be too far off. The Fourth Congress resolutions had marked a political victory by 'Abd al-Fattah Ismail and other leftist leaders, underscoring their support among party cadres and in the ranks of the Liberation Army. Qahtan al-Sha'abi's faction, however, still controlled the formal reins of state power, and could count on the loyalty of much of the regular army. They were merely waiting for an opportune moment to strike back.

On 15 March 1968, a week after the end of the Fourth Congress, the General Command held its first meeting. The conflict between Ismail and al-Sha'abi dominated the proceedings: the latter simply refused to yield on the resolution relating to collective leadership, and stuck to his position that the President was the supreme authority in the State. On the question of land reform, Ismail insisted on implementing the land reform resolution of the Congress which called for confiscation without compensation of lands belonging to sultans, tribal chiefs and ex-ministers. Al-Sha'abi insisted on compensating landowners, and limiting landownership to 25 *feddans* (about 26 acres or 10.5 hectares) instead of the planned 5 *feddans* (Hawatmeh, 1968, pp. 108–12). On 19 March the local leadership of the National Front in Aden called for a political rally to support Ismail and the resolutions of the Congress. Al-Sha'abi and the army opposed the rally and threatened to disband it by force.

On 20 March, less than two weeks after the Fourth Congress, the army launched a coup against the radicals. A military communiqué was issued, stating that firm action was needed to save the country from communism. A campaign of arrests was put into effect. Many prominent members of the leftist faction (including 'Abd al-Fattah Ismail and six others from the General Command) were detained; others were arrested but later escaped from jail. Supporters of the imprisoned leaders responded almost immediately with public demonstations against the coup. In the Western region, the Liberation Army surrounded local regular army units. Elsewhere, some army units mutinied against their own commanding officers and joined in opposing the coup. South Yemen was on the verge of another civil war (Hawatmeh, 1968, pp. 113–21).

Although al-Sha'abi was doubtless pleased with the army's blow against the radicals, his support for the coup itself was only lukewarm. Consequently, the army began to back down, and finally reached agreement with the President that they would return to barracks on condition that there were no purges or reprisals against the officers responsible. For his part, al-Sha'abi subsequently described the coup as an 'individualist, sincere, but misguided effort'. He blamed 'extreme leftist policies' as the cause of South Yemen's political troubles (Hawatmeh, 1968, pp. 122–3).

By a vote of 6 out of 41 members of the General Command, the President obtained a mandate of 'absolute measures' to face the crisis for a period of one month. On 23 March he proclaimed a new land reform which set the limit of ownership at 25 *feddans*, and allowed compensation for confiscated property. On 23 March the rest of the imprisoned leftist leaders were released. Qahtan obtained a resolution to rule alone, starting from April 1968 (Hawatmeh, 1968, p. 124). On 15 May 1968 a coup was attempted against al-Sha'abi by some of the leftist faction; it was suppressed, and the organizers were forced to flee into the hinterland. Fighting followed, in which the army initially gained the upper hand (Hawatmeh, 1968, p. 129).

At this point a recurrent theme in Yemeni politics—tribalism—intervened.

The army split over tribal loyalties between Dathina tribes (al-Sha'abi's allies), and 'Aulaqi tribes' (sympathetic to the Saudis). The two army factions clashed in June 1968. Salem Rubayi 'Ali, the leader of the leftist rebel forces in the mountains, decided to move his forces in support of the President against the Saudi-sponsored army mutineers. The 'Aulaqi mutiny was soon crushed, and reconciliation between the two wings of the National Front (briefly) secured. Al-Sha'abi agreed to the appointment of political officers in the army and the strengthening of the militia. Ismail (who had been in Bulgaria for 'medical treatment') and other leftist leaders returned to Aden.

The interlude was precisely that, however, and new and old disputes soon (re)emerged. Again the underlying issue was that of the power of the presidency, and its relationship to the party. Although Qahtan had resigned as prime minister in April 1969 in favour of his cousin (and close ally) Faysal, the left continued to attack the President's tendency towards individual authoritarianism. Matters came to a head in the summer of 1969 when, following a disagreement between them, al-Sha'abi sought the resignation of Muhammed 'Ali Haytham, Minister of the Interior (and, like the President, from the Dathina tribe). This was opposed by the NF General Command who declared the dismissal of ministers to be its own prerogative. In response to this reassertion of party primacy the President issued a constitutional declaration granting himself wide powers, including the power to dismiss ministers. Haytham, Muhammed Salih Al-'Aulaqi (the new Minister of Defence) and other party moderates joined with the radicals in opposing al-Sha'abi's authoritarianism, thus undermining the President's remaining support bases in the army, party and among tribal elements. (The political value of al-Sha'abi's allies in the army command—already tarnished by their involvement with the British in the Federal Army—had already declined as growing evidence of their links with Saudi Arabia and other conservative groupings emerged.) At the same time, the left wing of the NF was increasingly successful in winning over junior army officers to their cause. They were now aided in this by Haytham's strong influence among soldiers from his home region (al-Safir, 13 July 1980, p. 14).

Finally, on 22 June 1969 the radicals moved against al-Sha'abi, supported by the bulk of the party, Liberation Army, militia, and army lower ranks. The President was forced to resign and then imprisoned. Many top army officers were purged, or fled to North Yemen where they found Saudi Arabia and other conservative regimes only too willing to support intrigues against the new People's Democratic Republic of Yemen. Inside South Yemen Salem Rubayi 'Ali became Chairman of the Presidential Council, the new body of collective leadership, and Assistant Secretary-General of the National Front.

'Abd al-Fattah Ismail was appointed Secretary-General of the Central Committee of the National Front, and Chairman of the Supremen People's Council. Haytham became Prime Minister; 'Ali Salem Al-Bidh occupied the post of Minister of Defence, while 'Ali Antar became Commander of the Army (Hawatmeh, 1968, pp. 123-9; al-Fattah, 1974, pp. 98-128; Omar, 1970, pp. 262-74; Sultan, 1979, p. 99).

From Liberation Movement to Socialist Vanguard: The Role and Structure of the Party in the PDRY

Although the party apparatus (won over in 1966) and the state apparatus (seized on 22 June 1969) were now firmly under their control, the leftist wing of the National Front could not immediately embark on the socialist transformation of South Yemeni society. Quite apart from the objective obstacles to such a task—tribalism, underdevelopment, hostile neighbours and recurrent threats to internal security—the party had not yet developed the ideology, organization and trained cadres necessary for the task. In the decade following the June 22 Corrective Step the National Front thus underwent a structural transformation of its own, with the aim of rendering the organization ready and able to act as the socialist vanguard of the Yemeni masses.

The first difficulty to be addressed was the immaturity of the National Front's revolutionary ideology, an ideology which (in its social and economic dimensions) has largely been constructed as a critique rather than as a coherent program of action. As 'Abd al-Fattah Ismail later noted (Hassan, 1974, p. 11):

The National Front was a petit bourgeois political organization which had begun to develop into a democratic and revolutionary organization. However . . . political and ideological maturity was limited to a small number of its members. The political organization [of the National Front] was to lead the people and the state. But how? There was no solid conviction within a common background.

In an effort to increase the level of ideological awareness and sophistication within party ranks, study and vigorous self-criticism were promoted among National Front cadres (*Le Monde*, 30 May 1972, p. 4). In 1971 a Higher School of Scientific Socialism was established to provide advanced ideological and organizational training, graduating some 3,000 party cadres by the early 1980s (Vasileva, 1980; Halliday, 1983, p. 58). Others were sent abroad (primarily to the Soviet Union and Eastern Europe) for this training. Party officials began to monitor and guide all aspects of government in the country.

Under the State Constitution of 1970 the National Front was formally recognized as the country's leading political organization (article 7).

The changes taking place within the National Front were institutionalized at its Fifth Congress in March 1972. New by-laws were adopted for the party. These set forth the basic principles of the National Front: the adoption of scientific socialism (which has in practice meant a sort of eclectic Marxism), and the struggle against imperialism, Zionism and reaction (article 1). Articles 2 to 4 respectively entrenched three important organizational principles within the party: democratic centralism, collective leadership, and the purge ('purging counter-revolutionary and decadent forces being essential for the organization to continue and to develop') (National Front, 1972, pp. 107–9). The old structure of the party, with its 'General Command' and other Arab nationalist trappings, was replaced by a new centralist structure based on the communist model (Figure 2.2).

The political programme adopted by the Fifth Congress established the basis of democratic national authority in the unity of the legislative and executive branches of government, co-ordination of the activities of those branches, and the adoption of planning as the way to develop Yemen. The programme advocated the policy of struggle against imperialism, colonialism, and the unity of Arab democratic forces, nuclear disarmament, and declared its support for the unity of the socialist camp as the natural ally of

Figure 2.2 Organizational structure of the National Front, 1972

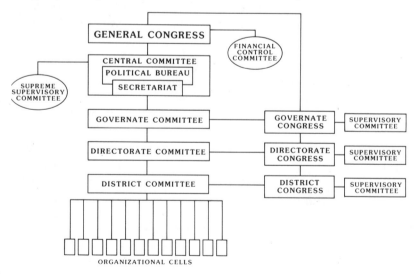

South Yemen (National Front, 1972, pp. 37–104). A new popular militia and popular defence committees (discussed in Chapter 3) were formed to defend the Yemeni revolution and encourage popular participation in it.

National Front General Secretary Ismail noted the changing role and task of the party in his speech to the Congress (cited in al-Ashtal, 1973, p. 278):

> The National Front is changing its status from being a mass organization destroying everything set up by the feudalists and colonial regimes and leading the broad masses through the national liberation stage into being a leading force in society directly responsible for authority, and drawing up programmes for the broad masses.

In other words, the measures adopted at the Fifth Congress—the reorganization of the party, the drawing up of a new political programme—were meant to signify the National Front's readiness to embark on the 'national democratic stage of the revolution'. In this stage the political preconditions for South Yemen's continued progress would be established, and the National Front itself would be prepared for its final evolution into a *bona fide* vanguard party. In the years which followed, the NF closely examined the revolutionary and party structure of other countries, paying particular attention to the Soviet, Cuban, Chinese and Algerian models.

The party moved a step closer to its goals in 1975. Following a Unity Agreement (February) and the NF Sixth Congress (March), the National Front formally joined the Popular Democratic Union (led by Abdallah Ba-Dhib, then Minister of Culture) and the Vanguard Party (led by the Minister of Communications, Anis Hassan Yahya) in forming a single transitional organization, the Unified Political Organization of the National Front (*al-Tandhim a-Siyasi al-Muwahad: al-Jabhah al-Qawiyyah*). Article 1 of the Constitution of the UPONF adopted at the Unification Congress (11–13 October 1975) described the organization as the 'political vanguard of the toiling masses' of the PDRY, 'guided in its work by scientific socialism' (UPONF, 1975a; UPONF, 1975b, p. 5). According to the Programme adopted at the same time, the UPONF marked a 'transitional stage towards the establishment of national democratic alliances' (UPONF, 1974c, p. 14). During this transitional stage true ideological understanding would arise alongside the spontaneity and experimentation of revolutionary action, and a party and leadership would be developed which would truly constitute a vanguard for the Yemeni people (UPONF, 1975c, p. 15). The organization adopted for the National Front at the Fifth Congress was essentially retained, the major structural change within the party being the formal integration of the PDU and vanguard parties within its ranks.

The transitional form of the UPONF continued for three years until, on 11

October 1978, the National Front was at last transcended by the desired vanguard party, the Yemeni Socialist Party (*al-Hizb al-Ishtiraki al-Yamani*). Although the basic organizational structure and leadership of the NF/ UPONF remained essentially unchanged, the new party title (as well as the Programme and Constitution adopted at the First YSP Congress in October 1978) signified the National Front's coming-of-age—a recognition and affirmation by party leaders and cadres alike that the organization was now ready to fulfill the leading role in South Yemen that it had achieved at independence in 1967. According to YSP Secretary-General 'Abd al-Fattah Ismail:

> The Yemeni Socialist Party is the vanguard of the Yemeni working class aligned with the peasants and other working segments of the population and revolutionary intellectuals. It is the living expression of this class consciousness—a consciousness of its real interests, future, and historic role. The aim of the Party is to transform the society in a revolutionary manner to consolidate the achievements of the national democratic revolution and the transition to socialism. [This transition] is guided by ... the theory of scientific socialism which takes into account local conditions of growth and the development of the national democratic revolution in our country [*al-Hadaf*, 29 October 1978, p. 6.]

In the contemporary Yemeni Socialist Party power emanates from the leadership along typical democratic centralist lines, though there is provision for lower-echelon cadres to criticize the party leadership within certain bounds. The General Congress is the supreme authority of the YSP, but on average it convenes for only three days every two to five years. At this time it elects the party Secretary-General, the Central Committee and the Politburo. It is the YSP Central Committee which runs the party between

Table 2.1 Party leadership, 1963–1986

NF Secretary-General	
Qahtan al-Sha'abi	1963–1969
'Abd al-Fattah Ismail	1969–1975
UPONF Secretary-General	
'Abd al-Fattah Ismail	1975–1978
YSP Secretary-General	
'Abd al-Fattah Ismail	1978–1980
'Ali Nasser Muhammed	1980–1986
'Ali Salem al-Bidh	1986–

congresses, meeting one or more times per year in plenary session. The Central Committee is the most powerful leadership institution in the party. The most powerful and important members of the Central Committee participate in the Committee's Politburo, headed by the party Secretary-General. It is the Politburo which makes immediate political decisions on behalf of the Central Committee. It is accountable to the Central Committee, however, and when the Congress is not in session (i.e. most of the time) it is the Central Committee which is the ultimate arbiter to which disputes and dilemmas are referred. On two occasions the Central Committee has ordered the removal of the President of the Republic (Salem Rubayi 'Ali in June 1975, 'Ali Nasser Muhammed in February 1986). The Central Committee also includes an Executive Committee (less powerful than the Politburo, despite its name), a Secretariat (which administers party business), an information committee, and an appeals committee. Prior to the YSP Third Congress (October 1985) which enlarged the leadership bodies of the party to include some of 'Ali Nasser Muhammed's leading opponents, the Central Committee consisted of forty-seven full and eleven candidate members. Its subcommittees were composed as follows: Executive Committee (eight full and three candidate), Politburo (seven), Appeals Committee (six), information Committee (ten), and Secretariat (five). It is this latter body, the Secretariat, which administers the party bureaucracy and oversees the activities of lower-level party and mass organizations. The Central Committee also includes the Secretaries of the six governate-level party organizations. The structure of the YSP Central Committee is shown graphically in Figure 2.3.

While the powers of the Central Committee in general and the Politburo in particular are immense, it should not be thought that YSP Congresses are

Figure 2.3 Organization of the YSP Central Committee, 1985

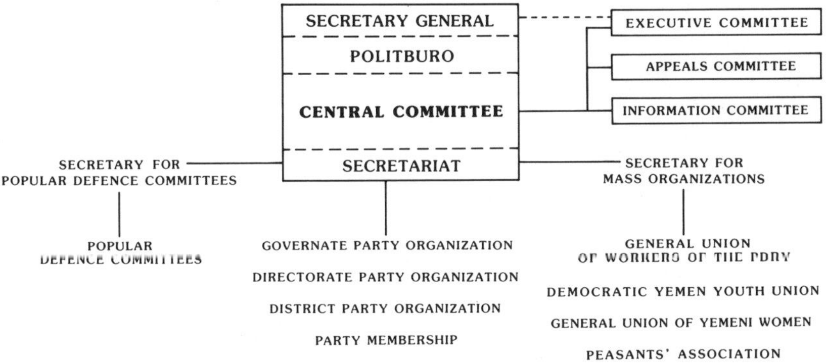

a mere rubber stamp of decisions taken at a higher level. Real political competition and policy debate can occur within Congresses, a fact evident at both the 1980 Extraordinary Congress (which demoted 'Abd al-Fattah Ismail) and the 1985 Third YSP Congress (which re-established his position and those of his party allies in the YSP leadership).

The YSP operates party cells throughout the country on a regional (town, district, governate) and economic (factory, collective or co-operative) basis. It also operates cells in the armed forces, youth and women's organizations, and trade unions. Most recruitment occurs through these mass organizations, and especially through the Democratic Yemen Youth Union. Everyone up to the age of 28 joins the party exclusively through the Union. Applicants must demonstrate literacy, as well as suitable commitment and ideological outlook. Once confirmed by the local Central Committee, members will serve a two-year probationary period before qualifying for full membership (subject again to approval by the local party Central Committee).

Reliable figures for total party membership are difficult to come by. One frequently-cited source suggests a total of 26,000 in 1977 (Naumkin, 1978, p. 66), or about 3.5 per cent of the adult population (Halliday, 1983, p. 69). Workers and peasants were said to account for 12 and 4.8 per cent of this total respectively. More recent and detailed figures for the Third Governate only

Table 2.2 YSP Membership by Occupation (Third Governate, 1982)

Occupation	% of party members
Office employees	36.0
Workers*	26.0
Peasants†	14.6
Military	12.3
Students	5.0
Independent householders	2.9
Intellectuals	2.0
Bedouin	1.0
Fishermen‡	0.9
Housewives	0.3

* Category includes agricultural workers on state farms.
† First-stage co-operative and non-cooperative peasants—12.9%. Second- and third-stage co-operative peasants—1.7%.
‡ Co-operative fishermen—0.5%. Independent fishermen—0.4%.

provide a more detailed view of the occupational backgrounds of typical party members (see Table 2.2.)

One notable feature of these figures is the relatively low proportions of workers in party ranks. Even in urban areas, such as Aden's industrial al-Sha'ab district, workers comprise a minority of members—400 out of 950, with the remainder being students and white-collar employees. A number of factors are responsible for this, the most important being the low proportion of workers in South Yemen as a whole, the high rate of working–class illiteracy, and the political evolution of the party. In the latter case, YSP officials admit that rivalries between the National Front and the urban-based PSP before independence, and political infighting in the party leadership after independence, have had a negative impact on party recruitment (Rybakov, 1982, p. 44).

The low proportion of the vanguard class in the PDRY's vanguard party has been a matter of concern for some time (Ismail in *al-Hurriyah*, 23 October 1978, pp. 20–1). In January 1981, following the YSP's 1980 Extraordinary Congress, the party Central Committee called for a general membership campaign with particular emphasis on recruiting workers (Muhammed, 1981, p. 26). In order to increase the rate of worker participation in the party the probationary period for prospective working-class YSP members has been set at one rather than two years.

What little evidence is available suggests that the campaign has met with significant but not overwhelming success. In Ghail Bawazir District of the Fifth Governate (which includes the city of al-Mukalla), for example, the YSP now boasts a party membership of 1,000 (out of a total population of 125,000), of whom 34 per cent were workers (Rybakov, 1982, p. 48). The overall increase in YSP members as a result of the membership drive has most likely been in the 10–20 per cent range.

3 The Political System II: Government and Politics

Constitutional and Government Structure

The present formal political structure of the People's Democratic Republic of Yemen is set forth in detail in the State Constitution of the Republic. This constitution was drafted by leading party and government members (particularly 'Abd al-Fattah Ismail), with technical assistance from both Egyptian and East German experts. It was promulgated on 30 November 1970, on the third anniversary of independence and some seventeen months after the June 22 Corrective Step. Minor constitutional ammendments were later made in 1978 to allow for the replacement of the National Front by the Yemeni Socialist Party, and these were duly approved by the Supreme People's Council on 31 October 1978.

The Constitution consists of six parts:

Part I: Foundations of the National Democratic Social System and the System of State (three chapters, articles 1–32).
Part II: Citizens and Their Organizations (two chapters, articles 33–61).
Part III: Organization of State Authority (four chapters, articles 62–115).
Part IV: Democratic Law and Justice (one chapter, articles 116–24).
Part V: National Defence and Security (one chapter, articles 125–30).
Part VI: Interim and Final Orders (one chapter, articles 131–5).

Chapter 1, Part I sets forth the political foundation of the State. It contains three important themes. First, it declares the PDRY's commitment to Yemeni unity (articles 1, 12), to the struggle against imperialism, colonialism and 'local reactionary feudalism' (article 13), and to the 'complete elimination of exploitation of man by man' (article 8). Second, it declares that the State is based on a class alliance between the working class, farmers, the intelligentsia, and the *petit bourgeoisie*, ultimately led by the workers (article 7). Third, this alliance is expressed through the agency of the National Front (now the YSP), which 'on the basis of scientific socialism lead political activity of the public and public organizations in order to develop the society in a manner which achieves national democratic revolution following a non-capitalist course' (article 7). The public participates in this through elections to local People's Councils or the Supreme People's Council (articles 9–10).

Chapter 2 specifies the economic foundations of the State. The State is mandated to 'develop the national economy' and 'ensure a fair distribution of the fruits of society between its citizens' in accordance with the principle of social justice (article 14). Thus, while the right to private property is guaranteed (article 18), it is not unconditional.

The articles contained in this chapter envisage a biased, mixed-market economy—'market' in the sense that the broad right to own and transfer property continues, 'mixed' in the sense that government spending and planning predominates, but is not universal; 'biased' in the sense that the bounds of property ownership are limited by the principle of public welfare (article 18, clause 2). Elsewhere in this chapter, the Constitution upholds the nationalization of foreign companies and the redistribution of land in accordance with the Agrarian Reform Law of 1970 (article 15, 19). The State is granted a monopoly over foreign trade (article 21). Economic development occurs under the aegis of a development plan prepared by the State, which has the force of an overriding law (article 17).

Chapter 3 of Part I commits the State to developing its citizens through education, promotion of the sciences, arts, and culture, and protection of the family and South Yemen's 'Arab and Islamic legacy'. (Later, in article 46, Islam is recognized as the state religion.) Particular emphasis is placed on combatting the 'corrupt concepts' spread by colonialism and tribalism (article 31).

Part 2 addresses the rights and duties of both the public and of mass organizations. All citizens enjoy formal equality. The list of formal rights granted to them is impressive: work, education (also a duty), personal freedom, court trial, nationality, sanctity of home, secrecy of communication, freedom of religion and of artistic, literary and cultural expression; the right to assemble 'within the spirit of the constitution'; medical care; freedom of movement within the boundaries of the State. Duties comprise the defence of the domestic order and of the Republic's frontiers, public service, and the payment of income tax. Under article 55 the government is given the right to grant asylum to those struggling for national and social liberation abroad. In the past this has often been invoked in granting shelter to Palestinian guerrilla groups and other liberation movements. Chapter 2 defines the purpose and legal status of trade unions, women's and youth organizations, and agricultural co-operatives.

Legislative and Executive Authority

The formal political organization of the State is dealt with in Part III of the Constitution. Chapter 1 outlines the structure and role of the People's

Supreme Council (PSC), the formal State legislative body and source of sovereign authority. It consists of 101 members elected triennially through general, equal, and direct elections in the governates. The electorate may, by petition, demand the recall of their members. In 1978 an eleven-person Presidium was added to the PSC, bringing its total membership to 111. The chairman of the Presidium (the President) is the formal Head of State.

The PSC issues legislation covering the whole range of state business. It debates and establishes guidelines for the Council of Ministers in foreign and domestic policy. It must ratify foreign treaties, the national development plan, and the annual state budget. Finally, the People's Supreme Council elects from its ranks all members of the Presidium (formerly the Presidential Council) and a majority of the members of the Council of Ministers. The Prime Minister must himself be a member of the PSC, to which he is accountable through a vote of confidence.

The senior executive of the People's Supreme Council until 1978, the Presidential Council, was established under Chapter 2 of the Constitution. It consisted of at least three and not more than six members. (In practice its membership usually embraced the President, who acts as its chairperson, the Prime Minister, and the Secretary-General of the party.) It was this body which was responsible for actually executing state policy and overseeing the

Table 3.1 State Leadership, 1969–1986

June 1969– August 1971	Salem Rubayi Ali (President) Muhammed Ali Haytham (Prime Minister)
August 1971– June 1978	Salem Rubayi Ali (President) Ali Nasser Muhammed (Prime Minister).
June 1978– April 1980	'Abd al-Fattah Ismail (President) 'Ali Nasser Muhammed (Prime Minister)
April 1980– February 1985	'Ali Nasser Muhammed (President) (Prime Minister)
February 1985– January 1986	'Ali Nasser Muhammed (President) Haidar Abu-Bakr al-Attas (Prime Minister)
February 1986–	Haidar Abu-Bakr al-Attas (President) Yaseen Saeed Numan (Prime Minister)

work of government. Unlike the PSC, its powers were concrete, specific, sweeping and real. Article 92 of the 1970 Constitution charged it with:

(1) representing the Republic at home and abroad;
(2) fixing dates for PSC and local People's Council elections;
(3) nominating the Prime Minister and Cabinet;
(4) appointing members of the Supreme Council for National Defence;
(5) proposing draft legislation (although most legislation in fact originates with the PSC, and in particular with the Council of Ministers);
(6) promulgating laws passed by the PSC;
(7) appointing and discharging leading state officials;
(8) appointing and discharging leaders of the armed forces;
(9) appointing and discharging Supreme Court judges and the Attorney-General;
(10) awarding decorations;
(11) approving treaties not requiring ratification by the PSC;
(12) appointing and discharging the Republic's diplomatic representatives;
(13) accrediting representatives from foreign governments;
(14) granting amnesty;
(15) granting asylum;
(16) declaring a state of emergency and general mobilization;
(17) declaring a state of national defence.

The Presidential Council was the real focus of power in the PDRY. The Council was expected (although not required) to present its views on foreign and domestic policy to the PSC, and to periodically ask the Prime Minister for reports on specific programmes. The Council also initiated debates in the PSC and proposed legislation on specific matters.

In 1978 the Presidential Council was abolished, and replaced by the Presidium of the Supreme People's Council. The Presidium consists of a Chairman, a Deputy Chairman, and a Secretary, with a total membership of eleven. The Chairman of the Presidium is the Head of State of the PDRY and President of the Republic.

The Presidium, as an institution, has never wielded the executive power held by its predecessor. Rather, state power has shifted to the President and PDRY Council of Ministers. The Council of Ministers, established under Chapter 3 of the 1970 State Constitution, consists of the Prime Minister and the various Cabinet ministers (article 101). It is now the highest administrative and executive body of the state. Each minister is separately responsible for his/her department to the Prime Minister, and the Council as a whole is responsible to the PSC (article 102). Under Article 103 the Council of Ministers is charged with:

(1) proposing the broad lines of government policy;
(2) submitting draft legislation to the PSC;
(3) preparing and executing the state economic plan and national budget;
(4) appointing members of the Supreme Council for National Planning;
(5) auditing the final accounts of the state;
(6) approving the form of treaties and agreements before submitting them to the PSC and Presidential Council;
(7) safeguarding internal and external security;
(8) directing, co-ordinating and supervising government departments;
(9) appointing, discharging and punishing leading State officials.

The content and distribution of portfolios in a typical Council of Ministers is shown in Table 3.2.

In addition to the major institutions of legislative and executive authority discussed above, a system of functional Supreme Councils has grown up since the 1970s. Two of these (the Supreme Planning Council and the Supreme Council for National Defence) are mandated under the Constitution (article 103; 128) to deal with development planning and national security planning

Figure 3.1   National government structure, PDRY

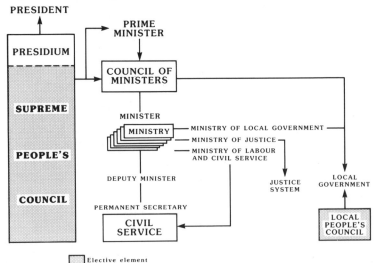

respectively. Other Councils established include the Supreme National Council (which dealt with local government) and the Supreme Supply Council (FAS, 1977, p. 102), both apparently abolished in 1978. The Supreme Councils have generally acted as supervisory and co-ordinating bodies in a given area, with membership drawn from among the ministers and senior officials of relevant departments, the Presidium, experts and party officials. Local versions of the Councils have also been established in some cases at the governate level.

As might be expected in a country as poor, illiterate and inaccessible as South Yemen, the operationalization of the formal government structure envisaged in the Constitution has taken some time. Lacking a comprehensive census of the country, the first members of the SPC were nominated. Elections from a selection of candidates were held in 1978, both directly (eighty-six seats) and indirectly via mass organizations. Most of those elected were drawn from the YSP but about forty were elected from outside party ranks. By-elections for the SPC were held in June 1981, with the government reporting that some 771,763 people (or 94.6 per cent of the eligible electorate) had voted.

The present government of the PDRY was established in the aftermath of the overthrow of President ʾAli Nasser Muhammed in February 1986. Following a series of meetings by the YSP Central Committee and Politburo, interim Head of State Haidar Abu-Bakr al-Attas was confirmed as President and a new eighteen-member Council of Ministers established, headed by Prime Minister Yaseen Said Numan.

Civil Service

The government structure described above would mean little in the absence of an organized civil service through which government policies could be carried out, and in fact this was precisely the situation that existed in South Yemen at independence, when the British and Indian colonial officials who occupied the bulk of middle and upper-ranking government administrative positions left the country. Still others left after the 22 June 1969 Corrective Step. This, and the general lack of educated cadres in the country, left South Yemen devoid of experienced administrators. Moreover, many of the civil servants who remained were corrupt or politically unreliable, having served as part of the British colonial administration. Since the education necessary to join the colonial service had only been available to the rich before 1967, most civil servants were of elite backgrounds and could hardly be expected to commit themselves to the objectives of the new revolutionary government. To deal with this situation (and to make best use of what few cadres were

Table 3.2 Government of the PDRY, February 1986

Head of State	President Haidar Abu-Bakr al-Attas
Prime Minister	Yaseen Said Numan
Labour & Civil Service	
Deputy Prime Minister	Salih Montasser al-Siyali
Interior	
Deputy Prime Minister	Salih Abu-Bakr Bin Hussainoun
Minerals & Energy	
Defence	Salih Obeid Ahmad
Foreign Affairs	'Abd al-Aziz al-Dhali
State Security	Said Salih Salem
Finance	Mahmoud Said Mahdi
Planning	Faraj Bin Ghanem
Housing & Construction	Muhammed Ahmad Salman
Industry, Trade & Supply	Abdullah Muhammed Othman
Communications	Salih Abdullah Muthanna
Fisheries	Othman 'Abd al-Jabbar Rashid
Justice & *Waqfs*	'Abd al-Wasei Abd al-Salem
Agriculture & Agrarian Reform	Ahmad Ali Muqbel
Culture & Information	Muhammed Ahmad Garhoum
Education	Salem Ba-Salem
Health	Said Sharaf
Minister of State for Unity Affairs	Rashid Muhammed Thabit

available), central control over allocation, reallocation, training and promotion was placed in the hands of the Ministry of Labour (later the Ministry of Labour and Civil Service). The civil service was thoroughly purged. Special management and training institutes were established, including the Institute of Statistical Training (1970), the College for Economic and Management Studies (1974), and Aden University (1975). Others were sent abroad for training in Arab countries or Eastern Europe. Throughout this process great efforts were made to assure the growth of an effective and reliable civil service. The principles of hiring by qualification (primarily educational achievement) and promotion by merit were adopted by the Ministry of Labour and Civil Service, the agency responsible for all civil service employment. In order to prevent the emergence of a privileged class of state administrators, civil servants are paid at the same rates, and enjoy the same benefits, as other employees. Special supervisory committees have been established in all ministries to ensure that financial irregularities do not occur. A Central Board of Audit, responsible solely to the Prime Minister, was formed in 1972 to provide further financial safeguards. The penalties for wrongdoing in government service are severe (Halliday, 1983, p. 51).

These and other similar measures have been quite successful in building for the PDRY a relatively efficient government bureaucracy. By 1977 the number of people employed by central government had grown to 32,183, more than twice the 13,274 employed in 1970. Of these, some 14 per cent were unskilled workers, 48 per cent clerical and skilled workers, and 38 per cent managers and executives (World Bank, 1979, p. 71). At the head of the civil service are Cabinet ministers, and beneath them one or more politically-appointed deputy ministers. There is also in each ministry at least one permanent secretary, who remains with a department and hence provides continuity despite changing ministerial leadership. Senior bureaucrats are said to be devoted and well motivated. According to a World Bank study team (1979, p. 72), however, the commitment to work declines at lower levels. (The government is trying to deal with this through incentive bonuses.) In contrast to many other developing countries, bureaucratic corruption is rare. The greatest problem remains the shortage of trained staff, a shortage which is acute at senior levels. Another problem has been the inflexibility of government operations introduced by centralized administration and control of government operations. In many cases (such as education) policy implementation has been devolved to governate level in an attempt to counteract this problem.

The Judicial System

Prior to independence, the legal system of South Yemen was a small, colonial-designed one largely limited to Aden and its environs. The entire system had a clear political bias: court proceedings took place in English, and legal personnel were largely drawn from the (European and Indian) colonial elite. Outside Aden, tribal 'urf and Islamic shari'ah legal systems predominated.

Little legal reform occured in the years immediately following independence, other than court proceedings now took place in Arabic and appeals to the (British) Court of Appeal for East Africa and the Privy Council were ended. After the June 22 Corrective Step, however, a major revision of the legal/judicial system was undertaken by the revolutionary government. The judiciary was purged and work was initiated on a new legal structure (PDRY, 1977a, pp. 72-4).

As a first step, People's Courts and land reform tribunals were established in the early 1970s alongside the nascent socialist system of justice. These courts were intended to facilitate popular participation in the legal system and to dispense revolutionary justice, such as the confiscation and redistribution of large landholdings, or legal proceedings of a local, political, or security nature. Certainly the justice administered by them could be characterized as haphazard and even brutal, but they nevertheless served an important purpose at a time when the central judicial system had not yet been established. The need for People's Courts diminished as the regime consolidated its position and a new judicial system emerged, and they were consequently abolished in 1979.

Responsibility for overseeing the development and operation of a new judicial system in the PDRY was given under the 1970 Constitution to the Minister of Justice, who was also empowered to establish courts for special purposes such as military and arbitration tribunals. The Minister of Justice appoints the Attorney-General (article 118). Three levels of court were established: a Supreme Court, based in Aden; governate courts, in each of the country's governates; and local magistrates' courts. The magistrates' courts deal with minor criminal, traffic, and by-law offences, family matters and civil disputes involving less than YD1,000 in local areas. The governate courts deal with serious crime (murder, manslaughter, rape and gross indecency, arson, sabotage, etc.) inheritances, larger civil cases, appeals from magistrates' courts, and other matters referred to them by the Attorney General. The Supreme Court deals with constitutional matters, and is the final court of appeal in the PDRY. By 1980 some ninety courts at various levels existed within the PDRY (PDRY, 1977a; *al-Madinah*, 20 July 1980, p. 19; Shamiry, 1985). A Secretary of Justice in each lower-level court monitors the judicial process on behalf of the Ministry.

Parallel with this restructuring of the judicial system, the basis of a new legal system was being established, drawing upon appropriate tribal, Islamic and Crown Colony law as well as revolutionary legislation. A Public Prosecution Law was promulgated in 1973, a Personal Status (Family) Law in 1974, a Penal Code in 1976, and a Civil Code (consisting of some 1,930 sections) in 1983. Equality before the law, presumption of innocence, the right to legal defence and a fair and public hearing, and freedom from arbitrary arrest and detention were formally guaranteed (United Nations, 1981). In order to deal with a severe shortage of trained legal personnel, an Institute for Legal Studies was established in 1972, and a training school for judges the following year. In 1978 a Faculty of Law was opened at the University of Aden. In order to guarantee that the benefits of the South Yemen's new legal system would be extended to all, an enlarged legal aid programme was instituted in 1977.

Despite the abolition of the People's Courts in 1979, popular participation has remained an important theme in the judicial system of the PDRY. In 1977 voluntary judicial bodies known as 'Social Justice Organizations' were set up to deal with petty offences and minor domestic disputes in residential neighbourhoods. At present these only exist in Aden and Abyan governates. Mass organizations have been brought into the legal process too. People awaiting trial may now be released into the custody of mass organizations, which also have the right to representation in the trial process itself (Shamiry, 1984).

Local Government

Since 1968 South Yemen has been divided into a number of governates (six since March 1980) for the purpose of local government. These in turn are divided into directorates and subdivided into districts. Local government boundaries have been deliberately designed to cross-cut tribal boundaries, thus weakening tribal identities. Also, the governates were to be known by number only, in another effort to weaken the geographic dimension of tribalism. Eventually in 1980 the Supreme People's Council changed this policy and gave formal names to the governates, in a more realistic appraisal of tribalism's power and the best ways of combating it (Halliday, 1983, p. 50). (The size and population of the current governates of the PDRY are given in Chapter 1.) Approximately 3,000 people are employed in local government (1977).

Two (often contradictory) principles underlie local government. The first of these is centralization, a principle enshrined in Chapter 4 of the Constitution. In an effort to maintain central government control over outlying areas and to promote national integration, a pyramidal power structure has been implemented. Within each governate an Aden-appointed governor holds central authority; commissioners and assistant commissioners administer the directorates and districts respectively. The governor retains final authority over the smaller units, while local government as a whole is supervised by the Council of Ministers under the authority of Article 104 of the Constitution. From 1976 until 1978 responsibility for this was assumed by a Supreme National Council, chaired by the Minister of Local Administration (FAS, 1977, pp. 103-5; PDRY, c1981, pp. 26-7). In January 1978, however, the Ministry (and possibly the Council) were abolished, and control over local government was placed in the hands of the newly-created General Department for the Administration of Local Government, headed by a director who was appointed by and responsible to the Council of Ministers. This Department was upgraded to a Ministry of Local Government by presidential decree in May 1981. The ministry disappeared, however, in the Cabinet reorganization which followed the downfall of 'Ali Nasser Muhammed in February 1986, and the present status of local government administration at the ministerial level is unclear.

The second principle constitutionally mandated in local administration is that of popular democracy. Under Article 114 the establishment of local People's Councils was called for. The power and responsibilities of these bodies are vague. Nevertheless, in 1976–7 local elections were held for them, first in the Fifth Governate in the summer of 1976 and then in the rest of the country the following year. Some 204 members were elected, twenty-one of them women. Local executive bureaux were then selected by decree of the Council of Ministers on the recommendation of local Councils. These bureaux were charged with preparing the local budget and supervising local administration under the scrutiny of the local People's Council (FAS, 1977, pp. 105–6). Further local elections were held in eighty-six constituencies in June 1981.

In practice, 'democratic centralization' has proved to be an uneasy mix, and it has generally been the latter element (centralization) which has won out. Local People's Councils seem to have little real power, which rests in the hands of centrally-appointed (and supervised) administrators. The possibility that democratic autonomous local government bodies could be used to build up an independent power base within the country has only increased the tendency towards centralization. There is, of course, a major precedent for

Figure 3.2 Local Government Structure, PDRY

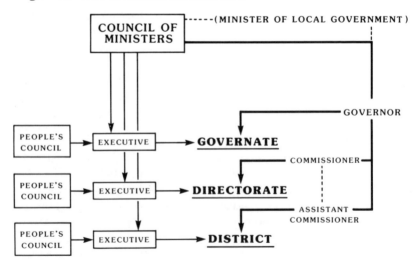

this fear: the radical wing of the NF did, after all, first build up its power in Hadhramawt in the period 1967-9. More recently, the late 1970s saw Ja'im Salih (a Salem Rubayi 'Ali supporter) build up a considerable political fief in the Third Governate through his positions on local councils and in the local party Politburo (*14 Uktubar*, 18-20 July 1978). Salih was toppled (and executed) in June 1978 during the overthrow of Rubayi 'Ali, but the lesson remains.

Party-State Relations

In theory, the Yemeni Socialist Party serves as the political vanguard of the Yemeni people, formulating revolutionary policies which are then implemented by the state. This relationship has been borne out in practice, with Five (and Three) Year Plans, proposed legal codes, and major foreign and domestic policy decisions all being approved (if not formulated) by the YSP Central Committee or Politburo long before being passed on the PSC for legislation and the Council of Ministers for implementation. As in many other Marxist regimes, the close integration of the state and party mechanisms in the PDRY, and the subordination of the former to the latter in all major policy matters, is fostered and maintained through a variety of organizational mechanisms.

First, the leading role of the party is enshrined in the state *Constitution*. This provides a legal basis for party supremacy. Second, there exists substantial *overlapping of party/state membership*. All government ministers and senior bureaucrats are party members, as are many junior civil servants and military ranks. Typically, the most senior ministers (Prime Minister, Deputy Prime Minister, Minister of Defence) and the State President are members of the YSP Politburo, while other ministers, important deputy ministers and governors are members of the party Central Committee. Until its abolition in 1978, the party Secretary-General usually sat on the Presidential Council. A majority of the People's Supreme Council are party members, as are most civil servants and military officers. The principle of *representation* —that is, the involvement of YSP officials at all levels of state decision-making—is applied throughout, from government ministries and departments to local production councils at the workplace. Moreover, even where party members constitute a minority (as they did in the first, appointed, People's Supreme Council), the *positioning* of these members in leadership positions or on key committees guarantees party control (Hudson, 1977, p. 361).

A third mechanism of party primacy has been evident in the *monitoring* and *control* functions performed by the party bureaucracy under the control of the YSP Central Committee Secretariat. It is these party agencies which administer the important task of 'training, selecting, and placement of the personnel who are entrusted with the task of implementing and checking the implementation of the party line' (Muhammed, 1983, pp. 70–5). For example, within all government ministries, a personnel committee consisting of party, union and management representatives must approve all transfers and promotion of personnel before these are submitted to the Ministry of Labour and Civil Service. Similarly, candidates for election, and appointments to the military and mass media are all vetted by the party. The existence of a parallel party structure and bureaucracy allows government actions to be closely scrutinized for their adherence to party/State policy.

Finally, the *mass organizations* (discussed below) play an important part in integrating party and State. On the one hand they are directed by and tied to the YSP through the Secretary for Mass Organizations. On the other hand they participate directly in the implementation of State policy, and provide representation of their various constituencies (workers, women, youth, peasants, etc.) within the State structure.

Taken together, these different integration mechanisms have rendered both party and State, two parts of a single party/State system, closely integrated at all levels. This is not to say that differences or divergences

Figure 3.3 Party–State Linkages

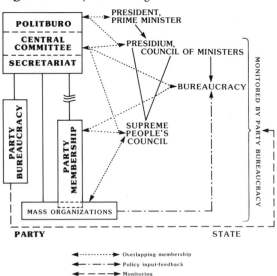

between the two elements cannot arise: there has been, for example, a clear pattern of South Yemeni Presidents and non-government members of the YSP Central Committee conflicting over the prerogatives and imperatives of the State versus those of the party (al-Sha'abi, Salem Rubayi 'Ali, Ali Nasser Muhammed). Similarly, the Army and its commanders have sometimes resented or resisted party control. While party–State tensions are real and sometimes important, however, they should not overshadow the fact that the party is clearly dominant. Invariably, in every party–State conflict to arise since 1969, it has been the principle of party supremacy which has triumphed. As Abdalla al-Ashtal (South Yemen's Ambassador to the United Nations) once expressed it, the PDRY truly represents a case of 'politics in command' (al-Ashtal 1973).

Mass Organizations

An important part in South Yemen's party/State system is played by the country's mass and quasi-mass organizations. These organizations are effectively controlled by the YSP, through the Central Committee's Secretariat for Mass Organizations. They are integrated into both the party and State structure at all levels. One or more representatives from each mass organization sits on each party central committee (district, directorate,

Figure 3.4   General Union of Yemeni Women

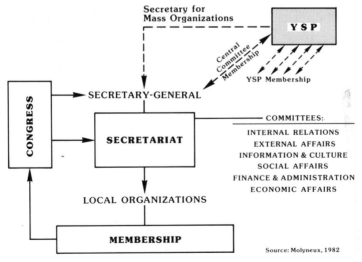

Source: Molyneux, 1982

governate and national). The mass organizations are also assured of representation in local People's Councils as well as the Supreme People's Council, electing a small proportion of the members of these themselves. The structure and State/party links of a typical mass organization—the General Union of Yemeni Women—can be seen in Figure 3.4 (Molyneux, 1982).

Mass organizations (granted explicit recognition in Part II of the State Constitution) are intended to perform a number of important functions in the South Yemeni political system. First, they are to act as a major 'transmission belt' of State and party policy, working towards its implementation at the mass level and providing feedback on its effect. Second, they are to be instruments of revolutionary socialization, educating their members and others in the values and world view of the Yemeni revolution. Third, they are intended to function as important avenues of party recruitment. A fourth function—that of advocacy—is also intended, but in a limited way. Mass organizations are encouraged to call for the adoption of new policy or the revision of old, but only provided they do so within the bounds of acceptable political discourse: criticism should be constructive, limited, and voiced quietly, usually in closed-door meetings with appropriate party and State officials.

All four of these functions—policy transmission and feedback, socialization, recruitment, advocacy—are performed by mass organizations in the PDRY. Overall, however, they have not been performed to the satisfaction of many members of the party leadership. Central Committee member (and Secretary) Anis Hasan Yahya, for example, has complained that 'unions [and other mass organizations] are still playing a marginal role in economic and social life' in the country (14 Uktubar, 18 December 1983, p. 3). This failure is especially evident with regard to the feedback and advocacy functions, and the failure of mass organizations to provide valuable input into State economic and social planning has in the past been singled out for particular criticism.

The three mass organizations discussed below—the General Union of Workers of the PDRY, the Democratic Yemen Youth Union, and the General Union of Yemeni Women represent the largest and most important such groups in the PDRY. There are many others, ranging from professional groups to the General Union of Yemeni Students. Surprisingly (in view of the PDRY's large agricultural population), national peasant conferences were not initiated until the latter part of 1971, and a mass organization for peasants (the Democratic Yemen Peasants' Union) was not established until October 1976. There are a variety of reasons for this. The political consciousness of the peasantry is often low. There has been a tendency to involve younger farmers in the Youth Union rather than in local peasants' associations. Finally, the agricultural co-operatives perform many of the same functions as do mass organizations at the local level, and their existence has hence obviated much of the need for a mass peasant organization. Even today, a decade after their initial creation, the peasants' associations are yet to play a prominent role in the socio-economic life of the PDRY.

The three other organizations examined here—the Popular Defence Committees, the People's Militia, and the armed forces—are not mass organizations in the sense of the others (although the first two were in large part designed as such). In many ways, however, their roles and relations to the party/State structure parallel those of the genuine mass organizations. For this reason they are also examined below.

General Union of Workers of the PDRY

The General Union of Workers of the PDRY (*al-Itihad al-'Am li 'Umal Jamhuriyat al-Yaman al-Dimoqratiyah al-Sha'biyah*) was established soon after independence, replacing the Aden Trade Union Congress and all other labour organizations in existence at that time. Under article 57 of the 1970 State Constitution it is charged with 'the protection of [the workers'] interests and increasing the democratic consciousness of their members', 'mobilizing their members for the realisation of the economic plan', and participating in wage negotiations and the operation of nationalized and public enterprises. Under the Fundamental Labour Law (Law No. 14) of 1978 employees are guaranteed the right to form and join unions (article 93). Unions are further guaranteed the right to participate in development and production planning, as well as in the resolution of industrial disputes (articles 94–6).

Local unions thus represent workers locally in the labour–management production committees which have been established at all industrial workplaces. Regionally, the Union takes part in local People's Councils, government committees, and in the local YSP party organization. At the national level the Union provides input and feedback (but rarely criticism) to government ministries, and helps to co-ordinate and facilitate the implementation of government policy at all levels. It also publishes a weekly magazine, *Sawt al-'Umal* (The Voice of the Workers). Internatio nally, the General Union of Workers of the PDRY maintains friendly ties with trade unions in some Arab countries, Ethiopia, Cuba, North Korea, Vietnam, Eastern Europe and the Soviet Union, and is a member of the Prague-based World Federation of Trade Unions.

Leadership of the Union rests with a Secretary-General and Central

Council who in 1977 administered a full-time staff of ninety-six union officials. Most Union leaders are YSP members, with the Union Secretary-General sitting on the YSP Central Committee. At the local level, union officials are almost invariably represented on local party committees. The Central Council (consisting of sixty-one full and six candidate members in 1981) and its powerful supervision and control committee (eleven members) are elected by delegates at periodic General Union congresses. The background of Congress delegates provides us with perhaps the best available data on the membership of the organization as a whole. Of the 617 who attended the 1981 Congress 46 per cent were workers and 54 per cent salaried employees. About 14 per cent of the delegates were women (*al-Hurriyah*, 5 October 1981, p. 32).

Membership for most South Yemeni workers in the General Union is automatic. Its total strength has been estimated at 84,000 (Molyneux, 1982, p. 18), of whom up to one-third are reportedly women. However, the socio-economic and political role of the Union in the PDRY has been limited—a fact which, in view of the historic role assigned to the working class, has been of some concern to YSP leaders. According to Yahya:

> The unions constitute the principal power for the party of the working class, which cannot continue its struggle to develop socialism in the presence of weak unions whose role in economic and social life is still marginal. Of course our colleagues in the union movement may be disturbed by what we are saying, but it is a fact that the union's contributions to the improvement of economic conditions and implementation of the state's economic and social plans are still very modest and do not reflect the role [assigned to the unions] in economic and social life [*14 Uktubar*, 18 December 1983, p. 3.]

This weakness parallels (and is caused by many of the same factors as) the weakness of worker representation in the YSP itself.

Democratic Yemen Youth Union

The Democratic Yemen Youth Union (*al-Itihad al-Shabab al-Yamani al-Dimoqratiyi*, commonly known by its Arabic acronym *Asheed*) is another mass organization whose formation was mandated by Part II of the 1970 Constitution. According to article 59:

> The youth organization shall unite students, young workers, farmers and the educated. The youth organization shall cover training, education, culture and the general struggle of the working people to fulfill the national democratic revolution.
>   It shall promote the political consciousness of its members in accordance with the

national democratic revolution and shall support their scientific, technical and recreational training.

It shall participate in solving the general problems of the people.

It shall use its maximum capacity in removing illiteracy and backwardness and shall ensure that its members employ their spare time in the service of the people and solving their problems.

Further legal basis for the organization was provided by Law No. 2 of 1980 which consolidated its existence as a legal entity. Its membership stands at approximately 31,000.

In many ways, *Asheed* is the most important mass organization in the PDRY. Part of the reason for this is purely demographic: approximately one-quarter of South Yemen's young population are between the ages of 16 and 28, the Youth Union's recruiting constituency. Above and beyond this, however, the YSP has found the youth of the country most open to ideas of social reform and change. Consequently, the Union has become the best organized, most dynamic and progressive mass organization in the PDRY (*14 al-Uktubar*, 18 December 1983, p. 3). It has come to play a special political role, being recognized in the party constitution as the YSP's main reserve and assistant (Rybakov, 1982, p. 43). As noted earlier, people up to the age of 28 join the YSP exclusively through the Union.

General Union of Yemeni Women

The General Union of Yemeni Women was founded in February 1968, and is a recognized mass organization under article 58 of the 1970 Constitution. When first established, the Union's activities were confined to the major population centre of Aden, Lahej and the Hadhramawt. By the time of its first full Congress in 1974, however, it had grown to be a genuinely national organization, with a formal organizational structure embracing all governates. As shown in Figure 3.4, the Union's leadership consists of a thirty-five member (1977) general secretariat, which in turn forms functional committees to deal with different Union responsibilities (internal and external relations, information and culture, social affairs, finance and administration, and economic affairs). Total reported membership stands at 14,926. Most (about 89 per cent) are 'housewives'. Of the remainder, 915 (6.1 per cent) are industrial workers, 528 (3.5 per cent) rural workers, 253 (1.7 per cent) civil servants, and some students. Wage-earning members pay a monthly membership fee of 100 *fils*, while non-earning members pay 50 *fils* (*al-Siyasah*, 18 September 1981, p. 11; Molyneux, 1982, pp. 20-1).

The General Union of Yemeni Women (GUYW) sees its main role as integrating women into the economic life of the country, through education and technical training. In 1976, for example, the Union established six training centres in various parts of the country, training an average of 1,500 women per year. It has also played a leading role among women in the Republic's anti-literacy campaign. In 1975–7 alone, a reported 59,065 Yemeni women attended literacy courses (*14 Uktubar*, 22 October 1980, p. 2). The Union sponsors radio and television programmes on the changing role of women in Yemeni society, and publishes its own magazine, *al-Nisa* al-Yaman* (the Yemeni Women).

Like the other mass organizations discussed above, GUYW plays a significant if limited role in formulating and implementing State policies which affect women, and in providing informational and decision-making input to State officials. According to Maxine Molyneux's detailed and insightful examination of the status of women in the PDRY, the General Union of Yemeni Women does not 'see itself as a feminist organization . . . existing principally to further the interests of women *per se*; rather it acts as part of the state's political apparatus . . . [M]easures which could be taken to improve the position of women are considered in the context of other long-term objectives' (Molyneux, 1982, p. 21). YSP Central Committee members suggest that even within this limited mandate there is considerable room for improvement—indeed, that 'the women's organization in Democratic Yemen may be the most backward organization . . . [playing] no effective role in our economic and social life' (Anis Hasan Yahya in *14 Uktubar*, 18 December 1983, p. 3).

Popular Defence Committees

Like many other Third World Marxist regimes (Nicaragua, Ghana, Benin and Ethiopia, to name a few), the PDRY has been attracted to the system of Committees for the Defence of the Revolution first established in Cuba. These committees involve the population in a variety of revolutionary, education, mobilization, control and security tasks at the local level, and they have been (in Cuba at least) an important mechanism of mass participation in revolutionary government. Following a study visit by two Central Committee members to Cuba in the early 1970s, the first Yemeni Popular Defence Committee was established in an area of Sheikh Uthman (near Aden) on 30 May 1973. Subsequently they were set up in other urban areas. The Committees are controlled by the party through the Secretary of the Organization of Popular Defence Committees, a member of the party Central Committee. The Committees themselves are organized at the housing unit/neighbourhood level, with higher leadership bodies at the district, directorate, governate and all-Republic levels. Membership is open to all citizens over the age of 16.

The functions of the Popular Defence Committees are varied. They include:

(1) maintaining the night-time security of the neighbourhood and safe-guarding economic installations;
(2) monitoring possible counter-revolutionary elements in the local population;
(3) carrying out volunteer work;
(4) distributing ration cards;
(5) participating in district health and anti-illiteracy campaigns;
(6) controlling local housing and combatting housing fraud;
(7) solving simple family and social problems, and establishing social justice boards (in Aden) in order to lighten the burden on the courts and the civil service;
(8) providing community input into schools through local parents' councils;
(9) organizing solidarity campaigns;
(10) helping to implement the Military Service and Personal Identity Card laws (al-Hurriyah, 12 June, 1983, p. 86).

In practice, however, the Popular Defence Committees—intended by the party to be one of its strongest and most broad-based mass organizations—have not been very successful. The security function has come to dominate the Committee's other (social and educational) roles. Moreover, public participation in the committees is reportedly low (Halliday, 1983, p. 58).

Popular Defence Forces and People's Militias

While defending national security is the primary task of the Popular Defence Forces (regular armed forces) of the PDRY, it is not their sole one. Because young men from all class and tribal backgrounds are conscripted for several years' service in its ranks, the armed forces have provided the State/party with an unequalled opportunity to break down tribal and other sub-national loyalties, to provide basic education and training, and to instill support for the revolution and its aims among this important demographic group (14 Uktubar, 30 April 1980, p. 2). In this way the Popular Defence Forces comprise an important socialization and policy implementation mechanism not so different from that carried out by the 'true' mass organizations.

Like the mass organizations, the Popular Defence Forces are closely integrated into the party/State structure. Firm political control is exercised over them by the apparatus of both party and State. Indeed, it is a fundamental party tenet that the 'party direct the rifle' rather than vice versa. In the Ministry of Defence political control is provided by the Ministry's Political Department. Generally, both the Minister of Defence and the Deputy Minister in charge of the Political Department are members of the party Central Committee, the former also being a member of the powerful party Politburo. The YSP organizes party cells at all levels of the Popular Defence Forces, with the usual division of the party structure (district/directorate/governate) being replaced by one more appropriate to military life (brigade/armed forces branch/armed forces).

Ideological instruction for all ranks of the military is intensive, and support for the revolution and its aims is an important prerequisite for promotion. Political officers are appointed to all military units. In some cases political training goes beyond the theoretical to include a pioneering role in social reform. In the early 1970s, for example, the army led the drive towards agricultural collectivization by establishing and operating a number of state farms (al-Jundi, 14 October 1971, p. 6, 19).

The political reliability of the armed forces was not always so secure. As 'Ali Antar (Commander of the Popular Defence Forces and later Minister of Defence) recounted to the Army journal al-Jundi (14 October 1971, p. 19);

[The armed forces] used to be composed of the sons of sheikhs, amirs, and big land-owners, and were formed on tribal lines. In fact, they were formed from a specific tribe, even if other tribes were represented, and their tribe, for example, would be predominant in the command of the army and the armed forces. This structure did not come about by accident, rather, it was designed [by the British] to break down the unity of the country through tribal conflict.

Even after independence, no apparent change was allowed in the structure of this organization because the middle-of-the-road forces in the revolution, by virtue of their bourgeois mentality and political dominance, were afraid of radical change.

After the Corrective Step of June 22, 1969 the revolutionary leadership . . . purged the army of elements wishing to preserve their old political and class privileges, and we began to construct our armed forces on new bases which would allow the sons of workers, peasants, nomads, and fishermen to occupy a role in these forces. From among the ranks of these participating classes we prepared technical and administrative leadership cadres so that they could participate in the building, protection, and support of the revolution.

Hence

the expansion of political awareness among the ranks of our armed forces and the expansion of scientific socialist awareness among our soldiers and officers are tantamount to the safety [mechanism] that enables the soldiers and the officers to adopt firm principled positions toward their revolution [and party] [Ismail in *14 Uktubar*, 29 March 1978, p. 8.]

The need for such a safety mechanism was deeply engrained in the party in the period 1967-9, when al-Sha'abi used the Army against the left in his struggle to retain power. At that time (during the Zinjibar Congress, to be precise) the party called for the formation of a popular militia to act as a counterweight to the army. The construction of this militia was begun soon after the Corrective Step, initially under Chinese guidance and later with help from Cuban advisers. Today, the People's Militia of the PDRY numbers some 15,000 members, organized on a local basis. Party influence among many militia members is strong and at all levels YSP control is closely integrated into the command structure. Militia members receive literacy and other education in addition to basic military and other training. In September 1983 a Military Intelligence Department was reportedly established with the militia, further strengthening its role as a political counterweight to the regular armed forces (*al-Wahdah*, 15 September 1983).

Not all the political difficulties associated with the armed forces have been solved. In the past tensions have arisen over the relative role of the Popular Defence Forces and People's Militia, and over promotion policy. Great popularity among Army ranks ('Ali Antar) or influence over local militia command structures (Ja'im Salih in 1978) has sometimes allowed individuals to construct personal powerbases in the armed forces despite safeguards. In times of political crisis (1978, 1986) some units have reacted or split along tribal lines. However, in contrast to many (if not most) developing countries, the armed forces of the PDRY exercise little political influence in and of their own. According to 'Ali Nasser Muhammed (then Minister of Defence), 'Democratic Yemen has overcome the danger of coups, because the revolution's measures have . . . radically touched military organizations . . . [so that] . . . it has become impossible for our soldiers' rifles to be directed at the hearts of their people or threaten their country's independence' (*14 Uktubar*, 1 September 1975). The militarization of the party or State seems to be an unlikely possibility.

Political Dissent

Political dissent in the PDRY comes in several forms, each of which has been met with a slightly different response.

The first form of dissent comprises those who have accepted the basic outlook and goals of the revolution, but who differ on questions of tactics and minor policy. Such criticism is accepted, even valued, provided it remains within the bounds of the party/State structure and acceptable political discourse—hence the National Front's tolerance (and eventual merger with) the PDU and PVP, groups with consonant but not identical ideological orientations.

At the same time, when criticism goes beyond acceptable limits in either content or form (questioning the basic direction of the revolution, for example, or violating the tenets of democratic centralism), reaction by the party is swift. In 1975, for example, the PDRY's Ambassador to Cairo was reportedly arrested at Aden airport and imprisoned for what was perceived to be excessive criticism of State economic planning (Amnesty International, 1976, p. 193-4). Purges have been commonplace in the NF/YSP since independence, and have been upheld as a legitimate and necessary political mechanism by successive party constitutions. While the usual consequence of a purge is demotion, reassignment, or loss of party membership, arrests and executions have taken place—particularly in the wake of major internal political crises, such as those of 1969 and 1978. In the case of the January 1986 turmoil, however, appearances are that the YSP (acting in the interests of party unity) has been relatively lenient in the aftermath of what was a very costly and bloody conflict. Although some fifteen-hundred supporters of deposed President 'Ali Nasser Muhammed were arrested in the wake of his downfall in January 1986, the bulk of these (approximately one thousand) were released within a month. A general amnesty for the remainder (and for many past opponents of the regime) was later announced at the end of March.

A second form of dissent in the PDRY consists of apolitical resistance to government policy on the part of affected individuals or groups. The most common form of this has been tribal resistance (sometimes armed) to central government authority, particularly in the early years of independence. This resistance has generally been both sporadic and politically disorganized, particularly as government policy increasingly weakens tribal cohesion. Sometimes, however, a degree of coherence to tribal uprising has been provided from without, either by party members mobilizing fellow tribes-men in support of their political position (e.g. 'Ali Nasser Muhammed's attempts to raise the Dathina in support of his presidency in February 1986), or by outside powers hostile to the South Yemeni revolution (for example Saudi Arabia support for the 1969 'Aulaqi rebellion).

This latter situation introduces the third variety of dissent present in the PDRY: organized counter-revolutionary opposition to the regime, usually externally based and funded (internal counter-revolutionary activity has been all but rooted out). In the late 1960s the remnants of SAL and FLOSY sought to overthrow the regime from bases in North Yemen. Support came from among the up to 500,000 former colonial civil servants, conservative military officers, business interests, tribesmen, traditional leaders and others who for economic or political reasons are said to have left South Yemen in the aftermath of independence and the June 22 Corrective Step. Support also came from the North Yemeni government (within which Abdullah al-Asnaj later became Foreign Minister and Presidential Adviser), from Saudi Arabia, and allegedly from the United States (with which Aden broke diplomatic relations in 1969). Counter-revolutionary armies—the 'Army of National Unity' in North Yemen, the 'Army of National Salvation' in Saudi Arabia— were established and financed. Later, in the early and late 1970s respectively, Egypt and Iraq also joined in sponsoring South Yemeni *émigré* groups.

Counter-revolutionary activity against the PDRY has been shown in periodic bombings, assassinations and economic sabotage. Although these actions never came close to toppling the regime (and have steadily declined over the years as the party has consolidated its position), they have incurred their cost. Real economic damage has been done on occasion, and the political and financial cost of maintaining internal security (discussed below) has been high. Moreover, the external support it receives has prevented counter-revolutionary opposition to the regime from disappearing altogether.

Today the largest exile group opposing the South Yemeni government is the National Grouping of Patriotic Forces in South Yemen (NGPF), established under Iraqi auspices in Baghdad in May 1980. The NGPF brought together within its framework representatives from a number of opposition movements. These include: the United National Front (led by former Adeni chief minister and FLOSY leader 'Abd al-Qawi Makkawi), the Yemen Unity Front (led by former PDRY Prime Minister Muhammed 'Ali Haytham, who narrowly escaped assassination by South Yemeni agents in Cairo in 1975), the remnants of the South Arabian League, and the June 26 Group (supporters of deposed President Salem Rubayi 'Ali). These different groups set up a Constituent Council with Makkawi as Secretary-General and Haytham as Assistant Secretary-General to oversee the development of the Grouping into a fully-fledged, organized political movement (*al-Ray' al-'Amm*, 7 April 1980; Muscat Domestic Service, 18 December 1980, 19.00 GMT). In a statement issued at the conclusion of this first meeting, the NGPF Constituent Council called for a 'revolutionary and radical change in the politics and actions' of the South Yemeni government through:

(1) the establishment of a national democratic regime truly representative of the Arab masses of South Yemen;
(2) the release of all political detainees;
(3) the extension of democratic freedoms and safeguards;
(4) respect for human rights;
(5) the purging and reorganization of the state structure;
(6) support for Yemeni unity;
(7) liberation from foreign (i.e. Soviet) influence and a commitment to pan-Arabism;
(8) renunciation of imported ideas (i.e. Marxism) and a return to South Yemen's spiritual and cultural heritage;
(9) independence, sovereignty and non-alignment (text in *al-Jumhurriyyah*, 14 May 1980, pp. 1, 11).

The NGPF subsequently formulated a National Charter, which was ratified by the Grouping's first Congress on 15–19 January 1984. At this time the transitional Constituent Committee was replaced by a National Assembly and Executive Committee. 'Abd al-Qawi Makkawi was confirmed as NGPF Secretary-General at the same time (*al-Wahdah*, 15 February 1984, pp. 4–6).

Since its establishment in 1980, the National Grouping of Patriotic Forces in South Yemen has primarily acted to promote opposition to the current regime on the part of other Arab countries, particularly in the face of improving relations between Aden and the conservative Arab Gulf states. In support of these activities the NGPF publishes a monthly information journal, *al-Wahdah* (Unity), from Cairo. Its activities within the PDRY, however, would appear negligible and thus far easily contained by the regime. In 1982 thirteen South Yemenis were arrested for attempting to sabotage key economic facilities, including the refinery at Aden. These individuals claimed to belong to the 'National Liberation Army', a previously unknown anti-government group; the government claimed that the plotters were acting as agents of Saudi Arabia and the United States Central Intelligence Agency. Of the group, ten were executed and three sentenced to fifteen-year prison terms.

Internal Security Apparatus

In the face of external and internal threats to the regime a formidable and multi-faceted security and intelligence apparatus has been constructed in the PDRY. Its main elements are the thirty-thousand-strong Public Security Forces, established soon after independence under the Ministry of the Interior; and the Revolutionary Security Service, under the control of the Ministry of State Security since the latter's establishment in November 1974. These two forces perform regular and secret police functions respectively. Their roles are supplemented by the Popular Defence Forces, the People's Militia, and the Popular Defence Committees, as well as by the constant monitoring and control over the State exercised by the YSP. Because of external interference in South Yemeni affairs, the admission to and movement of foreigners in the country is closely controlled, and in 1975 a stringent anti-fraternization law was introduced.

The security forces reached a peak of brutal efficiency under Muhammed Said Abdullah ('Muhsin') Shajabi, Deputy Minister of the Interior until 1974, when he assumed the newly-created position of Minister of State Security. It was during his reign that the anti-fraternization laws were issued, together with detailed directives limiting what could—and could not—be discussed by students with foreign teachers, or by civil servants with foreign technical experts. All dissent was ruthlessly suppressed: in 1977, for example, eight farmers were sentenced to death for their part in a protest against government restrictions on the production of the narcotic plant *qat*. (The sentences were later commuted to imprisonment by the President.) Other government critics simply disappeared or died under mysterious circumstances, including some exiled outside the country. Amnesty International (1977, pp. 315-17) reported that prisoners were being held under oppressive conditions (including the use of torture) at the al-Fatah detention camp in Aden. The legal safeguards included in the country's Constitution, penal code and other legislation were simply ignored.

Upset both by Muhsin's flaunting of socialist legality and his growing political power, the party eventually acted to curb the worst of his excesses. In August 1979, Muhsin came under political attack from fellow YSP Central Committee members for the atmosphere of a police state which his activities had created throughout the country. The criticism was particularly intense from the powerful Minister of Defence, 'Ali Antar, who was angered by Muhsin's ministerial empire-building and his attempts to extend the security services' power into, and at the expense of, the regular armed forces. Muhsin was removed from office, and a collective committee was established to oversee internal security affairs (*al-Dustur*, 29 October–4 November 1979, pp. 16–17). Subsequently the anti-fraternization laws and some of the more stringent aspects of the state security system he had constructed were reportedly weakened or repealed (*Le Monde Diplomatique*, October 1982, pp. 22–3).

Political Dynamics

In theory (and to a considerable extent in practice), the South Yemeni state is directed by the party—a party whose internal decision-making is governed by the twin principles of democratic centralism and collective leadership. These two principles represent a 'fundamental internal party tenet' (Ismail in *al-Hurriyah*, 23 October 1978, pp. 20–1), and they have both been enshrined in party doctrine since the Fourth Congress of the National Front (1968) as a means of ensuring political stability and a smooth and effective policy process. In the words of 'Abd al-Fattah Ismail, collective leadership is 'a safety barrier meant to prevent the revolution falling once again into the hands of an individual leader. . . . No individual . . . can be either the substitute for the collective, or singlehandedly bear the responsibility for an entire historic phase' (Ismail, 1977, p. 7).

It is true to say, however, that since the triumph of these principles in the June 22 'Corrective Step', South Yemen's political history has been punctuated by serious (and often bloody) struggles for power within the party/government leadership. Notable among these have been the execution of Salem Rubayi 'Ali in June 1978; the sustained power struggle between 'Ali Nasser Muhammed, 'Abd al-Fattah Ismail (exiled 1980–84), and 'Ali Antar, which followed Rubayi 'Ali's overthrow and continued until January 1986; and the January 1986 civil war which saw Muhammed deposed, Ismail and Antar dead, and the emergence of a new party and government leadership. Extreme political violence has been a constant companion of major political succession or change; at a lower level, many assassination incidents attributed by the government to counter-revolutionary forces may have actually stemmed from internal political disputes. Yet, at the same time, the leadership and control of the NF/UPONF/YSP has never been seriously questioned or threatened since 1969.

The Rise and Fall of Salem Rubayi 'Ali

Following the June 22 Corrective Step and the establishment of a Marxist regime in South Yemen, political authority in the country passed from the hands of deposed President Qahtan al-Sha'abi to the new five-person Presidential Council chaired by South Yemen's new President, Salem Rubayi 'Ali. Other members of the Council were 'Ali Nasser Muhammed, 'Ali Antar, 'Abd al-Fattah Ismail (NF Secretary-General) and Muhammed 'Ali Haytham, the moderate Prime Minister.

Over the next two years 'Ali, Ismail and others on the leftist wing of the party gradually isolated Haytham from real decison-making and political power in the emerging People's Democratic Republic of Yemen as they asserted the primacy of the party over the State. In August 1971, following the promulgation of the new Constitution (November 1970) and the appointment of the first People's Supreme Council (March), members of the Presidential Council and all other government bodies were asked to resign so that they might be formally reappointed by the PSC. When the new Presidential Council was reappointed, however, it consisted of only three members, all party stalwarts: Salem Rubayi 'Ali, 'Abd al-Fattah Ismail and 'Ali Nasser Muhammed (who replaced Haytham as Prime Minister). Haytham's tribal support, so significant in his 1969 confrontation with al-Sha'abi, was effectively neutralized by his replacement by a fellow Dathina.

Despite the removal of Haytham and the final consolidation of the National Front's left wing in power, new tensions soon arose, particularly between 'Ali and Ismail. 'Ali tended to favour the Chinese over the Soviet revolutionary model, and was suspicious of the party reorganization then under way. He argued for mass democracy instead of centralization, the importance of spontaneous revolutionary action (such as the peasant uprising during the 1970 land reform) and the need for ideologically-dedicated (rather than technically competent) cadres. He opposed party reforms, which, in his view, would render the party rigid and bureaucratic. He also opposed NF integration with the PDU and PVP on the grounds that these parties were small and narrowly-based (Halliday, 1983, p. 59). In the international sphere 'Ali increasingly advocated a normalization of relations with the PDRY's conservative neighbours, diversification of foreign aid sources, and less dependence on the Soviet Union. Ismail, by contrast, advocated an ideologically militant approach and close alliance with the socialist camp, rejecting any moderation of the revolution's aggressive foreign policy approach. Ismail was also the primary architect of the new party structure then in formation. Both leaders and sets of positions had different supporters in the Cabinet and the National Front. The individualistic, power-orientated elements tended to coalesce around 'Ali, who also fostered support among his Dathina co-tribesmen, from his home region, and from former members of the Liberation Army (many of whom were now serving in senior positions in the regular army). The more ideologically-orientated elements tended to support Ismail, who if less populist was more imposing as a party figure and theorist. Ismail also enjoyed good relations with the PDRY's closest ally, the Soviet Union.

The split polarized over the issue of leadership. Increasingly, 'Ali sought to centralize power in his hands (thus ignoring the fundamental party principle of collective leadership), subordinating the Council of Ministers to a secondary role and ruling through presidential decree. In response, the YSP Central Committee met in mid-June and passed a series of resolutions limiting the power exercised by the President in the absence of the Prime Minister. Some of Salem Rubayi 'Ali's supporters and relatives in middle-ranking party posts were reportedly removed from their positions (*14 Uktubar*, 25 June 1978, p. 5).

Matters came to a head a few days later when, on 24 June 1978, President Ahmad al-Gashemi of the Yemen Arab Republic was killed by a bomb planted in the suitcase of Salem Rubayi 'Ali's personal envoy. Suspicion immediately fell upon 'Ali among others (see Chapter 6). The President, however, refused to answer questions on the matter from the party Politburo. This, and 'Ali's implication in the original act, led to the holding of an emergency meeting of the YSP Central Committee on the night of June 25–26. 'Ali refused to attend; instead he submitted his resignation as President, which was accepted by a majority vote of the Central Committee with only four objections. The Central Committee also stripped him of all party posts.

A few hours later, while the Politburo and some Central Committee members were discussing how best to handle Salem Rubayi 'Ali's departure from power and the situation in the country, troops loyal to 'Ali opened fire on the party headquarters building where the meeting was being held. Fortunately for those inside, the meetingroom was sheltered by surrounding trees and buildings and the fire was largely ineffectual. At the same time, 'Ali's supporters in the Third Governate attempted a *coup d'état*. Fighting flared both there and in Aden, but most militia and regular Army units (including 80 per cent of those in the President's home area of Abyan) remained loyal to the party and to Defence Minister 'Ali Antar (*Arab Report and Record*, 1–15 August 1978, p. 568). Artillery and air power gradually reduced 'Ali's defences around the presidential palace, and within two days Salem Rubayi 'Ali, Ja'im Salih and fellow conspirator (and Central Committee member) 'Ali Salem La'war had been captured. They were all executed shortly afterwards (*14 Uktubar*, 27 August 1978, supplement).

The Struggle for Power, 1975-85

Salem Rubayi 'Ali's downfall confirmed the leading position of three other prominent liberation-era figures in South Yemen politics: 'Abd al-Fattah Ismail, 'Ali Nasser Muhammed and 'Ali Antar. Ismail became the new Head of State of the PDRY following the June events; Muhammed and Antar retained their positions as Prime Minister and Minister of Defence respectively. Both Ismail and Muhammed were appointed Brigadier-Generals in the Popular Defence Forces in an effort to further consolidate party control over the military. The supporters of former President 'Ali—now described as an unrepentant individualist who had forged secret ties with Saudi Arabia and other reactionary regimes—were purged from the government and party.

Although they had co-operated in bringing down 'Ali, ideological, political and personal conflict between these three leading figures was not long in coming. Each looked to a distinct base (or bases) of support. Ismail enjoyed his greatest popularity among ideological party cadres. He could also count on support in the burgeoning state security sector through his protégé (and relative) Muhsin. Muhammed found supporters among tribal elements (particularly from his Dathina tribe and in his home region of Abyan) and former members of the Liberation Army. He also drew significant support from the armed forces, having served as Defence Minister before gaining the prime ministership in 1971. Antar also enjoyed tribal support (among the Dhala and around Lahej) and in the Liberation Army. His popularity in the Army was immense.

The political drama which followed was played out in five acts. The first pitted 'Ali Nasser Muhammed and 'Ali Antar against Muhsin, the Chief of State Security. As noted earlier, Antar was critical of Muhsin's attempts to extend the power and purview of the security services into and at the expense of the armed forces. Muhammed supported the Defence Minister on the issue, apparently seeing it as an opportunity to reduce one of Ismail's key pillars of support. When the dispute ended with Muhsin's removal from the State Security portfolio on the direction of the YSP Central Committee in August 1979, Ismail lost a major ally. At the same time a number of 'Ali Nasser Muhammed's allies in the party were promoted, and a new Director of the Ministry of Defence's Political Department, Lt.-Col. Ahmad Salim 'Ubayd, was appointed despite Antar's misgivings (*al-Dustur*, 29 October–4 November 1979, pp. 16–17).

The second stage of the power struggle saw a more direct confrontation between Ismail and his opponents. Increasingly, the President was criticized for being excessively theoretical and doctrinaire. At a time when serious questions regarding the value and effectiveness of Soviet aid were arising within government and party ranks, Ismail was seen as being too closely tied to the Soviet development model. His internationalism and position *vis-à-vis* Yemeni unity were, it was suggested, too militant given the PDRY's limited foreign policy resources. This, and Ismail's North Yemeni background, left him open to implicit charges that the President showed insufficient concern for the imperatives of the South. Foreign Minister Muhammed Salih Muti' figured prominently among those critical of Ismail and his policies. Muhammed supported Muti', but seemed content to let the other assume leadership of the anti-Ismail campaign.

By April 1980 Muti', Muhammed and others had finally secured sufficient support within the YSP Central Committee to force Ismail's resignation as both President and party Secretary-General. As consolation, the former President was invited to assume the meaningless position of 'Honorary' Chairman of the YSP. 'Ali Nasser Muhammed was appointed as the new party chief. A few days later the People's Supreme Council ratified Ismail's resignation and appointed 'Ali Nasser Muhammed Chairman of the Council Presidium. In October an Extraordinary YSP Congress was held at which Muhammed's party positions were confirmed and a new YSP Central Committee elected. Ismail went into self-imposed exile in Moscow.

A further strenghtening of Muhammed's position came in August 1980 when Muti', Muhammed's erstwhile ally in the struggle against Ismail, was charged with spying on behalf of Saudi Arabia. The Foreign Minister was arrested and imprisoned after an unsuccessful attempt to flee to Ethiopia. He later died, in March 1981, 'shot while trying to escape'.

By the end of the 1980 YSP Congress 'Ali Nasser Muhammed's personal power within the party/State structure had reached heights unparalleled in the history of the PDRY. He now occupied all three of the leading positions in the regime—President, Prime Minister and YSP Secretary-General. His only remaining rival of any great political importance was 'Ali Antar, whose enormous popularity among the ranks of the armed forces doubtless made the President uneasy. Fortunately for Muhammed it also made other Central Committee members sufficiently uneasy for the President to engineer the removal of Antar from the Defence portfolio and to replace him by Salih Muslih Qasim in May 1981.

The effects of this move were far-reaching, ushering in a fourth phase in the on-going struggle for power in South Yemen. Muhammed had tried to lessen the blow to Antar occasioned by his removal from 'his' Ministry of Defence through a series of countervailing appointments as Minister of Local Government, Deputy Prime Minister, and Deputy Chairman of the Presidium. Nevertheless, the former military chief was clearly antagonized by Muhammed's manœuvre. A *de facto* alliance between Antar and Ismail was not long in coming.

Soon after this, Muhammed began to come under fire for his domination of power. He was also criticized by party ideologues for his moderation of the regime's domestic and foreign policy: Ali Ba Dhib, for example, was heard to question the nature of 'this pragmatism which these days is being called for in more than one form and under more than one screen' (Cigar, 1985, p. 790). The President's support in the party Central Committee began to weaken. In May 1984 the Central Committee appointed five new members to the Politburo (including some of Muhammed's critics), and brought Muhsin back from exile in Addis Ababa to serve as Minister of Housing. Muhammed was now reportedly being accused of ideological impotence by fellow Central Committee members (*al-Siyasah*, 28 June 1984). Calls for the return of Ismail were voiced, and later that year Ismail did in fact return from Moscow. In February 1985 the YSP Central Committee made further Politburo appointments and brought Ismail back into its ranks as a member of the Central Committee secretariat. Either under pressure from his colleagues or in an attempt to allay criticism of his hold on power, Muhammed resigned as Prime Minister a few days later in favour of Haidar Abu-Bakr al-Attas. In the summer factional fighting between Muhammed and his opponents was said to have been averted only by the diplomatic intervention of Soviet and Palestinian officials (*Middle East Economic Digest (MEED)*, 2 November 1985, p. 48).

Further evidence of Muhammed's declining popularity came in October 1985 at the YSP Third Congress. Although Muhammed was re-elected as Secretary-General of the party, other steps were taken to limit his power. The Central Committee was expanded from forty-seven to seventy-seven members to include many of the President's opponents. Similarly, the Politburo was expanded to sixteen by the election of three new members— Ismail amongst them (*MEED*, 1 February 1986, pp. 4–6).

The Overthrow of 'Ali Nasser Muhammed

The tripartite power struggle in South Yemen entered its fifth and final phase with the conclusion of the YSP Third Congress. The Congress seems to have been the last straw for Muhammed, indicating to him that only by bold and decisive action could he hope to retain his hold on power much longer. With his party support evaporating, only violent action remained to him—a replay of Salem Rubayi 'Ali's desperate moves of June 1978.

According to subsequent South Yemeni accounts, the President called a Politburo meeting for 10 a.m. on 13 January 1986. When the members of the Politburo duly arrived for the meeting they were ambushed by members of the President's personal guard. A wild gunbattle between the ambushers and Politburo bodyguards ensued in which a number of Politburo members were critically wounded. Meanwhile, the President fled to Abyan where he and his supporters (including the Governor of Abyan, Muhammed 'Ali Ahmad) tried to raise Army, militia and tribal support for a march on Aden (*Globe and Mail*, 1 February 1986).

The ambush in Aden and attempted insurrection in Abyan proved the signal for widespread fighting throughout the Republic. Opposition to Muhammed had been largely preempted by his initial attack on the Politburo: 'Abd al-Fattah Ismail, 'Ali Antar, Defence Minister Salih Muslih Qasim, Politburo members 'Ali Shal Hadi and 'Ali Asaad Muthina, Minister of State for Unity Affairs Muhammed Abdullah Osheish, and several other Central Committee members and leading state officials were killed in the ambush or the subsequent fighting. The remaining members of the Central Committee held an emergency meeting, stripping Muhammed of all State and party offices. A number of State and party officials were expelled because of their implication in Muhammed's coup attempt, including the Ministers of the Interior, National Security and National Health, a Deputy Minister of Defence and two Deputy Ministers of National Security, the Army and Air Force Commanders; the Governor of Abyan Governate, and several Central Committee members. A new collective leadership was established, with Prime Minister al-Attas (who had flown from India to the Soviet Union on hearing of the crisis) appointed as interim Head of State (*MEED*, 1 February 1986, p. 51). Desperate attempts were made to communicate the situation to and to secure the loyalty of Army, Air Force, Navy and militial units, many of whom had received contradictory orders from the renegade President.

Despite the confusion (and the death of many important party leaders), the party and government gradually gained the upper hand. Naval units remained loyal throughout; other units began responding to State orders. After two weeks of bloody and intense hand-to-hand fighting, first Aden and then outlying regions were secured. Thousands were killed. Muhammed made quick trips to Ethiopia and North Yemen in an effort to secure support, but to no avail. By the end of the month the former President had been forced to seek refuge in neighbouring countries—escaping the execution that had befallen Salem Rubayi 'Ali, but no more successful in his attempt to gain personal control of the party/State machinery. A new State and party leadership was confirmed following YSP Central Committee meetings in early February. Al-Attas was confirmed as the Republic's new President; Yaseen Said Numan became Prime Minister; Politburo member 'Ali Salem al-Bidh was appointed YSP Secretary-General. Six new members were appointed to the sixteen-person YSP Politburo. Officially, Muhammed was now classed as a mere stooge of imperialism,' a man who 'never was and never will be a scientific socialist, and [who] is of that ilk of politicians who mix revolutionary cards with rightist reactionary cards' in the foreign and domestic arenas (Yaseen Said Numan, quoted in *MEED*, 15 February 1986, p. 34).

Party, Politics and Power in the PDRY

In all the cases examined above a variety of political and social factors can be seen at work aggravating existing tensions and producing new ones, against a backdrop provided by the hard choices and difficult decisions faced by any South Yemeni leader. The most important of these factors are those of ideology, party/State conflict, the domestic and regional/international environment, and the persistence of personal conflicts within the leadership elite.

Ideological differences. Tensions within the South Yemeni regime have commonly revolved around ideological differences among the regime's leadership, despite the triumph of the left wing of the National Front in 1969. In some cases such disputes have, in the hands of less ideological figures such as 'Ali Antar, merely provided a theoretical camouflage for attacks of a more personal or political nature. At other times issues have arisen which cut to the core of the South Yemeni revolution, issues ranging from basic disagreements over the model of socio-economic development to be followed, to foreign policy, to the structure and organization of the party.

State/party tensions. Although party and State are closely integrated in the PDRY, tensions between the two elements can and do arise. Usually one or both of two basic issues are involved: pragmatism and collective leadership. Both involve ideological and structural dimensions alike. Party leaders have generally tended to stress the value of ideological purity, and have adopted an ideological position on issues confronting the regime. By contrast, state executive officers, faced with the day-to-day realities of the PDRY's domestic and international position, have often become increasingly flexible on policy issues over time.

With regard to collective leadership, a parallel divergence has been evident: successive state presidents have sought to centralize power in their own hands (partly for its own sake, partly to facilitate quick and flexible decision-making), while party officials have resisted this trend. Both divisions reinforce themselves over time. Those in favour are appointed to important government posts and seek to maximize their power there. Those out of favour or opposed to the state leadership, on the other hand, have generally turned their energies towards the party—particularly since any challenge to the status quo must necessarily win party legitimation to succeed.

Domestic environment. Politics and political conflict in South Yemen are naturally shaped by the social milieu within which they occur, a milieu that includes the persistence of tribal and other sub-national loyalties. Because of this the background of political leaders has often assumed considerable importance. Leaders from tribal backgrounds (Salem Rubayi 'Ali, 'Ali Nasser Muhammed) have often used their background to mobilize political support in their own home districts—their ideological rejection of tribalism notwithstanding. Former members of the Liberation Army (Salem Rubayi 'Ali, Antar) have similarly found this a marked political asset, winning them significant support among the ranks of the armed forces and former guerrilla fighters. Finally, there are those political leaders ('Abd al-Fattah Ismail) whose roots lie in North Yemen. Lacking a natural South Yemeni constituency, they have tended to assume an internationalist and ideological position. Consequently they have tended to be more militant on international issues, especially the issue of South Yemeni support for lefitst forces seeking to overthrow the San'a regime.

The influence of such factors has led some Western observers to suggest that South Yemeni socialism is nothing but a façade, behind which tribalism and traditionalism lurk (for example, Countryman, 1986). Certainly, it is true that the domestic environment has an important impact on politics in South Yemen (as it does in all countries), that leaders have sought to build power-bases in the traditional sector, and that traditional loyalties have been appealed to in times of crisis. At the same time it should be noted that at no time have such powerbases proved decisive. Appeals to tribalism have generally been issued by *losing* parties. Sustained large-scale tribal uprisings (such as those that afflicted the British and the early days of PROSY) have been unknown since the early 1970s. Moreover, there has been a steady decline in the importance of these factors as tribalism is weakened, the leaders of the 'Liberation Army' era are replaced by a more technocratic breed, and the remaining North Yemenis in the regime disappear from view.

Regional/international environment. Political conflict in South Yemen is also shaped by the international environment within which it takes place. The Soviet Union and other socialist allies of the PDRY, for example, are commonly identified as playing a prominent role in South Yemeni internal politics—to the point of alleging Cuban and Soviet military involvement in the 1978 overthrow of Salem Rubayi 'Ali (Cigar, 1985, pp. 787-8). The evidence for such direct involvement, however, is scanty to say the least, largely based on dubious reports in the *émigré* and Saudi press. A sober appraisal of Soviet influence over South Yemeni politics confirms instead that while such influence is real, it is also indirect (Chapter 6). The Soviet Union may let it be known that it favours a given individual or faction, thus boosting the political power of that group within South Yemen to some degree. At the same time, the Soviet Union has been careful to maintain an air of formal neutrality, supporting the leadership in power until a new one emerges. Indeed, as Halliday (1984a, p. 221) has pointed out, and the experience of 'Abd al-Fattah Ismail suggests, Soviet support can be a two-edged sword for South Yemeni leaders.

A very different—and possibly more important—effect on South Yemeni domestic politics has been provided, paradoxically enough, by the conservative regimes of the Arab Gulf. These countries have long sought to bring about a moderation of the regime in Aden, either by the promise of reward (development aid) or by threat of reprisal (support for counter-revolutionary groups). While the process has not been a steady one—Salem Rubayi 'Ali, and to a lesser extent 'Ali Nasser Muhammed were both in part overthrown because of their cautious positive response to such overtures—there can be little doubt that the impact of these Arab countries on South Yemeni politics and policy has been very real.

Personal conflicts. Finally, political conflict within the PDRY leadership has been exacerbated by the degree to which it has assumed personal overtones. Individuals have tended to become identified with political positions and vice versa, and the tensions of past disagreement have been perpetuated within the ranks of a leadership group which has been relatively stable in composition since the Corrective Step. Because patronage and nepotism—important political processes in most countries, but particularly in the Middle East—have not yet been entirely eliminated from the political process, such personal conflicts have been extended throughout the party/State system as leaders appoint followers and relatives to positions of power.

Looking to the future of South Yemeni politics, one possible interpretation of events suggests that the resurrection of tribalism in times of
political crisis may serve to undermine efforts to weaken tribal loyalties, and
will lead to a gradual (re)tribalization of South Yemeni politics. Likewise, the
use of force in initial political dispute (the June 22 'Corrective Step', the
overthrow of Rubayi 'Ali) has tended to set a precedent, and to establish
violence as an accepted (if not approved) weapon in the armoury of South
Yemeni political leaders. Such analysis suggests that both *'urf* and the *lex
talonis* have passed into the common law of South Yemeni politics.

A contrasting assessment points to the important changes wrought by
South Yemen's most recent political crisis, the overthrow of 'Ali Nasser
Muhammed. The crisis itself was a triumph of the party/State machinery
over the intrigues of any one group of political actors, a victory of organization over opportunism. This suggests a certain maturity and stability in the
South Yemeni political system, political violence notwithstanding. Moreover, and equally importantly, a new party and state leadership appears to
have emerged from the wreckage of recent civil war. Ismail, Antar
and other members of the old guard are dead; the new leaders of the
PDRY are generally younger, more technocratic, and less tied to historic
disputes and powerbases in the Liberation Army, tribes, or regular armed
forces. Only time will tell how this group will deal with the recurrent political problems of the PDRY. They may find, however, that together with the
more prominent of the Liberation era leadership, many of the tensions that
had gripped the country since independence also died in the fighting of January 1986.

4 The Economic System

The People's Democratic Republic of Yemen, with a per capita GNP of only $510 (1983), ranks as one of the world's poorest countries. Put in context, however, the PDRY's economic achievements have been substantial. Despite its lack of natural and trained human resources, poverty and the onset of a severe economic downturn at independence, the country has achieved one of the highest economic growth-rates in the world. Moreover (and perhaps more importantly) this economic growth has not occurred at the cost of other economic and social objectives. In the nearly two decades since independence the regime has made major advances in the nationalization and integration of the economy, redistribution of income, the provision of social services, and in fundamentally restructuring the economic base of social life in the country.

The Economy at Independence

At independence South Yemen's new leaders found themselves faced with a fragmented and largely underdeveloped economy gripped by the most severe depression the country had known in modern history. Indeed, to speak of South Yemen as having a national economy at all is misleading. At independence economic activity in the country took place within two distinct spheres, largely unrelated to one another. The first was a modern, internationally-orientated sector based on the port and the now-departed colonial administration in Aden. In sharp contrast to this, local subsistence-level agriculture predominated throughout the rest of the country under primitive and exploitative conditions. A mere 22 km. of metalled road existed in the entire countryside, a testimony to colonial interest in keeping the hinterland of South Yemen weak and divided.

In Aden the most important single factor in the post-independence economic crisis was the withdrawal of direct and indirect British support for the local economy. Prior to independence the Protectorate's expenditure had generally outstripped revenue by as much as two or three to one. The British had made up this difference with a direct grant of up to £20 million in 1967, a significant portion of national income. The sudden interruption of this at independence caused havoc. Moreover, the collapse of the South Arabian Federation as the vehicle of South Yemeni independence had preempted the possibility of continued British civil or military aid after 30 November 1967. The British naval installations in Aden (which had accounted for as much as one-quarter of its GNP) were closed on the eve of independence at a direct cost of between fourteen thousand and twenty-five thousand jobs. Convinced that the city had no economic future, a further eighty thousand people (many of them skilled professionals in the trade and services sector) left Aden. The closure of the Suez Canal, through which most of Aden's maritime business flowed, came as a further blow. The number of ships calling at the port dropped from 650 to 100 per month. This drastically cut port revenues, repair and servicing charges worth in excess of YD12.5 million annually—or about one-fifth of GNP. National income decreased by 20 per cent and foreign exchange receipts by 40 per cent in the first years of independence (Mansfield, 1973, pp. 178–81; al-Sha'aibi, 1972, pp. 140, 145–6; PDRY, 1977c; World Bank, 1979, p. 2).

Above and beyond these immediate factors, the South Yemeni economy also faced a number of major structural problems. In Aden the service sector was disproportionately large, accounting for over 52 per cent of 1968 GNP (al-Sha'aibi, 1972, p. 141). It was also closely dependent on the now-severed colonial relationship. The industrial sector was almost non-existent, except for Aden's British-owned refinery. Consequently, the majority of finished good were imported. Most service and industrial concerns were foreign-owned. At the same time there was little new foreign investment or aid forthcoming; most investment dried up when the British departed.

Economic conditions in the hinterland were no better. Land ownership and control over irrigation was often concentrated in the hands of a few, generally tribal sheikhs, sultans, or *sayyids*. In Lahej, Abyan and the Hadhramawt as much as 80 per cent of the land was cultivated by tenent farmers. Peasant life was marginal at best, unbearable at worst. Conditions were especially bad for sharecroppers and agricultural labourers who suffered the greatest degree of exploitation. Periodic famines were commonplace. A similar pattern of subsistence-level semi-feudal production existed in the coastal fishing sector, where some thirteen thousand private fishermen were dominated by the fish merchants and local chiefs who owned many of the nets, larger boats and other means of production (World Bank, 1979, pp. 2, 31).

The agricultural sector was also backward in terms of productivity. Of the 1,440,000 acres available for cultivation in 1954, for example, only 175,000 acres had actually been cultivated. What cultivation did exist was often inefficient (al-Habashi, 1968, pp. 210–13).

Economic Policy since the Corrective Step

Immediately on independence severe austerity measures were imposed by the new government in an effort to deal with the economic crisis. Civil service wages were cut by between 6 and 60 per cent. Government expenditure was sharply curtailed. Hoping to return economic activity to pre-independence levels, President al-Sha'abi and his supporters made no attempt to restructure the South Yemeni economy for fear that such action would only cause further economic dislocation. Consequently, from 30 November 1967 to 22 June 1969 little real change took place in the economic situation of the country.

This changed, however, with the Corrective Step. Following the overthrow of al-Sha'abi in June the new revolutionary government embarked on a series of radical measures designed to restructure, integrate and expand the national economy. In 1969 and 1970 respectively sweeping nationalization and land reform measures were implemented. Comprehensive economic planning was also instituted to fully mobilize the human and economic resources of the Republic in the interests of national economic and social development.

Nationalization

The regime's first major economic policy initiative following the Corrective Step was the nationalization of most foreign-owned enterprises in South Yemen on 27 November 1969. The nationalization laws, subsumed within the Law for the Economic Organization of the Public Sector and National Planning (Law No. 37 of 1969) set out to realize 'the minimum stage of eradicating economic dependence', liberate and sustain national productive forces, and establish a private sector to enable the state to control, direct and lead the national economy. For this purpose, the law (text in National Front 1969, pp. 140-1) called for:

(1) nationalization of all foreign banks and financial institutions;
(2) nationalization of all 'big imperialist commercial corporations';
(3) nationalization of all insurance companies, bringing the insurance sector fully under public control;
(4) nationalization of all companies offering port and bunkering services, and the creation of a free trade zone in Aden port;
(5) nationalization of all 'imperialist companies' that distribute petroleum products;

(6) national planning in the public sector and national direction of the
private sector.

The principles of national control and public ownership of the South Yemeni
economy were also enshrined in the 1970 State Constitution, which declared
nationalized and public corporations to be 'vital pillars in the development of
the national economy' (article 15).

Under the provisions of the 1969 law (and the provisions of the Law for
the Organization of Foreign Trade of 1971 and the Banking System Law of
1972) a National Bank of Yemen was formed by the nationalization and
amalgamation of eight banks (seven of them foreign-owned). The Insurance
and Reinsurance Company was likewise formed from twelve nationalized
insurance companies, and the National Corporation for Foreign Trade,
National Home Trade Company and Yemen National Oil Company from
five nationalized trading companies and five nationalized petroleum distribution companies. Port service companies were taken over by the newly-
created Aden Ports Board (PDRY, 1977b, pp. 28, 41; World Bank, 1979, p. 3).
In 1971 the free port status of Aden was revoked, and replaced by a small
duty-free transit zone. Three years later, the Nasr (Victory) Free Trade
Company was established to administer the hard-currency sale of duty-free
commodities to tourists, transit visitors and diplomatic personnel (PDRY,
1977b, p. 48). Aden's largest industrial concern, the British-owned refinery,
remained under foreign control until May 1977 when ownership was
voluntarily passed to the PDRY. British Petroleum has continued to operate
the refinery, but now under contract to the South Yemeni government.

Initially, South Yemeni nationalization was not accompanied by similar
restrictions on new foreign investment, which Prime Minister Muhammed
'Ali Haytham sought to attract (Bidwell, 1983, p. 247). After Haytham was
eased from power, however, his more radical National Front colleagues
moved to control what they saw as the potentially distortive impact of
foreign capital on South Yemen's socio-economic revolution. Severe foreign
investment restrictions were introduced in 1971, and amended in 1972.
According to the State Constitution, such investment would only be allowed
in so far as it was compatible with national development and the aims of
South Yemen's national democratic revolution (article 24).

While such actions were successful in establishing national control over
the South Yemeni economy, they also had the effect of cutting the PDRY off
from much-needed sources of foreign exchange and investment capital (al-
Shahari, 1972, pp. 158–65). The Housing Law of 1972 (which nationalized all
absentee property), for example, led to a sudden drop in expatriate remit-

tances to South Yemen, much of which had traditionally been used for house construction in native towns and villages. Similarly, outside commercial investment in the country virtually ceased in the first decade of independence.

Eventually, however, recognition of the negative effects of this policy, coupled with growing pragmatism and confidence in the ability of the nationalized economy to withstand the drawbacks of foreign investment, led to a gradual relaxation of investment policy. First, restrictions on expatriate remittances were slackened. Then the 1971–2 laws were superseded in October 1981 by a new Investment Promotion Law (Law No. 25) which offered guarantees and tax concessions to potential investors. The PDRY also began stressing its membership in the Arab Organization for Investment Surety and the Arab Investments Office in an effort to buoy up investor confidence (*al-Masar*, 1 May 1983, p. 7–9; *al-Tali'ah*, 1 February 1984, pp. 42–5). Particular attention is now being paid to attracting expatriate investment: an expatriates' organization (complete with a magazine, *Nida' al-Watan* (Homeland's Call)) and periodic expatriate conferences have been fostered, and expatraite deposits enjoy a concessionary rate of interest (approximately three times that offered to domestic depositors). As a result of such measures the value of expatraite remittances to South Yemen has increased from $56 million in 1975 to approximately eight times that level a decade later, representing no less than one-fifth of GNP.

Agrarian Reform

A second area of priority for the revolutionary government in the wake of the Corrective Step was agrarian reform. The social and economic importance of this measure cannot be overstressed: the entire semi-feudal social order which the left wing of the NF sought to overrun was rooted in rural conditions and the patterns of rural land ownership, control and usage. Rural social conditions were, for the most part, highly exploitative: tribal sheikhs used their traditional control over grazing rights and land allocation to personal advantage and to maintain social control; while in the more densely settled areas the dominant system of land and water rights, rent/sharecropping and money-lending clearly favoured landowners over tenants.

South Yemen's first agrarian reform law had in fact been promulgated by President al-Sha'abi on 25 March 1968. It had called for the redistribution of all lands in excess of 25 *feddans* (irrigated) or 50 *feddans* (un-irrigated) per individual. Large landowners were to be compensated for confiscated land. Because of al-Sha'abi's obvious lack of enthusiasm for land reform (and the machinations of local power elites and corrupt civil servants) the law was irregularly and often inequitably applied. It was also bitterly opposed by the left wing of the National Front, which argued instead for a law that would (in keeping with the resolution of the National Front's Fourth Congress) set lower ownership limits, confiscate without compensation the land of sultans, sheikhs and other members of the hinterland elite, and mandate the restructuring of the agricultural system in South Yemen along socialist lines through the creation of collectives and state farms. As noted in Chapter 2, differences over the pace and nature of land reform provided a major political backdrop to the power struggle between al-Sha'abi and his radical opponents in the years immediately following independence. After the Corrective Step, sweeping agrarian reform was one of the first promises made by the new revolutionary government on 22 June 1969.

The second Agrarian Reform Law (text in PDRY, 1978, pp. 7-19) was subsequently issued on 5 November 1970. Its guiding principles were enshrined a few weeks later in the State Constitution, article 19 of which states:

The properties of the Sultans, Amirs, Sheikhs and rulers of the expired regime and the properties of all persons stated in the agrarian reform law shall be sequestered without compensation. The land shall be utilized by farm workers, poor farmers and citizens migrating from the towns and deserts.

The extent of land ownership shall be defined by law.

Land distributed by agrarian reform to farm workers, poor farmers and citizens migrating from towns and deserts, shall enjoy the special protection of the State. No person shall take possession of such land.

The State shall ensure the enforcement of agrarian reform in the shortest possible time in all parts of the country according to the principles of social justice and with the participation of farm workers and workers.

The Sate shall encourage agricultural cooperative societies and shall establish State farms.

The State shall also administer waqf lands and properties.

The Agrarian Reform Law itself (Law No. 27 of 1970) had a number of new and important features which had been absent from its 1968 pre-decessor. First, it confiscated the land of former protectorate officials and the hinterland elite without compensation (article 3), as well as religious endowment (*waqf*) lands. All irrigation and water supply installations were nationalized (article 35). Second, it limited landholding to 20 *feddans* of irrigated land or 40 *feddans* of un-irrigated land per individual and to twice this amount per family (article 4). While this was only 20 per cent less than the individual maximum set under the first law, most land was parcelled out in considerably smaller lots—5 to 10 *feddans* per family on average. Third, the 1970 law created agricultural co-operatives on confiscated land, with membership compulsory for all those who had gained land through land reform (article 30). Moreover, the State was mandated to establish state and model farms to 'encourage peasants and co-operative societies to undertake collective work' (article 31). All exploitative mortgages taken out more than five years previously were cancelled. Finally, a State agricultural corporation, the Directorate of Agricultural Co-operation and Land Reform, was established to oversee and foster the entire land reform process (PDRY 1977b).

Land reform itself began in South Yemen on 23 October 1970, two weeks before the formal promulgation of the Agrarian Reform Law. Hundreds of armed peasants began arresting landlords and redistributing land in party-fomented uprisings. As the takeovers spread throughout the country, however, it soon became a golden opportunity to settle personal and tribal scores under the cloak of spurious revolutionary legality. Faced with a mounting public outcry, the government moved to control the excesses through the Ministry of Agriculture and Agrarian Reform and the authority given it by articles 19-22 of the 1970 law. Disputes over land redistribution were dealt with by a three-person judicial committee composed of a representative from the Ministry, a representative from the National Front, and one other member. Elective subcommittees consisting of agricultural labourers and poor peasants were established at the district level (article 23), and following redistribution these became the organizational nuclei of the agricultural co-operatives which the State was to support.

As a consequence of the second Agrarian Reform Law, large-scale land ownership in the PDRY was virtually abolished by 1973. Some 124,319 *feddans* (nearly one-half of the country's cultivated land) were redistributed among some 25,778 landless or near-landless families. Moreover, the very scope and violence of the takeovers served an important political purpose in South Yemen by further hastening the collapse of the old order. According to Salem Rubayi 'Ali, a leading proponent of spontaneous revolutionary action:

The land does not give itself away. It has to be taken. The National Front encouraged the *intifadhat* [popular uprisings] and other popular revolts, because revolutionary violence is the only way to produce a definite break [between] the large landlords and the workers ... this policy also had some major consequences: the peasants, fishermen and workers have set up militias to defend, arms in their hands, both their social gains and the power that made them possible [quoted in al-Ashtal, 1976, p. 279.]

Similarly, 'Abd al-Fattah Ismail characterized the agrarian reform laws of 1970 as having 'grant[ed] revolutionary legitimacy to the peasants so they could be liberated from . . . feudalism and re-acquire the land by organizing their ranks and venturing into a class war against their class enemies' (*14 Uktubar*, 22 June 1978, supplement).

Under the PDRY's land reform legislation and the Co-operatives Law of 1972 three forms of agriculture have emerged. The first of these are three varieties of peasant co-operatives. In first-stage co-operatives individual holdings are not merged, but worked separately. Irrigation is managed collectively, however, and fees for this and other co-operatively-supplied services are paid by each farmer to the co-operative. In second-stage co-operatives lands are merged and worked semi-collectively. After the deduction of co-operative costs, profits are distributed among peasants on the basis of land and labour contributed. In third-stage co-operatives all land and services are owned by the co-operative and managed collectively. Profits are distributed on the basis of labour contributed (Hasan, 1974). As of 1980 there were a total of forty-four co-operative farms in the PDRY, accounting for approximately 70 per cent of cultivated land in the country (Halliday, 1983, p. 45). Most of these are of the first or second variety, and the government has thus far been unsuccessful in its efforts to develop these into the higher type, first by 1982, then by 1985.

State farms represent the second form of agriculture in the PDRY. There were thirty-five of these in 1978, accounting for about 10 per cent of cultivated land. State farms are, according to the South Yemeni government, designed to perform three major functions:

(1) the extension of cultivation through land reclamation, and increased agricultural and livestock production;
(2) the supply of foodstuffs both for domestic consumption and export;
(3) improved productivity through agricultural and livestock research and experimentation, to be passed on to the co-operative sector (PDRY, 1977b, p. 15).

State farm labourers (approximately three thousand in 1978) are treated like any other public sector employee, receiving set wages and benefits for their work, and an additional share in the net profits of the farm.

Peasant freeholdings dating from before 1970 represent the third form of agriculture in the PDRY. Such farming continues primarily in remote areas where, for one reason or another, small peasant farms rather than large-scale land ownership existed before the revolution, and where the land reform measures consequently had little effect. Private holdings now account for

Table 4.1 Structure of agriculture, PDRY (1977)

	Area (acres)		Population	
	Total	Cropped	Total	Labour
State farms	29,400	18,000	20,000	4,000
Agricultural production co-operatives	214,000	100,000	189,000	36,300
Private farms	23,000	4,000	7,500	2,500
Nomads	–	–	180,000	36,000
Agricultural service* co-operatives	–	–	80,000	16,000
Machine rental stations	–	–	5,500	1,100
Fisheries co-operatives**	–	–	37,500	7,500
Poultry complex	–	–	4,000	800
Total	266,400	122,000	523,500	104,200

* 31 co-operatives.   ** 13 co-operatives.   Source: World Bank, 1979.

about 20 per cent of the cultivated land of the Republic. Livestock, for the most part, is also privately owned.

In addition to the agricultural sector itself, co-operatives have been fostered by the government in all other aspects of rural life. Under the 1972 Co-operatives Law agricultural service (irrigation, seasonal loans, equipment, etc.), social services, livestock, craft and fishery co-operatives have been established. In the case of the latter, by 1977 some seven thousand five hundred fishermen had been organized into over a dozen co-operatives, accounting for approximately two-thirds of the fishing sector. A State-controlled fishing industry has also been established under the Ministry of Fisheries, consisting primarily of large offshore boats producing for the export market (PDRY, 1977b, pp. 21-4; World Bank, 1979, pp. 30-32, 119).

The scope, depth and social implications of the PDRY's agrarian reform policies have been tremendous. The restructuring of the rural economy led to a marked improvement in the material standards of living of South Yemeni agricultural workers: most collectives now offer medical care and other previously unavailable social services, while in the state farm sector the daily wage for agricultural labour had risen to 900 *fils* by the mid-1970s—an increase of 450 per cent over that paid to farm workers prior to independence (PDRY, 1977b, p. 18). Even more importantly, agrarian reform has transformed the social structure which underlay much of the rural poverty and exploitation of pre-revolutionary south Yemen:

The old power holders—petty sultans, privileged clans, and clerics—have been displaced at the local as well as national level. Through a series of spontaneous and violent uprisings, power has been seized by the lowest, least powerful strata— peasants, fishermen, and labourers. Land reform and marketing co-operatives have set in motion a signficant redistribution of wealth [Hudson, 1977, p. 351.]

Economic Planning

Although a Supreme Council for National Planning was established in South Yemen as early as 1968, it was not until after the Corrective Step and the Law for the Economic Organization of the Public Sector and National Planning (1969) that the framework for comprehensive economic planning in the country was established. As with nationalization and agrarian reform, this third pillar of economic policy was firmly entrenched in the 1970 State Constitution, which declares that the 'national economy shall be wholly directed in accordance with a development plan prepared by the State' (article 17), a plan which overrides all other non-constitutional laws. By this planning the PDRY hopes to make best use of its scarce resources and to maximize the effectiveness of its economic policy.

Development planning in the PDRY is conducted by the Ministry of Planning, created in 1973 from the Central Planning Commission, which in turn had replaced the Planning Board established under the Law for the Economic Organization of the Public Sector and National Planning of 1969. Insight into how this agency frames and implements development plans in association with other government (and party) agencies has been provided by a World Bank study team which visted Aden in 1978. According to their report (World Bank, 1979, pp. 57–67) the initial political guidelines for development planning are drawn up by the Politburo of the party Central Committee. These are then passed on to the Ministry of Planning for elaboration and operationalization in association with the party's Economic Secretariat. Development projects and requisite background information are solicited from both regional (governate) and sectoral (economic and social service ministries and public corporations) agencies. These proposals are then screened and co-ordinated into programs by the Ministry of Planning, with particular attention to the availability of funding for them. Further (political) review is provided by the Politburo and by the Supreme Council for National Planning (economic review). When the final plan has been formulated by the

Table 4.2 Central Government Expenditure, 1977

	Expenditure (YD)	Percentage
General administration	5.63	12.7
Defence and security	18.93	42.5
Local administration	1.22	2.7
Public works, communications	0.77	1.6
Finance and economy	3.89	8.7
Health	2.45	5.5
Education and guidance	8.26	18.6
Agriculture	0.93	2.1
Pensions	0.44	1.0
Other	1.97	4.4
Total	44.49	
Development investments	57.00	

Source: World Bank, 1979, p. 104.

Ministry of Planning it first receives political approval from the party Central Committee. It is then passed on via the Supreme Council for National Planning to the Council of Ministers, which formally issues it and submits it to the Supreme People's Council for legislation. An essentially similar procedure is followed in drawing up annual investment budgets within the development plan. Policy implementation is carried out by the relevant sectoral and regional agencies. They are monitored in this by the Ministry of Planning and the party's Economic Secretariat, and corrective action is ordered when and where necessary.

The development investments thus formulated account for over one half of all central government expenditure in the PDRY (Table 4.2). They are funded through a special fund established for the purpose (Table 4.3), as well as through the banking system (domestic borrowing), self-financing by public corporations, and loans and grants from external agencies (Table 4.4). Most development investment funding—about 75 per cent—ultimately comes from external sources.

The first development plan implemented in the PDRY was the Three Year Plan of April 1971–March 1974. This plan envisaged total investments in the South Yemeni economy of YD40 million. Because of the severe employment, supply and foreign exchange shortages facing South Yemen, these investments were primarily directed at labour-intensive development projects (such as road-building) in the productive sectors of the economy.

Table 4.3 Sources of Development Fund, 1974–1977

	YD ('000)	Percentage
External sources	58,927	78.7%
Expatriate contributions	144	0.2
Grants	654	0.9
Loans (commodity)	6,652	8.9
Loans (cash)	5,900	7.9
Other	45,577	60.8
Domestic sources	15,974	21.3%
50% net profits of		
public corporations	11,385	15.2
contributions from civil		
service salaries	2,374	3.2
government transfers	2,215	3.0

Source: World Bank, 1979, p. 107.

Most of the money actually allocated (47.4 per cent) was hence directed at agricultural and industrial projects, or to much-needed economic infrastructure (37.9 per cent). While economic and planning difficulties (coupled with the failure of some foreign donors to meet aid commitments) led to only 77 per cent fulfilment of plan objectives, significant progress was made in improving South Yemen's dire economic circumstances.

Table 4.4 Actual Sources of Total Development Investments, 1974–1977

	YD ('000)	Percentage
Development Fund	76,772	56.5
of which external	61,834	45.5
Banking system	11,454	8.4
Self-financing	7,337	5.4
External agencies	40,384	29.7

Source: World Bank, 1979, p. 106.

Figure 4.1 Development plans, PDRY

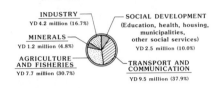

THREE-YEAR PLAN 1971-1974
(Expended : YD 25.1 million)

INDUSTRY
YD 4.2 million (16.7%)

MINERALS
YD 1.2 million (4.8%)

AGRICULTURE
AND FISHERIES
YD 7.7 million (30.7%)

SOCIAL DEVELOPMENT
(Education, health, housing,
municipalities,
other social services)
YD 2.5 million (10.0%)

TRANSPORT AND
COMMUNICATION
YD 9.5 million (37.9%)

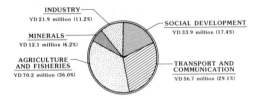

FIRST-FIVE YEAR PLAN 1974-1978
(Expended : YD 194.8 million)

INDUSTRY
YD 21.9 million (11.2%)

MINERALS
YD 12.1 million (6.2%)

AGRICULTURE
AND FISHERIES
YD 70.2 million (36.0%)

SOCIAL DEVELOPMENT
YD 33.9 million (17.4%)

TRANSPORT AND
COMMUNICATION
YD 56.7 million (29.1%)

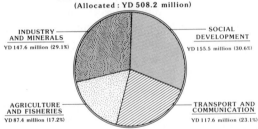

SECOND-FIVE YEAR PLAN 1981-1985
(Allocated : YD 508.2 million)

INDUSTRY
AND MINERALS
YD 147.6 million (29.1%)

SOCIAL
DEVELOPMENT
YD 155.5 million (30.6%)

AGRICULTURE
AND FISHERIES
YD 87.4 million (17.2%)

TRANSPORT AND
COMMUNICATION
YD 117.6 million (23.1%)

The first Five Year Plan covered April 1974 to December 1978 (the financial year was revised part way through to coincide with the calendar year). It initially proposed investments of YD75 million. As new resources became available, however, spending targets were repeatedly raised, finally to YD274.7 million. Some YD194.8 million was actually expended. With the immediate economic crisis now over, this plan embraced capital-intensive development and important substitution projects in the agricultural and industrial sectors, and health, education and other social development projects in the social sector. Indeed, the proportion of funds for the latter nearly doubled, from 14.8 per cent (10.0 per cent expended) in the First Three Year Plan to 22.6 per cent (17.4 per cent expended) in the First Five Year Plan. Overall, a 71 per cent implementation rate was achieved (PDRY, 1974).

The succeeding Second Five Year Plan was originally intended to cover the period 1979-83. In 1980, however, it was abandoned, revised and rescheduled for 1981-5 to allow for the consolidation of the previous plan and the reformulation of development objectives. At the same time light was shed on the various deficiencies and problems which had become evident in the course of the first two plans. At the planning level these included the absence of necessary statistics, the paucity of financial resources, a failure to fully mobilize the human resources of the country, and insufficient construction capacity. At the level of implementation the weakness of construction and financial resources (particularly the failure of some donors to live up to commitments) were again identified as major problems by the Ministry of Planning, as well as a general absence of implementation schedules, failures to receive material and equipment on time, and a lack of housing for foreign experts which in some cases caused delay in important projects (*14 Uktubar al-Iqtisad*, 18 July 1978, pp. 6–7). In framing a new plan greater attention was paid to these difficulties, as well as to feasibility studies, the integration of investment projects at the planning stage, and the strengthening of economic accountability and management skills (*al-Thawri*, 26 April 1980, pp. 1, 4).

Moreover, the emergence of a Revised Second Year Plan at this time coincided with, and was affected by, the replacement of 'Abd al-Fattah Ismail as President by the more pragmatic 'Ali Nasser Muhammed. Under the new plan a more flexible approach to investment capital emerged, with expatriate investment and all sources of foreign aid enjoying new encouragement. The proportion of funds allocated to industrial development rose to 29 per cent, and those allocated to social development to 31 per cent. An average GDP growth-rate of 11 per cent per annum was projected over 1981–5, with real output growth of 18 per cent per annum in the industrial sector, 12 per cent in agriculture, and 9 per cent in fisheries predicted. The plan also envisaged continued growth of the public/co-operative and mixed sectors of the economy. An 88.7 per cent implementation rate was achieved in the first year of the plan, possibly reflecting the new planning process adopted (Arif, 1983, pp. 118–22; Halliday, 1983, pp. 44–6).

A Third Five Year Plan (1986–90) was originally intended for ratification by the Supreme People's Council in early 1986. Political turmoil in the preceding months (culminating in the removal of President 'Ali Nasser Muhammed from power in January), however, served to delay its formulation and announcement.

Sectoral Development

As a result of the general policies outlined above, the PDRY has achieved in substantial measure both economic restructuring and economic growth.

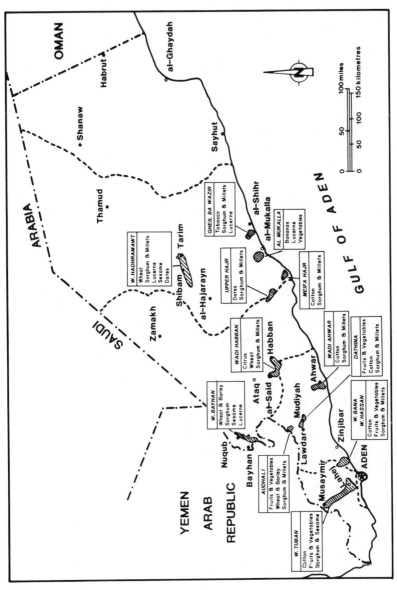

Map 4.1 Major areas of agricultural production, PDRY

National income has increased at a high average rate of 8.7 per cent per annum (1970–81). Public and co-operative ownership of the economy was scheduled to rise to 72 per cent by the end of the 1981–5 development plan.

Economic growth has been greatest in the service and industrial sectors. Industry accounts for 26 per cent of (1981) GDP, and has been growing at an average annual rate of 12.1 per cent. Services have also expanded steadily, now accounting for 61 per cent of GDP (17 per cent trade, hotels, restaurants; 13 per cent transport, storage, communications; 4 per cent finance, insurance, real estate; 1 per cent business and personal services; 26 per cent government services). Growth has been lowest in the agricultural sector (13 per cent of 1981 GDP), wherein the 2.1 per cent per annum growth rate experienced over 1970–81 has failed to match the rate of population increase. The consequence of this has been a growing dependence on imported foodstuffs, with cereal imports rising from 149,000 metric tons in 1974 to 205,000 metric tons by 1983 (World Bank, 1985, p. 184). Approximately two-thirds of South Yemen's food requirements are now imported.

Agriculture and Fisheries

South Yemen's agricultural difficulties arise from several factors. The first and most obvious set of these are the adverse physical conditions under which agriculture must operate in the country. Arable land represents only 0.6 per cent of the Republic's total surface area. Of this the vast bulk is watered by unreliable and meagre rainfall or intermittent *wadi* irrigation.

In an effort to expand the area under cultivation (and the reliability and productivity of land already under cultivation), approximately 60 per cent of the government's agricultural investment has been directed at irrigation projects (World Bank, 1979, p. 27). This has included the construction of a major dam at Abyan, as well as numerous smaller dam sites elsewhere in the country; many kilometres of new irrigation canals; and an average (1972–7) of ninety-two new groundwater wells drilled each year. The area of land under irrigation has correspondingly risen from 53,000 hectares in 1974–6 to 70,000 hectares in 1981. There has also been substantial investment in agricultural mechanization and other inputs (fertilizers, pesticides, etc.). By 1982 an average of six tractors and approximately 11,000 kg. of fertilizer were available per 1,000 hectares of arable land in the PDRY, compared with one tractor and 5,000 kg. in the Yemen Arab Republic (FAO, 1985a).

The Wadi Hadhramawt project—the largest in the country—has been fairly typical of the approach taken to agricultural development in South Yemen. In its $7 million first phase (1977–82), agricultural machinery, fertilizers and pesticides were made available by the State to local co-operatives and state farms through subsidized prices and low-interest loans. Two water-processing plants were established at Shibam and al-Qatm irrigation networks were extended, and groundwater studies undertaken throughout the valley. To support agricultural activity and aid marketing, a date-processing plant and 120 km. of secondary access roads were built. The second phase of the project (1984–8) envisages a doubling in the area of annual cultivation and an increase in groundwater irrigation from 52 to 93 per cent, resulting in expansion of both productivity and absolute production. Some 56 new deep wells are to be dug; 105 open wells improved; and 20 wells electrified. Trucks, plows, irrigation sprinklers and technical experts are to be provided for local farms. The project will be funded by a $9 million loan from the International Development Agency (IDA), $11.7 million from the Kuwaiti Monetary Fund, and $12.2 million from the Arab Fund for Social and Economic Development (*14 Uktubar*, 24 September 1983, p. 2).

Such measures, combined with active land reclamation, have resulted in a steady increase in the area of land under cultivation. They have not resulted, however, in the expansion of agriculture outside the dozen or so *wadis* where it is traditionally practised. In part this is because it is in existing agricultural

Table 4.5 Agricultural Production, PDRY

	1973	1983
Crop *		
Sorghum and Millet	72	80
Wheat	15	15
Barley	4	2
Sesame	3.8	4
Cotton lint and seed	15	9
Livestock †		
Cattle	96	120
Sheep	225	1,000
Goats	900	1,350
Asses	30	170
Camels	40	100

* Thousand metric tonnes.
† Thousand head.
Source: FAO estimates.

areas that investment is most productive; in part it is because most of the land of the PDRY is simply useless from an agricultural viewpoint. According to one survey conducted by the Ministry of Agriculture and Agrarian Reform, even under optimum conditions (irrigation of all suitable lands—something well beyond South Yemen's current financial resources) the area that could be cropped would still represent less than 2 per cent of the total (World Bank, 1979, p. 117).

Moreover, despite an absolute increase in the area under cultivation due to expanded irrigation, the level of agricultural production in South Yemen has seen unsteady growth in recent years (Table 4.5). In 1985 the Food and Agriculture Organization estimated that total crop production had increased only 8 per cent and food production only 2 per cent over 1974–6 levels, while per capita food production had actually declined (FAO, 1985b). This declining productivity is rooted in the structure and operation of the new agricultural system set up by agrarian reform and co-operative legislation—a system which, although having achieved a substantial improvement in the social conditions of the rural population (Chapter 5), has generally failed to stimulate agricultural production beyond immediate post-independence levels.

At the local level, the initial impact of agrarian reform has tended to disrupt the social organization of agricultural labour, undermining traditional work patterns along with traditional work relations. The development of new modes of work, organization and rationalization is a process of experimentation in the revolutionary situation of the PDRY. As a result of the problem of building new relations of production while dismantling traditional ones, agricultural production in the public sector in particular has lagged behind objectives. On third-stage collectives the problem is exemplified by the precipitate formation of such farms from lower-level co-operatives where the necessary political and social consciousness has yet to emerge among the peasantry. On first- and second-stage co-operatives (which are significantly more productive), the assessment of state taxes, social insurance payments, co-operative and pump fees as a percentage of absolute production has been seen as penalizing the most productive farmers. In many cases peasants seek to avoid taxation by retaining produce for personal consumption or sale on the black market, or by concentrating their attention on the small private plot which each co-operative family is allowed to tend. Overall, the gains from agriculture have often been too low (compared with wages in the industrial and service sectors) to keep farmers on the land (*14 Uktubar*, 16 December 1983, pp. 3, 5). Compounding this, the large size of co-operatives (which may have a thousand or more members) often reduces what is intended to be a popular democratic institution to a faceless bureaucracy, resented by those attached to it (*Le Monde Diplomatique*, October 1982, pp. 22–3).

In addition to the question of local organization, agricultural production in the PDRY has also been constrained by poor management and the weakness of agricultural support organizations. This has been particularly evident in the case of the numerous machine-renting stations established in rural areas, which government and party officials freely admit have suffered serious problems. These stations lack equipment, spare parts and trained personnel, and as a result have only managed to achieve 65–70 per cent of their work allocations (*14 Uktubar*, 16 December 1983, pp. 3–5).

Finally, the system of agricultural marketing and pricing adopted in the PDRY has had an adverse impact on agricultural productivity. In the case of marketing, until 1980 two public organizations—the National Corporation for Home Trade (cereals) and the Public Corporation for the Marketing of Vegetables and Fruit—held a monopoly over the distribution of agricultural produce. The distribution networks they manage have been plagued by bottlenecks, shortages and wasteful transport and storage techniques. In the past surplus produce has rotted away in the fields because these agencies have been unprepared to handle it (*14 Uktubar*, 20 November 1980, p. 2). At other times these organizations have found themselves left with no legal recourse when other public and co-operative institutions fail to deliver contracted production.

Agricultural prices are also centrally controlled (by the Ministry of Agriculture and Agrarian Reform). They often bear little resemblance to the costs of production, supply, or demand—even where these are known. The result has been the distortion of agricultural production from year to year, and its decline in the long term.

Numerous attempts have been made to deal with these problems over the years, each reflecting the political atmosphere and leadership of the time. Salem Rubayi 'Ali, deeply suspicious of the bureaucratization of the revolution, sought to improve agricultural productivity through the promotion of revolutionary spontaneity, enthusiasm and socialist emulation in the countryside. After his downfall his policies were widely blamed for having only hampered agricultural efficiency. 'Abd al-Fattah Ismail preferred very different policies, favouring greater central control of agriculture by the party and State. Under his leadership the YSP Central Committee called in 1979 for sterner work discipline, better planning and more efficient technical support (*14 Uktubar*, 21 December 1979, p. 3).

As the problems of central planning emerged, however, 'Abd al-Fattah

Ismail's policies were criticized as being too bureaucratic. Following Ismail's downfall in 1980, 'Ali Nasser Muhammed introduced in their place a number of new reforms designed to increase flexibility, incentive and professional competence in the agricultural sector. Under a 1980 law peasants were allowed to distribute up to 40 per cent of their fruit and vegetable production independently, at up to 150 per cent of the official price. Incentive bonuses and piece-work wages were introduced on state and collective farms, and some co-operatives reorganized into a series of smaller production brigades. Consideration was also given to reducing the size of co-operatives, and to replacing the existing taxation system (based on production) with one based on actual service costs and the area of the co-operative—thus rewarding increased production. In December 1982 further initiatives to improve agricultural productivity proposed by 'Ali Nasser Muhammed included increased farmgate prices for fruit and vegetables; improved wages on state farms and at machine-renting stations; improved transportation and storage facilities; and the provision of trained agricultural economists to state farms and co-operatives (*14 Uktubar*, 14 December 1983, p. 3).

At present the effectiveness of these reforms is unclear. It is also unknown whether the reforms (opposed by many of the more ideological members of the party) will continue in the aftermath of Muhammed's downfall. In February 1986 the new South Yemeni Prime Minister, Yaseen Said Numan, commented that Muhammed 'deviated from our party's economic policy, towards the extreme right, and pursued a devastating economic policy that permitted without limit parasitic economic activity', suggesting that he and many other senior party and government leaders had serious misgivings about the economic reforms instituted by the former president (*MEED*, 15 February 1986, p. 34). On the other hand, it is evident that some reform of the agricultural system in the PDRY is imperative if the country is to reduce its increasing dependence on imported foodstuffs and the resultant drain on already scarce foreign-exchange reserves. Given this, the agricultural issue may once again provide a major area of dispute between pragmatic party technocrats attempting to boost productivity and their more doctrinaire colleagues committed to the social and economic model of agricultural production established in the 1970s.

In contrast to agriculture development in the PDRY's fisheries sector has been much more successful. Indeed, the fisheries contribute to South Yemen's GDP an amount roughly equivalent to that made by the larger but less productive agricultural and livestock sectors. The total catch, although fluctuating as a consequence of economic, climatic and biological factors, has expanded steadily. Tuna, sardines, mackerel, shark, cuttlefish, lobster and

Table 4.6 Fisheries Production, PDRY*

1974	1975	1976	1977	1978	1979	1980	1981	1982	1983
39.3	36.8	64.1	63.9	48.1	51.6	89.7	78.0	69.7	74.1

* Thousand metric tonnes.
Source: FAO estimates.

squid are the most important species fished. A significant portion of production (about one-third) is sold on the foreign market, and fish have become the country's single largest non-petroleum export.

The structure of fisheries in the PDRY is essentially similar to that of agriculture. The public sector, which now consists of seventeen large Soviet, Chinese and Japanese-build deep-sea boats operated by the Ministry of Fisheries, accounts for approximately 10 per cent of fish production (1976). Joint South Yemeni–Soviet and South Yemeni–Japanese fishing companies account for another 10 per cent. The remainder (80 per cent) is produced by co-operative sector. Some private fishing also takes place, but it is a small-scale enterprise generally carried out in remote areas from one-person boats for subsistence purposes. It is not included in government production statistics.

The fishing industry is supported by two canneries (at Mukalla and Shukra), a fishmeal factory and a fish freezing factory (Mukalla). Danish contractors completed a new $33 million fishing port at Nishtun in 1984. Similar upgrading of facilities is currently under way in Aden (with Soviet contractors) and at Mukalla (with Libyan financial assistance).

Industry and Resources

The industrial sector in South Yemen comprises four major components: light industry, water and electricity, minerals and oil, and construction. The first two of these are under the purview of the Ministry of Industry. The third has been administered since 1969 by the Petroleum and Minerals Board and its subsidiaries (the Yemen National Oil Company and Aden Refinery Company) on behalf of the Ministry of Industry. In February 1985, however, it was given its own Cabinet portfolio in the form of the Ministry of Minerals and Energy. Light industry, water, electricity, minerals and oil collectively account for 10 per cent of GDP (1981). The construction subsector, under the Ministry of Construction, accounts for another 16 per cent.

Since independence the PDRY has placed strong emphasis on industrial growth in all these areas, seeing in such growth the basis for reduced external dependence and a strengthened national economy. State investments in industry have been correspondingly large, and are growing: from YD4.2 million (16.7 per cent of expenditure) in 1971-4, to a planned YD147.6 million (29.1 per cent) in 1981-5. Industrial production has expanded accordingly, rising from YD15.4 million in 1973 to YD81.8 million a decade later (World Bank, 1979, p. 35; Arif, 1983, p. 119; *14 Uktubar*, 28 December 1983, p. 1).

The growth in industrial activity which has taken place in South Yemen since independence is particularly evident with regard to light manufacturing and processing. Before 1967 a soft-drink plant, ship repair, tuna processing, and a few small cotton gins represented the only significant industrial operations in the country, excluding the Aden refinery. Today, under the stimulus of state investment and import substitution policies, the PDRY boasts some fifty-two public, co-operative, mixed and private light industrial establishments involved in textiles and leather production, chemicals, building materials, machinery and appliance manufacture, and food processing.

The largest of these establishments, the Chinese-built textile factory in Aden, employs thirteen hundred people. Plagued by maintenance difficulties and obsolete equipment, the government is hoping that a maintenance agreement with Czechoslovakia signed in 1980 and a current $25 million expansion and modernization plan will boost production. Other light manufactures include agricultural implements, spare parts, plastics, tyres, liquid batteries, matches, bricks, sponges and paints. Tomato, flour, dairy, soft-drink, vegetable oil, and fish processing are also carried out. In 1985 a French company was contracted to build a 1,200 ton-per-day cement factory at Batays at a cost of $85 million. Work, however, was delayed in early 1986 by the political turmoil surrounding the downfall of ʾAli Nasser Muhammed.

Parallel with (and in support of) this growth in domestic manufacturing capability there have been significant advances in the provision of water and electricity. The value of production in this area in fact more than doubled between 1969 and 1977, from YD1.95 million to YD4.53 million (World Bank, 1979, p. 141). Energy consumption has increased at an average annual rate of 7.1 per cent (1973-83). At present South Yemen's Public Water Corporation is seeking funding for phase two of a $32.2 million water supply programme for Greater Aden. This project will involve the provision of 10.5 million cubic metres annually to the capital and its environs. Water projects worth another $21.3 million are under way at al-Mukalla, Shagrah, Seiyun and nearly forty other sites throughout the country in 1985 (*MEED*, 13 July 1985, p. 32). Major thermo-electric power generation construction programmes are under way on Socotra Islands, and along the coastal area east of Mukalla. In the long term the Public Corporation for Electric Power hopes to link Aden with Abyan governate by high voltage transmission lines as a first step towards building a South Yemeni national grid (PDRY, 1977a, pp. 48–56; *14 Uktubar*, 20 July 1983, p. 2).

Within the minerals and oil subsector economic growth has been less steady. Salt and limestone are at present the only mineral resources exploited in the PDRY. In an effort to expand this sector (and the foreign exchange earnings it could potentially earn), the government has made an increasing commitment to finding and exploiting new mineral resources. State investments in prospecting have increased markedly, from $1 million in 1971–4 to $34 million in 1981–5. The PDRY currently has a mineral exploration agreement with North Yemen and prospecting agreements with the Soviet Union, East Germany and Czechoslovakia. The Abu Dhabi Fund for Arab Economic Development has provided $1.8 million for mineral exploration activity.

Moreover, attracted by lack of financial cost to the PDRY of such contracts (and unhappy with the slow pace and productivity of Soviet prospecting), the government began opening up the country to exploration by Western oil companies on a concessionary/cost-share basis in the 1980s. As of early 1986 exploratory drilling for oil was being conducted by Brazil's Braspetro and France's Elf Aquitaine at Hurin-Ghayada and Balhaf respectively; by the Kuwaiti Independent Petroleum Group east of Aden; and by the Soviet Technoexport at Shabwa. In 1985 it was announced that the latter area too would be opened to Western companies.

Falling world oil prices, however, coupled with disappointing results from the wells drilled so far, are likely to lead to a slackening in petroleum exploration activity. Indeed, the Italian state-owned company Agip has now abandoned its activities at the offshore Sharmah field 600 km. east of Aden where South Yemeni oil was first discovered in potentially commercial quantities in 1980 (*Middle East Economic Survey*, 3 February 1986, p. A9). Other mineral discoveries have also yet to appear viable, although there is some hope that gold reserves discovered by Soviet prospectors in the Meddan area of the Hadhramawt might allow production by 1988.

In the absence of significant mining activity the minerals subsector thus continues to be dominated by the operations of the Aden refinery, which employed approximately eighteen hundred people and accounted for 9 per cent of total industrial production in 1977 (World Bank, 1979, p. 35).

Table 4.7 Aden Refinery Production, 1964–1985*

1964	1967	1970	1973	1976	1979	1982	1985
6.8	6.2	6.2	2.8	1.6	1.8	3.9	(3.9)†

* Million tons.
† estimate.

Production at the refinery steadily dropped in the first decade of independence, only slightly rising in the 1980s (Table 4.7). Indeed, despite an increase in the absolute price of this production brought about by rising oil prices, the refinery has operated at a loss, maintained only by politically-motivated evergreen oil supply contracts with Iran, Kuwait and the Soviet Union. A similar crude oil refining agreement with Algeria was signed in 1983. Current production stands at about 82,000 barrels per day (bpd)—roughly half of the refinery's capacity of 170,000 bpd. Of this, 10,000 bpd is refined for the Kuwaiti Petroleum Company, 12,000 bpd for the Soviet Union, 50,000 bpd for Iran, and 10,000 bpd for local consumption (*MEES*, 3 February 1986, p. A9). This is slightly more than the refinery's (1978) estimated break-even output of 3.4 million tons per year.

The refinery's difficulties are in part due to political factors, with many Arab countries having cut off oil supplies in the late 1970s in protest over the PDRY's foreign policy. Even more so, however, are they attributable to age and obsolescence. Completed in July 1954, the eight-million ton-per-year capacity refinery still uses the older 'hydro-skimming' production process rather than the more modern 'hydro-cracking' process. As a result it produces proportionately more low-grade fuel oil distillates (50 per cent as compared to 30 per cent with the newer process), and proportionately less high distillates (25 per cent, compared with 40 per cent). The docking and loading facilities are also old, and unable to accommodate large modern tankers. The refinery thus suffers in competition with others in the region. Even bunkering in Aden port by foreign companies is in large part done with fuel oil imported from the companies' own refineries outside the PDRY (World Bank, 1979, pp. 35–7).

In an effort to bolster the productivity and profitability of refinery operations the government announced a major $25 million modernization scheme in 1983. This includes a new 10,000 bpd vacuum distillation unit, an asphalt plant, a 40,000 bpd expansion in Liquid Petroleum Gas (LPG) facilities and new LPG storage tanks. The Italian firm Techipetrol, which is the main contractor for the project, expects completion early in 1986. Aden port expansion (discussed below) has included dredging and expansion of tanker facilities at the refinery. A $23 million contract for this work was signed in December 1985, with completion expected in July 1988 (*MEED*, 15 February 1986, p. 35).

Transport and Communication

At independence South Yemen's transportation and communication infrastructure was severely underdeveloped outside the international port and colonial administrative centre of Aden. The total length of metalled roads in the Republic did not exceed 470 km. of which only 22 km. lay outside urban areas. Road transport to the Fourth, Fifth and Sixth Governates from the capital was virtually impossible. Telephone services only existed in Aden. Aden also boasted the country's only modern air and sea ports, the latter in serious decline as a result of the closure of the Suez Canal (PDRY, 1977a, pp. 36–7). This lack of basic transport and communication facilities not only hampered economic growth but also posed a serious political challenge to national integration. The Republic could hardly be united behind developmental and political goals while its population lay beyond the reach of central government, isolated by geography and divided by distance.

Recognizing that 'transport and communications are vital elements in the socio-economic development of the country' (PDRY, 1977a, p. 37), the PDRY has allocated a large proportion of its development expenditure to infrastructural investment. The First Three Year Plan 91971–4) placed particular emphasis on labour-intensive infrastructure projects (such as road-building), investing YD9.5 million (37.9 per cent of expenditure) in this area. The sum later rose to YD56.7 million (29.1 per cent) in 1974–8 and to a planned YD117.6 million (23.1 per cent) in 1981–5.

In transport these investments have led to a tripling of the metalled road network and a doubling of the unpaved road network since independence, to over 1,781 km. and 10,291 km. respectively (Fisher & Unwin 1986; *14 Uktubar*, 23 October 1980, p. 2). New roads between Aden and Ta'iz, al-Mukalla and the Hadhramawt, Aden and al-Mukalla, and Shihr and Sayhut have now been completed, the last two with Chinese assistance. In 1985 the IDA agreed to contribute $14.4 million to a $39 million highways project which will link the last important agricultural area, Wadi Bayhan, with the metalled road network. OPEC and the Kuwaiti Fund for Arab Economic Development are also contributing to the undertaking. With the expansion of the road network there has also come a steady expansion in the volume of

Table 4.8 Metalled Road Network, PDRY

1969	1973	1976	1978	1980
470km.	559km.	620km.	1,346km.	1,781km.

Source: World Bank, 1979, p. 150; *14 Uktubar*, 23 October 1980.

road traffic. Some 32,800 motor vehicles were registered in the Republic in 1980, up from 24,500 in 1978. In 1980 a Republic-wide Yemen Land Transportation Corporation was formed to manage commercial transportation (trucking and busing), replacing the numerous semi-autonomous public transport corporations which had been created in each governate.

Under the PDRY's Civil Aviation Administration a similar expansion has taken place in air transport. Facilities at Aden (Khormaksar) International Airport (and at the Republic's other modern airport at al-Mukalla) have been continuously upgraded, most recently through the addition of a new runway and international terminal at the former. Hinterland air facilities have also been established or upgraded. There are now an estimated forty-eight regular airstrips in the country, four with permanent surfacing. The Democratic Yemen Airlines Company (Alyemda), created in September 1970, operates a dozen or so aircraft on regular domestic and international flights. About a dozen foreign airlines (including Air India, Ethiopian Airlines, Middle East Airlines, Yemen Airlines, Aeroflot, Saudi Airlines, Kuwait Airlines, Air Djibouti, and Air France) serviced Aden International Airport in 1985.

Aden port—one of the finest and best-placed natural harbours in the region—has undergone a recovery in recent years, particularly since the reopening of the Suez Canal in 1975 (Table 4.9). In the face of changing transport patterns (especially the Cape routing of modern supertankers),

Table 4.9 Aden Port Activity, 1966–1980

	1966	1969	1974	1976	1978	1980
Number of ships	6,246	1,568	1,233	2,336	2,215	2,436
Displacement*	31.4	8.1	5.1	9.9	9.6	12.6
Oil bunkers†	3,486	387	303	638	413	573

* Million registered tonnes.
† Thousand metric tonnes.

regional competition, and ageing facilities, port activity has not returned to its peak mid-1960s level—nor is it likely to do so.

In an effort to increase traffic volume a number of improvements to Aden harbour were made under the First Five Year Plan, including the expansion of deep-freeze capacity, repair facilities and coaster fleet, and the acquisition of a 4,500-ton capacity floating dock. A further $100 million expansion of the port is currently being planned by the Yemen Ports and Shipping Corporation and its subsidiaries (the Port of Aden Authority, the National Shipping Company and the National Dockyards Company). The project will involve the addition of four new deep-water berths (for a total of five), and a 60,000 ton grain silo and berth. A second floating dock has also recently been added by the Ministry of Fisheries—much to the chagrin of the existing National Dockyards Company facility which has complained bitterly of the competition (*14 Uktubar*, 17 July 1983, p. 3; Fisher & Unwin, 1986, pp. 854, 859, 862).

In the field of telecommunications, the Ministry of Communications, in conjunction with the Ministry of Information, has established a national and international short-wave service, and a series of local medium-wave transmitters. Television service, first introduced in 1964, has also been expanded and there are now an estimated 150,000 radio and 31,000 TV receivers in the country. Since March 1978 international cable communications, formerly operated by the British-owned Cable and Wireless station at Aden, have been under the control of the Yemen Telecommunications Company (YTC). The YTC hopes to replace the existing cable facilities with a satellite ground station in the near future if external funding can be secured (Fisher & Unwin, 1986, p. 854).

National Accounts

As noted at the beginning of the chapter, the withdrawal of British subsidies, the closure of the base, and the blockage of the Suez Canal in 1967 combined to create a severe foreign exchange crisis for newly independent South Yemen. Although the worst of this crisis was overcome by the early 1970s, the PDRY has continued to face a potentially precarious balance of payments situation.

The root cause of the PDRY's national account difficulties is the country's chronic visible trade deficit, which reached $793 million (excluding petroleum) in 1983. Quite simply, the country has little to offer in the way of exports: fresh fish (37 per cent) and petroleum (37 per cent) predominate, with cotton lint and seed (8 per cent), coffee (8 per cent), salt and hides also sold abroad. National development, on the other hand, necessitates the sizeable import of vehicles and machinery (35 per cent), food and live animals (23 per cent), petroleum (18 per cent), and basic manufactures (World Bank, 1979, pp. 94, 96). The PDRY's largest trading partners are at present the United Arab Emirates (UAE), Kuwait, Japan, the United Kingdom, France and China (Chapter 6). The volume of non-petroleum trade with African, Asian and socialist countries has steadily expanded in recent years, with the latter now accounting for about one-quarter of the total.

Both austerity and import substitution policies have been adopted by the government in an effort to reduce the commodity trade deficit and consequent drain on foreign exchange. Most foreign trade (about 90 per cent) is centrally administered by the state-owned Foreign Trade Company and the Ministry of Trade and Supply. Both organizations have a clear mandate to limit hard currency expenditure. The government has also sought to improve its balance of payments situation by building upon its successes in the services sector. The expansion of Aden's air and sea ports can be seen as part of this strategy, as can recent efforts to expand the tourist trade to thirty thousand visitors per year by the construction of new hotel facilities and the formation in association with the YAR of a Yemen Tourism Company in 1982. To meet short-term balance of payments difficulties, the PDRY commonly draws upon the International Monetary Fund.

While these trade measures have played a part in limiting (though not reversing) the growth of the PDRY's trade deficit, it has been two other sources of foreign currency that have allowed the Republic to attain a small overall balance of payments surplus in recent years: expatriate remittances and foreign aid. The first of these has grown dramatically since 1973 as a consequence of oil-boom job opportunities in the Gulf and a relaxation of investment regulations at home (Table 4.10). By 1984 the net value of private transfers (primarily workers' remittances) had reached $479.5 million, representing about one half of the PDRY's total GNP.

Foreign aid to the PDRY has also grown considerably in recent years. In the early 1970s the socialist countries dominated this aid, providing about 50 per cent or more of the total. A further 15 per cent came from the PDRY's radical Arab allies Iraq, Libya and Algeria; 15 per cent from other (bilateral and multilateral) Arab aid agencies; 10 per cent from international and United Nations aid agencies; and 10 per cent from the West and other sources. Today the quantity of aid given by the latter three sources has increased, both absolutely and relatively. As of the end of 1984 the PDRY had received some $94.34 million in aid from the Kuwait Fund for Arab Economic Development and $55.55 million from the Abu Dhabi Fund for

Table 4.10 Summary Balance of Payments, PDRY (US$ Million)

	1973	1977	1981	1982	1983	1984
Merchandise, exports	25.6	46.9	48.6	37.9	40.2	30.7
Merchandise, imports	−114.2	−344.2	−641.0	−690.8	−683.6	−824.6
Trade Balance	*−88.6*	*−297.3*	*−592.4*	*−652.9*	*−643.3*	*−793.9*
Exports of services	40.7	51.5	141.3	154.0	138.4	130.0
Imports of services	−36.6	−72.7	−169.4	−196.3	−210.8	−212.8
Balance of goods and services	*−84.5*	*−318.5*	*−620.5*	*−695.2*	*−715.7*	*−876.7*
Private transfers (net)	*32.9*	*187.3*	*378.7*	*429.7*	*439.5*	*479.5*
Official transfers (net)	*26.1*	*125.5*	*266.0*	*272.4*	*298.2*	*165.6*
Grants	0.5	59.1	121.9	126.5	43.1	29.5
Medium/long-term loans (net)	25.6	66.4	144.1	145.9	255.1	136.1
Misc. capital, errors and omissions	*27.0*	*18.8*	*−12.9*	*3.4*	*−15.5*	*233.3*
Overall balance	*1.5*	*13.1*	*11.3*	*10.3*	*6.5*	*−8.3*
Allocation of SDRs	−	−	5.3	−	−	−
Counterpart to valuation changes	6.3	2.5	−19.9	−15.9	−17.1	−23.6
Exceptional financing (IMF)	−	4.3	0.5	0.2	0.1	−
Monetary authorities	−	−	31.6	23.5	7.8	2.9
*Total change in reserves**	*−8.3*	*−19.9*	*−28.8*	*−18.1*	*2.7*	*29.0*

* − Signifies increase in reserves.
Source: IMF.

Arab Economic Development, making these two countries the two largest Arab aid donors to South Yemen. Total Arab agency aid (excluding direct government-to-government transfers) by the end of this period was valued at no less than $508.1 million, with even erstwhile arch-enemies Saudi Arabia and Oman having contributed $34 million each (*MEES*, 6 May 1985, p. B5). However, it is the socialist countries (especially the Soviet Union and the People's Republic of China) which are the PDRY's most important source of financial and technical assistance. At the beginning of 1985, for example, the Soviet Union announced its approval of a long-term aid program to the PDRY worth approximately $400 million (*MEED*, 29 June 1985, p. 36).

The Economic Outlook

Given its lack of resources and general economic underdevelopment, the PDRY has achieved much in two decades of independence. In its first phase of development (roughly 1969-74) the country established national control over the economy through nationalization, restructured the economic base of rural society through agarian reform, and set about constructing the communications, transport and planning infrastructure necessary to unite the country and establish the foundations for long-term economic expansion. In the second phase of development (1975-85) the PDRY's productive capacity was enlarged through capital investment in both the industrial and social sectors, much of it financed by an improved balance of payments situation which allowed the Republic to increase commodity imports beyond bare necessities. The results were evident in a steady rate of economic growth.

As the PDRY enters the second half of the 1980s there are indications that this second phase of development is coming to an end. The Arab oil boom which directly or indirectly financed investment has collapsed amid excess production and falling world oil prices, leading to a contraction of both foreign aid and expatriate remittances to South Yemen. This in turn will place severe pressure on the country's balance of payments, forcing a curtailment of capital investment projects, reduced importation of needed materials, asuterity measures and/or deficit financing. As early as 1984 there were indications that this was already happening. South Yemen's external debt rose to $1,268 million (over 100 per cent of GNP!), a deficit appeared in the PDRY's overall balance of payments, and *émigré* sources began reporting a large deficit in the state budget (*MEED*, 11 January 1986, p. 30; *al-Wahdah*, 15 February 1985, p. 3). More recently, confirmation has come from the government itself, which in the aftermath of 'Ali Naser Muhammed's downfall has accused the former president of 'extravagance with public money and material' and responsibility for an 'increased deficit which reached a horrible figure, threatening the country with an economic crisis' (*MEED*, 15 February 1986, p. 35).

Future economic retrenchment in the PDRY does not equate with forthcoming economic relapse, however. The PDRY could, through continued borrowing, attempt to finance a rate of growth that would outpace its growing rate of external and internal indebtedness. Given the YSP's recent criticism of Muhammed and its historic reluctance to rely on outside forces, however, it is unlikely to risk bankrupting the revolution in this way. Alternatively, it can shift the fulcrum of its development strategy to a domestic focus, calling on the skills and abilities built up since independence to improve productivity and infrastructure, particularly in the chronically weak agricultural sector. The possible return of many South Yemeni expatriate workers with skills learnt abroad could conceivably provide the necessary basis for such development. If regional recession forces the PDRY to adopt such a strategy, it may even prove to be in the country's long-term interests: improved agricultural production would go a long way towards reducing the PDRY's large import bill, while self-reliance would reduce the risk that political independence and national control of the economy, so hard won over past decades, might be mortgaged through external debt. While the direction chosen will not be known until the Third Five Year Plan is released sometime in the near future, the latter of these two approaches thus seems most likely. South Yemen's record of economic development will continue, but at a more modest and more constrained pace.

5 Social Policy*

Social policy in the PDRY, like economic policy, relates directly to the State's objectives of transforming society from the conditions of tribalism, feudalism and colonialism to the conditions of socialism and sovereignty. Thus, social, political and economic objectives are strongly interrelated in state policies and difficult to disentangle. Nevertheless, social policy constitutes a distinct sphere of state activity. While social objectives are generally founded in the government's efforts to eradicate the structural conditions of poverty and inequality, social policy is specifically operationalized in the programme areas of health, education, housing and employment, as well as in policies targeted at particularly underprivileged groups (women and bedouins).

The Foundations of Social Policy

The party's view on the social importance of South Yemen's colonial past, and the relationship between that past and present social policy tasks, were fully discussed and explicated at the National Front's key Fifth Congress in 1972. According to the *Programme of the National Democratic Stage of the Revolution*:

Underdevelopment in Yemen was one of the effects of the British colonialist 'divide and rule' policy. This policy was widely practiced, deepening divisions and fragmentations . . . The British followed the same policy in trying to fragment the south geographically, economically and politically. . . . British colonialism was thus able to strengthen tribalism, to encourage internal strife, and in this way it kept the [sultanates and sheikdoms] busy, allowing no possibilty of social or cultural development. Under the influence of this policy, British imperialism was able to dominate each petty sultanate and sheikdom individually. The heavy burden we have inherited from colonialism confirms its ugly face wherever it exists. For 129 years they left our country, and especially our countryside, without the most basic features of modern life: roads and means of communications, schools, health units, and drinking water wells were virtually non-existent.

*This chapter is written by Jacqueline S. Ismael, with the collaboration of Alexandra Brynen, Research Assistant, Faculty of Social Welfare, The University of Calgary. The chapter is adapted from a forthcoming book, *Social Policy in the Arab World: A Comparative Perspective*.

The colonialists believed that keeping our people in the Middle Ages would ensure the perpetual survival of the colonial presence. This was the terrible situation of underdevelopment left behind by colonialism and its seriousness was further intensified by the colonialist support of outdated values and nonsensical cultures to put our people in a state of humiliation and subjection [PDRY, 1977a, p. 5.]

In other words, the leadership of the PDRY perceives a strong link between colonialism and underdevelopment, and between domestic social structure, collective welfare and national strength. Only by addressing the former (and in particular South Yemen's colonial and tribal legacy), they believe, can real social and national development take place:

An understanding of these factors clarifies the great responsibility placed on the shoulders of the revolutionary forces in changing the existing social and cultural situation.

The revolution believes that the deep-rooted economic changes it is implementing will have a far-reaching effect which will allow it to participate as far as possible in social and cultural struggle to eradicate the residues of colonial social and cultural formations [PDRY, 1977a, p. 5.]

The State's responsibility for bringing about social change and transformation is also set forth in the 1970 State Constitution. In article 26 of the Constitution, for example, the State is directed to 'protect the working class and shall raise its level in various economic fields'. Article 27 notes that 'general education is the basis of social progress and all sections of the people have a right to it'. The State is also mandated to combat illiteracy (article 30), support the family, women and children (article 29), and to 'relieve the society of corrupt concepts spread by imperialism and colonialism and of backward tribal and communal tendencies and so use national culture for serving the national democratic revolution' (article 31). Citizens are guaranteed equality of opportunity (article 34), social security and the right (and duty) to work (article 35), free education (article 37), and medical care (article 49). Special emphasis is placed on advancing the social position of women through education, technical training, maternity leave, and state provision of daycare facilities (article 36). South Yemen's taxation system is progressive by law and reflects socialist principles: 'each person shall contribute towards the public income according to his ability' (article 54). In Chapter 3 of the Constitution the role of mass organizations in social development is recognized. This often includes an explicit social welfare function, such as the participation of the trade-union movement in the administration of social security and the role of youth organizations in combatting illiteracy (articles 57, 59).

Health

Health, the most fundamental human need, is one of the most sensitive indicators of the state of welfare of a population. More than any other set of statistics, basic life expectancy indicators reflect the conditions and consequences of poverty in the PDRY before independence. United Nations and World Bank data for 1965, for example, provide the following comparison of the area subsequently known as the PDRY with other less developed nations on basic life expectancy indicators.

As these statistics reflect, the population of southern Yemen in 1965 ranked among the world's highest morbidity and mortality rates. In fact, there were only nine nations with worse life expectancy rates—Mali, Malawi, Guinea, Sierra Leone, Afghanistan, Bhutan, Mozambique, Yemen Arab Republic and Angola (World Bank, 1985, pp. 218–19). What the data reflect are the conditions of malnutrition, endemic disease and lack of basic health services that are the hallmark of absolute poverty. What the figures mask are the substantial urban–rural differentials within the population. While life for the urban poor in southern Yemen was precarious at best, life in rural areas (where 70 per cent of the population lives) was even worse. For example, even such a basic item as drinking water for animal and human consumption was scarce. Because of the absence of permanent rivers, underground water is the primary source of supply. Only in Aden were there sufficient deep wells to

Table 5.1 Indicators Related to Life Expectancy for Selected Less Developed Nations, 1965

	Life expectancy at birth		Infant mortality rate (under 1-year old)	Child death-rate (aged 1–4)
	Male	Female		
China and India	51	53	115	16
Sub-Saharan Africa*	42–41	45–44	156–150	35–32
Other low-income economies†	44	45	147	27
PDRY	38	39	194	52

* Sub-Saharan African states were divided into two groups in the data reported. The figures cited are the population weighted averages for each group.

† As grouped by 1983 per capital GNP.

Source: World Bank, 1985, pp. 218–19.

supply the population. Rural residents depended on hand-dug wells which were usually highly contaminated. As a result, the rural population lived with the periodic ravages of drought—decimation of herds, famine—as well as the relentless toll of malnutrition and disease.

The immediate tasks facing the revolutionary government were the eradication of malnutrition through improvement in the supply and distribution of basic foodstuffs, the eradication of endemic disease through improvement in water supply and sanitation and through public health measures (innoculation, pesticide use) and the provision of basic health care services (both preventive and curative). The problems of meeting these tasks with inadequate financial resources were compounded by the isolation and fragmentation of the rural population, the lack of transport and communication infrastructures into the rural areas, the lack of adequate human resources to plan, develop and implement the necessary services in the rural areas, and the general ignorance of the rural population regarding elementary nutrition, hygiene and health care.

Food and Nutrition

The structural problems related to the production and distribution of essential consumer goods (including foodstuffs) have been attacked through fundamental economic reorganization—agrarian reform, nationalization of resources, collectivization of production, centralization of planning. These were addressed in the previous chapter. As noted there, these measures have improved but not resolved the problem of adequate and equitable supply of basic foodstuffs. A World Bank mission to the PDRY in 1978 reported the following findings (World Bank, 1979, pp. 44–5):

1. The delivery mechanisms of essential goods (including foodstuffs) to consumers are either state-owned or state controlled. All 'essential goods' have about 6 percent mark-up and are sold at (the same) fixed prices at all retail outlets throughout the country (the Government absorbing transportation costs to all consumption centers). There is no official food rationing (except for sugar where the ration is 3 lb. per person per month); however, retail outlets (particularly the cooperative or public sector stores through which essential foodstuffs are marketed) keep an unofficial check on quantities of food purchased. On the national level, a 'Supreme Committee for Supply' chaired by the Prime Minister meets monthly to review the supply situation of essential foodstuffs throughout the country.
2. *Price Stabilization Fund.* This was established in July 1974 (with an independent budget) with the principal objective of stabilizing the prices of essential food commodities namely, wheat, flour, rice, sugar, milk powder, ghee and cooking oil. Prices of these food items have remained unchanged throughout the period July

1974 to date (June 1978). In 1977, tea was added to the list of commodities to be supported by the Fund. More recently, the Government has used the Fund to subsidize other commodities such as canned tomato products. Subsidized food is effectively 'rationed' . . . and available to each person in limited quantities only.

3. *The Cost of the Average Food Basket (at 1977 Prices)* was calculated by the mission to be about YD39.9 per capita (adult consumption) per annum in the urban areas and YD26.7 in the rural areas. . . . The lower estimate corresponds fairly closely with the results of a social survey by ECWA in 1976 which reported average monthly costs of food per household (5.4 persons including 3 children) at YD9.5, compared to the monthly average income of YD20 (the survey was conducted for slum dwellers living in uncontrolled housing). Given the current minimum wage of YD20 per month in the public sector it appears that food consumption in the urban areas is satisfactory. It is much less clear that with agricultural or rural family incomes ranging between YD74–148 per annum (1976) or YD6.12 per month, the entire food needs of the population are being met.

4. FAO estimates of food supplies per capital indicate that per capita caloric intake has actually declined over the period 1969–77. While these estimates (based on FAO data on gross estimates of imports, local production, change in stocks, etc.) are subject to a wide margin of error, they do indicate a tightening in food consumption. In addition, the United Nations is currently transferring about 6,000 tons of basic foodstuffs under the World Food Program to PDRY as emergency relief. The overall food picture therefore appears to reinforce the need for improved agricultural production and associated increase in rural incomes.

FAO indices on food production reflect a steady though fluctuating increase in food production between 1971 and 1982—from 92.43 in 1971 to 97.80 in 1982 (1974-6 − 100) (FAO 1983, p. 76). To fulfill the primary planning objective of meeting the basic needs of the population, local food production is supplemented by imports. About two-thirds of food requirements are, in fact, imported (Arif, 1983, p. 121). As a result of improved local production and imported foodstuffs, per capita dietary energy supplies in relation to nutritional requirements increased from 80 per cent in 1973–5 to 94 per cent in 1980–2 (FAO 1985c, Annex Table 16). There has thus been steady progress in the struggle against malnutrition. Furthermore, through continuous development of the transport and communication infrastructures, as well as food storage and handling facilities, there is substantially better distribution of food to remote rural areas where the problems of malnutrition were most acute (and not addressed at all prior to independence).

Public Health Measures

Public health measures include the development of safe drinking water in the rural areas, improvement in sanitation, mass innoculation against communicable diseases, and pesticide control of insect-borne diseases. The leading causes of morbidity are infectious and communicable diseases that could be brought under control with improved public health standards (United Nations, 1978, pp. 30–2). Because of this, the PDRY immediately initiated a range of public health programmes to alleviate the morbidity and debilitating conditions of the population.

One of the first measures undertaken was the establishment of the Public Water Authority with responsibility for administration, maintenance and development of all water projects in the country. Provision of safe drinking water without charge to the consumer is one of its primary responsibilities. Under the 1971/2–1973/4 Development Plan, existing water facilities throughout the governates were upgraded and expanded, forty-four new deep bore wells were drilled to supply clean drinking water to villages and towns, and assistance was provided to local community projects for the development of clean drinking water. The 1974–8 Development Plan initiated a number of new water development projects (PDRY, 1977a, pp. 51–6). Progress on the provision of clean drinking water throughout the State is steady but slow, hampered by the shortage of financial resources, the climate and the terrain. Furthermore, the need for water for development projects as well as for individual consumption strains the slow and expensive development of new resources. The scarcity of water in PDRY is one of the most serious handicaps to social and economic development.

The problems of adequate sanitation have received some attention, though there is very little information available. The Office of Preventive Medicine, established in 1968, includes an environmental health branch. In addition to providing public education on hygiene to reduce the risk of disease, it co-operates with other ministries and preventive medicine bureaux in the governates, as well as with local community projects, to improve sanitation (PDRY, 1977a, pp. 26–33). Reports indicate that Aden was the only major population centre in 1976 with even a primitive sewage system. A team from the Federal Republic of Germany conducted feasibility studies in 1976 to devise a more effective water and sewage system for Aden (FAS, 1977, p. 115). Work has progressed on this and sewage systems have been initiated in al-Mukalla, the State's second largest city (14 Uktubar, 19 December 1983), and in other major municipalities (14 Uktubar, 15 February 1984). In the rural areas, community and public education appears to be the main thrust of efforts in this area.

To bring endemic diseases under control, mass inoculation programmes for all children against poliomyelitis, smallpox, tuberculosis and yellow fever have been undertaken, assisted by the World Health Organization. Pesticide spraying against malaria and bilharzia has also proceeded vigorously. By 1978, a joint UNDP/UNDPA mission to PDRY reported that 'a prevention programme against cholera, smallpox, and malaria has been conducted quite efficiently' (United Nations, 1978, p. 33).

A final sphere of State public health policy in the PDRY has revolved around the consumption of *qat*, the narcotic leaf traditionally consumed by men throughout the Yemens. Quite apart from the danger to health posed by the substance itself, the practice has serious unwanted social consequences in so far as it may consume a significant portion of daily income and divert it from otherwise more productive activities. In 1975 the government successfully imposed restrictions on the consumption of *qat* during workdays and a ban on its production. In the early 1980s consumption was reportedly banned altogether (Halliday, 1983, p. 54; Bidwell, 1983, p. 326).

Health Services

State provision of free health services is a fundamental objective of PDRY, expressed in article 49 of the Constitution thus:

Medical care is a right for all citizens. The State shall ensure this right by establishing all types of hospitals and health institutions and by organizing the medical profession, expanding free health services and spreading health education among the population.

The problems of fulfilling this objective are enormous. At the time of independence, the country had only twenty-seven trained doctors, 1,623

Table 5.2 Health services by type, 1977

Governate	Hospitals	Health centres	Health units	Maternal and child health units
First	4	1	9	8
Second	4	1	51	5
Third	5	3	54	3
Fourth	3	1	51	1
Fifth	7	7	79	5
Sixth	1	1	8	1
Total	24	14	252	23

Source: United Nations, 1978, p. 58.

Table 5.3 Medical and Auxiliary Health
Staff by Type, 1977

	Total	Yemeni
Physicians	222	125
Dentists	8	5
Pharmacists	19	11
Medical assistants	332	332
Qualified nurses	131	120
Lab technicians	24	22
X-Ray technicians	17	16
Qualified midwives	7	7
Health inspectors	10	10
Community midwives	205	205
Practical nurses	1,142	1,142
Auxuiliary health staff	237	237
Others	108	108
Total	2,462	2,340

Source: World Bank, 1979, Table 12.12.

other trained medical workers, eleven hospitals and eighty-four clinics (PDRY, 1977a, pp. 25–8). Facilities were heavily concentrated in Aden, and services in the rural areas were virtually non-existent. The expansion of services, especially to the rural areas, the training of medical and paramedical professionals, and the acquisition of medical equipment and medicines have been the primary objectives of health service planning. Thus, all development plans—1971–4, 1974–8 and 1981–5—have placed great emphasis on strengthening the PDRY's medical infrastructure. Table 5.2 reflects the development of the health service throughout the governates by 1977.

The shortage of trained medical and paramedical staff has been met on a short-term basis by bilateral and multilateral assistance. At the same time, an Institute of Health Studies was established to gradually supplant reliance on foreign professionals with indigenous manpower. Table 5.3 reflects the increase in medical and paramedical personnel by 1977.

The 1981–5 development plan projected a continued expansion of health services, with 5.4 per cent of the plan budget allocated to health services (*14 Uktubar*, 15 February 1984). It included plans to upgrade existing facilities, add five new hospitals with 1,088 beds, five health centres, fifty-one health

Table 5.4 Life Expectancy Indicators—YAR and PDRY, 1960 and 1981

	YAR		PDRY	
	1960	1981	1960	1981
Life expectancy at birth	35.8	42.6	36.0	45.5
Infant mortality rate	211.6	190.0	209.5	142.9
Child mortality rate	60.4	50.0	59.4	29.3

Source: World Bank, 1983b, pp. 98–9.

units and eight outpatient clinics. The mobile dispensaries programme for remote rural areas was also to be expanded (Arif, 1983).

Life expectancy at birth in the PDRY increased from 38.5 in 1965 to 46 in 1983, reflecting the overall improvement in the general health of the population. The increase is consistent with trends in other poor states of the world and does not reflect a quantum leap. What life expectancy indicators do reflect, however, is the substantial closing of the gap between urban and rural people and between rich and poor. This is revealed by a comparison of the PDRY with the Yemen Arab Republic (a state with the same cultural background but without the revolutionary social objectives of the PDRY).

The infants and children of the poor are at highest risk of mortality in an unhealthy environment. The increased reduction in these rates in the PDRY, together with the greater increase in overall longevity, are a result of the PDRY's substantial effort to equalize conditions for the poor generally, and the rural poor in particular. Although indicators disaggregated by income level, urban–rural residence or occupation are not available to support this conclusion, it is nevertheless inferred by the difference between health policies that are targeted to reduce structural inequalities and those that are targeted to ameliorate the consequences of structural inequalities.

Education

In the ideology of the PDRY, the educational institution functions as a primary agent of social change and is central to the goals of transition from a tribal social structure to a modern nation-state. According to one former South Yemeni Minister of Education, the educational system of the PDRY seeks to support economic and social development; to expand education opportunities and hence contribute to 'national consciousness of social responsibilities'; to deal with all children equally, regardless of social background; to engender a sense of 'national unity, national values and international solidarity'; to eradicate class and other social distinctions; and to equalize opportunities throughout the Republic (al-Noban 1984, pp. 104–5). Similarly, 'Abd al-Fattah Ismail once characterized education as providing a basis from which the youth of the country could help 'struggle to build the new society of the revolution' (*14 Uktubar*, 22 June 1978, supplement).

Before such goals could be pursued, however, the government had to deal with the underdeveloped educational system it inherited at independence. A severe shortage of schools and teachers existed throughout the country, particularly in the hinterland. What schools did exist were often not centrally administered; rather they were the product of local philanthropy, missionary activity, and fragmented colonial policy. Economic and cultural barriers made education available to the elite alone. The illiteracy rate at independence exceeded 80 per cent, and 95 per cent in rural areas.

A first step towards restructuring this situation was taken by Law No. 26 of 1972, which reorganized the Ministry of Education and established the administrative basis for the expansion of educational services in the Republic. Eight years' schooling (ages 7–14) was made compulsory. All fees for state education were abolished. Under the Literacy Law of 1973 all illiterate adults were compelled to attend literacy classes by 1982. This attendance (or eight years' schooling) became a prerequisite for legal employment. Intensive programmes of school-building and teacher-training were instituted. State expenditure on education has averaged 7.4 per cent of GDP, in contrast to 4.4 per cent for developing countries generally (World Bank, 1979, p. 47).

As with other policy areas, the party principles of democratic centralism guided and continues to guide organization and decision-making. Policy decisions are only made after close consultation by the minister responsible with school administrators and representatives of relevant mass organizations. Once a policy decision is reached, however, it becomes binding throughout the system (al-Noban 1984, pp. 110–11). In an effort to adapt policy to local conditions, policy implementation has, since 1973/4, been devolved to education directorates in each governate. These directorates work in association with local People's Councils, and their activities are monitored by the central Ministry of Education to ensure that educational standards are maintained.

As a result of its attention to the educational field, the PDRY has made substantial advances in this area. Table 5.5 reflects the progress made between 1966 and 1977.

Table 5.5 Statistical Indicators of Education, 1966/7 and 1976/7

	1966/7	1976/7
Number of schools		
Primary	329	976
Preparatory	53	326
Secondary	7	25
Number of teachers		
Primary	1,744	9,018*
Preparatory	n.a.	
Secondary	165	532
Number of enrolments		
Primary	49,928	206,358
Preparatory	11,583	43,410
Secondary	2,992	10,946

* Primary and preparatory schools were combined into a unitary eight-year programme in 1976.
Source: World Bank, 1979, Table 12.4.

Also reflecting this expansion in education, the percentage of participation in school had increased from 51.0 per cent in 1970/1 for the 7–12 year age-group to 65.4 per cent by 1976/7; from 15.0 per cent in 1970/1 for the 13–15 year age-group to 40.1 per cent in 1976/7; and from 4.2 per cent in 1970/1 for the 16–18 year age-group to 12.8 per cent in 1976/7 (World Bank, 1979, Table 12.4). By 1982, enrolment in secondary schools as a proportion of the age-group had increased to 18 per cent (World Bank, 1985, p. 222). Furthermore, the 1981–5 development plan targeted an increase in the enrolment ratio of the 7–14 year age-group from 67 to 83 per cent (Arif, 1983).

The first eight years of school are geared to the general socialization of children. Beyond this, secondary education and an increasing network of vocational and technical institutes and programmes run by various ministries are geared to the manpower needs of a developing economy. On-the-job training programmes have also developed as a means of upgrading the skills of the labour-force.

At the level of higher education, the University of Aden was formally opened in 1975, combining existing post-secondary institutions under one administration. It encompasses faculties of education, economics, engineering, agriculture and medicine. Since opening, the university has rapidly increased its enrolment. The 1983 graduating class totalled 803, representing a 93 per cent increase over 1982 (*14 Uktubar*, 19 July 1983). In addition, scholarships to study abroad are available—primarily through bilateral educational assistance programmes. In 1977/8, 466 new scholarships were offered for study abroad (World Bank, 1979, Table 12.9).

The adult literacy campaign initiated in 1973 had only very limited success. In the period from 1973/4 to 1976/7, out of a total of 201,004 adults enrolled in literacy classes, only 52,514 graduated (World Bank, 1979, Table 12.10). To increase completion rates, beginning in 1975, all public establishments were required to hold literacy classes for their employees. At the same time, a system of incentives was developed—pay increases and promotion—to encourage completion. In the late 1970s, planning for a new literacy campaign for 1984 was initiated. Based on a more systematic plan, this campaign mobilized community resources in a grassroots integrated approach to adult education (*14 Uktubar*, 20 September 1983). It stressed the need for adequate literacy courses to accredit more than sixty thousand literacy instructors mobilized through student, teacher, union and community organizations (*14 Uktubar*, 18 April 1983). As yet, there is no information available on the success of this campaign.

Employment

The social dimension of labour policies in the PDRY relates to the State's efforts to eradicate unemployment, minimize income inequalities, and abolish exploitative labour relations. Widespread unemployment, aggravated by the closure of the British military base in Aden and the closure of the Suez Canal, was at crisis proportions in Aden at the time of independence. Furthermore, disguised unemployment in the rural areas reflected the primitive conditions of exploitation and underdevelopment that consigned the vast majority of the population to an inescapable cycle of absolute poverty.

Thus, an underlying objective of all development planning in the PDRY has been the elimination of unemployment through rural and urban development. These plans were discussed in the previous chapter. Their success in reducing unemployment was noted by the 1978 World Bank mission to the PDRY thus:

Table 5.6 Percentage Distribution by Sector of Employed Labour
Force, 1969, 1973 and 1976

	1969	1973	1976
Agriculture and fishing	52.3	47.1	45.4
Industry	3.0	6.2	6.8
Building and construction	1.1	4.6	7.0
Trade, restaurants and hotels	9.8	7.7	7.5
Transport, storage and communications	1.5	4.3	6.0
Finance, insurance and real estate	0.8	0.6	0.5
Other services (including public, social and personal)	31.4	29.4	26.8
Total	99.9	99.9	100.0
(N, '000)	(264)	(323)	(399)

Source: World Bank, 1979, p. 82.

Open unemployment, severe in 1967, has now virtually disappeared as a result of Government employment policies (including a rapid intake into the government sector) and migration abroad. In fact it now appears (given emerging manpower deficiencies in certain key sectors including construction) that manpower shortages may soon constitute a major constraint to the economic and social development of the country [World Bank, 1979, p. 43].

Table 5.6 reflects the changing sectoral distribution of the labour force in the PDRY betwen 1969 and 1976.

As the table reflects, there was a 34 per cent increase in the employed labour force between 1969 and 1976, together with the sectoral redistribution occasioned by economic development. The total labour force, both employed and unemployed, increased from 311,000 to 416,000 in the period, while unemployment dropped from 47,000 to 17,000 (World Bank, 1979, p. 81). What is not reflected in the statistics is the substantial reduction in disguised rural unemployment since this unemployment was not included in the 1969 statistics. Reviewing the success of the development plans in 1978, Secretary-General of the Central Committee, 'Abd al-Fattah Ismail, observed:

The three-year development plan and the first five-year development plan have made it possible to establish a number of productive projects under the leadership of the public sector and thousands of workers and employees who had been deprived of the right to work in the past have been enrolled in the labour force. The trend of economic development of the second five-year plan ... points to the growing influence of the public sector on the domestic economy and to increase in the labour race, and the five-year development plan projects are to absorb 100,000 workers and employees. The reality of economic development points to the elimination of unemployment in our society. [*14 Uktubar*, 22 June 1978.]

By 1981, 45 per cent of the labour force were employed in agriculture, 15 per cent in industry and 40 per cent in services (World Bank, 1985, p. 214). The average annual rate of growth of the labour force between 1970 and 1985 was about 3 per cent—a very high growth-rate that is expected to last over the remainder of this century (ILO, 1977, Table 5). Thus, provision of employment for an expanding labour force remains an important development objective. Nevertheless, with substantive resolution of the unemployment crisis, the second Five Year Plan (1981–5) expanded the development focus to include not only unemployment but also the economic problems of manpower development (Arif, 1983). The number of vocational and technical training programmes rapidly increased to upgrade the quality of labour—a factor recognized as essential to further improvements in the quality of life in South Yemen (*al-Tali'ah*, 1 February 1984).

The introduction of a minimum wage and salary reductions provided an immediate relaxation of wage inequalities. Fixed scales of remuneration, reducing the income differential from 1:11 in 1967 to 1:3.5 for most incomes, contributed to further reductions. By 1976, average annual wage rates ranged from a low of YD73.6 in agriculture and fishing to a high of YD355.5 in finance, insurance and real estate (World Bank, 1979, p. 83). To provide a labour policy framework consistent with constitutional principles of equality and non-exploitation, in 1978 the PDRY passed Law No. 14, the Fundamental Labour Law (text in PDRY, 1978).

Law No. 14 established minimum conditions of wage labour in all sectors of the economy (articles 3 and 6) and established a Labour Council (article 4) to formulate general policy and offer recommendations to the State in the following areas: contracts of employment and related disputes; regulation of working hours and rest periods; wages, incentives and compensation policy; training and instruction of the work-force; industrial health and safety; retirement pensions, accident compensation and health care; supervision of labour legislation. The law guarantees the right to work and equality of opportunity, prohibiting employment discrimination on the basis of sex, age, race, colour, creed or language (article 5). It establishes the priority of employee claims against the assets of employers as paramount, even over the State Treasury (article 8) and regulates employment procedures (section 3), delegating to state employment agencies exclusive authority to hire (article

14). Employment of minors (under 16) is forbidden and priority of employment opportunity is given to the following categories of unemployed: persons disabled as a result of service in the defence of the nation, and the offspring of martyrs; persons who have completed national service with honour and loyalty; skilled professionals; persons unemployed by reason of redundancy (article 18).

Section 4 of the law regulates contracts of employment, both individual and collective, as well as the conditions for termination of contracts. Section 5 addresses the organization of labour and procedures, stipulating employer and employee obligations, legal incentives, and disciplinary measures. Section 6 addresses working hours, limiting them to eight hours per day or forty-six per week; overtime work; holiday, vacation, sick leave and maternity leave entitlements. Wages and compensation are addressed in section 7. Under article 54, the Ministry of Labour is responsible for publishing wage scales, determined in accordance with 'prevailing economic conditions and the general standard of living of the country'. The Labour Council is charged with proposing minimum wage scales by industry and profession, with an absolute minimum wage as the benchmark for all employment (articles 55 and 56).

Section 8 establishes the responsibility of employers to provide training opportunities for employees, and the responsibility of the Labour Council to organize training programmes. Section 9 deals with industrial health and safety, and section 10 with job security. Supervision of the implementation of labour legislation is covered in section 11, and section 12 deals with the arbitration of labour disputes. Section 13 guarantees employee rights to organize and join labour unions of their own free will, the right of the Confederation of Trade Unions to call a general strike, the role of the unions in regard to setting standards of working and living conditions for employees, as well as participating in management decisions. Section 14 establishes the penalties for contravention of the labour law, and section 15, the supremacy of Law No. 14 over all existing labour legislation.

Thus, Law No. 14 deals comprehensively with the problems of unemployment, inequality and exploitation. While the conditions of labour in the PDRY are still very difficult by modern standards, Law No. 14 provides the legal framework for guaranteeing that the benefits of economic growth will go directly to labour—rather than indirectly through a trickle-down effect. By this law, the State has directly tied the welfare and quality of life of the working population to the state-run economy, in effect supplanting the tribal structure as the primary determinant of individual and collective social welfare.

Housing

At the time of independence, the housing situation in southern Yemen reflected the same inadequacies as other basic needs. In Aden, while the British left behind a stock of upper- and middle-income housing, this was unequally distributed and rents were exorbitant. The urban poor lived in shanty towns and makeshift shelters. In the rural areas, the housing situation was even worse, with mountain caves being used for shelter.

To alleviate the situation in Aden, the PDRY passed Law No. 32 in 1972 nationalizing all property and confiscating the property of absentee landlords. All rents were reduced by 25 per cent. A Ministry of Housing was created to supervise nationalized housing and the construction of popular housing under development plans. The first Five Year Development Plan allocated YD3.3 million for the construction of 1,370 dwellings, 74 per cent of them in Aden (PDRY, 1977a, p. 79). By the end of the Plan's term, 1,481 units had been built (*14 Uktubar*, 18 July 1978).

Because of maintenance problems in public housing, the government decided in 1976 to sell new housing units constructed in the public sector to private individuals for personal occupation. A revolving mortgage fund was created to encourage private home-ownership. In addition, the National Bank offered long-term low interest house-building loans to attract housing investments by the expatriate population sending remittances to relatives in PDRY.

Allocations to housing development have been modest, averaging less than one per cent per year under each of the Plan periods, reflecting the severe financial restraints on development planning in the PDRY. Constraints on construction—the availability of resources, materials and manpower—have further hindered progress in this area. These constraints have been progressively overcome, and the second Five Year Plan—1981-5—set the construction of six thousand new units as its target (*al-Tali'ah*, 1 February 1984). In 1983 alone, 2,682 units were completed, 15 per cent more than actually planned and 303 per cent more than built in 1982 (*14 Uktubar*, 15 February 1984).

Underprivileged Groups

Two groups in Yemen that have been particularly underprivileged by the traditions and institutions of tribalism, feudalism and colonialism are women and the bedouins. The PDRY has given special attention to attaining the political emancipation and social equality of both groups. The challenges facing the State in bringing them into the mainstream of society have been compounded by strong cultural resistance.

Resistance to female emancipation and equality is historically rooted in the division of labour and the patriarchical social structure. Reinforced by tribalism, feudalism and colonialism in southern Yemen, these patterns virtually isolated women from civil society. The PDRY has pursued the legal emancipation of women through constitutional guarantee (part 2, article 36) and through the passage of Law No. 1 of 1974, the Family Law. This law represents an attempt to abolish polygamy, child marriage, forced marriage, dowry and unilateral divorce, as well as to ensure that child custody is based on the best interests of the child. Furthermore, Law No. 14 of 1978 provides legal guarantees of equal opportunity in employment for women, sixty days maternity leave with full pay and child-care facilities for working women.

As noted in Chapter 3, the General Union of Yemeni Women represents the State's attempts to mobilize women to participate in political, social and economic affairs. With a membership of almost fifteen thousand, the Union provides the basis for female participation in local, provincial and national political bodies. By 1981, women held six seats in the Supreme People's Council and almost 10 per cent of the membership in the local people's assemblies in the governates (al-Siyasah, 18 September 1981). An important function of the Union is the organization of educational and training programmes for women. It also organizes day-care centres for working women (14 Uktubar, 22 October 1980). By 1981, there were twenty-three day-care centres throughout the country (al-Siyasah, 18 September 1981).

Another important dimension of State efforts to reduce fundamental social inequalities between the sexes came through education. Between 1966 and 1976, the number of females enrolled in primary education increased from 10,166 to 71,531 (World Bank, 1979, p. 157). Progress continued over the next decade, though female participation rates in compulsory education remain below 50 per cent (compared to over 90 per cent for males). In effect this reflects the persistence of traditional cultural barriers to the education of women.

Increases in female participation in education are reflected at the upper end of the educational hierarchy by the increasing number of women graduating from university. In 1976-7, there was a total enrolment of 479 women in the University of Aden, compared to 1,214 men (World Bank, 1979, p. 160). The 1983 graduating class of the university included 398 women, compared to 405 men (14 Uktubar, 19 July 1983).

Female participation in the labour-force has also expanded rapidly as part of the State's efforts both to provide women with economic equality and to recruit them into the economic development effort. In its needs assessment report on the PDRY in 1978, a United Nations mission to PDRY concluded:

Increased education, along with the shortage of manpower among other factors, has significantly raised female work participation. In a society where only a few years ago women observed strict purdah (the wearing of veils), the Government has succeeded in getting women to work side by side with men in cooperatives, state farms, and industrial establishments. Women's participation, particularly in teaching, nursing, and secretarial jobs has increased considerably during the last five years and special attempts are being made to improve the women's participation in these professions by increasing their enrolment in respective educational and training programmes [United Nations, 1978, p. 23].

Although the absolute number of women in the labour-force increased rapidly, as a proportion of the total labour force female participation only moved from 4.4 per cent in 1965 to 5.8 per cent in 1981 (World Bank, 1983b, p. 99). While more opportunities have opened up for women in the economy, women remain concentrated in unskilled and semi-skilled occupations. Furthermore, traditional attitudes towards women's role in the home and in the workplace continue to inhibit greater female participation in the labour force.

State intervention and radical reforms have substantively improved the position of women in PDRY, but fundamental sexual inequalities remain and are reflected in the low rate of participation of women in the labour force and the weak commitment of working women to the labour force. In a comprehensive study of female employment in the PDRY, Maxine Molyneux concluded that 'sexual asymmetry in the occupational structure still allocates the best jobs to men and many of the worst to women' (Molyneux, 1982, p. 80). She identifies the State's failure to attack the root of this problem—the sexual division of labour in employment—as the main factor inhibiting fuller female participation (p. 82).

The problems of bedouins as an underprivileged group are very different from those of women. Bedouins constitute about 10 per cent of the population of PDRY. They are heavily concentrated in the remote Thamud district of the Fifth Governate and in the Sixth Governate. As nomadic pastoralists in remote areas, the bedouins are insular in their social structure, a characteristic intensified by the geographic, social, economic and political detachment from the rest of the population. As the most economically deprived group in the PDRY, they constitute an intractable problem of social inequality compounded by isolation and cultural resistance.

In 1973, the PDRY initiated the Development of Northern Areas Project with financial and technical assistance from United Nations agencies. The project aimed at improving the standard of living of the bedouin population, providing a basis for the economic integration of the bedouin into the rural economy, and encouraging them to adopt a settled lifestyle. This multi-sectoral project focuses the development of social service centres at major watering points in the regular migrations of the bedouin communities. The services at these centres include improving the quantity and quality of water resources for animal and human consumption (which includes the transport of water to the centres during the dry summer months); establishing community development programmes for literacy and vocational education; developing consumer co-operative societies; and providing schools and modern health units. In the economic sector, the project emphasizes ranch development and improvement in facilities for animal health and breeding; development of a regular animal marketing system and training programme for local officials in regional planning, community development and animal husbandry (United Nations, 1978, pp. 26-7). There is, unfortunately, no information available on an evaluation of this comprehensive project.

Another dimension of the State's efforts to assimilate the bedouins into the mainstream of Yemeni life is the development of residential schools for bedouin children. In effect, the schools separate bedouin children from their families for the school year. By 1976/7, there were a total of twenty-seven primary and ten preparatory residential schools with an enrolment of 27,572 students (World Bank, 1979, p. 50). No further information is available on this potentially controversial programme.

6 Foreign Policy*

The People's Democratic Republic of Yemen exhibits virtually all the characteristics of a small state that, in the classic power politics paradigm of international relations, would render it a virtual prisoner of external forces beyond its control: it is weak, underdeveloped, surrounded by suspicious or hostile neighbours, and occupies a strategic position coveted by regional and superpowers alike. This, combined with the cold war lenses through which the Republic is commonly regarded, has led many analysts of the country to reject examination of the foreign policy of the PDRY in its own terms. Instead, explanations of its international behaviour are framed in terms of the interests and actions of the Republic's principal ally, the Soviet Union. Unlikely rumours—that 'the island of Socotra was being forcibly cleared of its inhabitants so that it could be turned into a home of a joint South Yemeni–Ethiopian task force under a Russian commander' (Bidwell, 1983, p. 329), for example—are cited as evidence of Soviet domination without the slightest substantiation. South Yemen is thus reduced to a 'Soviet outpost', 'client', 'proxy', or 'satellite', so thoroughly penetrated by Soviet influence that it is held to be incapable of genuinely independent action (e.g. Wrase, 1979; Cigar, 1985; for a critique of these formulations see Wenner, 1984).

Here a very different approach to the international relations of the People's Democratic Republic of Yemen will be taken. Drawing on an analytical framework for Arab foreign policies developed by 'Ali Dessouki and Bahgat Korany (Korany & Dessouki, 1985), this chapter will show that despite the constraints placed on it by the global and regional systems, domestic factors have played an equally important role in shaping the foreign policy of the PDRY. While this policy has, on the whole, been congruent with that of the Soviet Union (and undoubtedly influenced by it), it has ultimately remained the product of Aden's—not Moscow's—concerns, aims and aspirations.

* This chapter was co-authored by Rex Brynen, Doctoral Fellow, Department of Political Science, The University of Calgary.

The Domestic Environment

Within the domestic environment of the PDRY five sets of factors have had the greatest impact on the international orientation and behaviour of the regime: its geographical location, its historical-ideological evolution, available economic and military capabilities, and the nature of its political system. A recurrent theme across all these goals is the way in which apparent weaknesses in the country's regional and international position have been lessened (or even reversed) through a combination of revolutionary theory with policy praxis based on a realistic appraisal of international opportunities and circumstances.

Geography

Sited at the southern entrance to the Red Sea and controlling access to it from the Indian Ocean through the Bab el-Mandeb, South Yemen's geographical position has been and continues to be one of great strategic importance (Map 6.1). As a consequence, the area has attracted the attention of a long line of outside powers: the British, the Turks, the Persians, the Ethiopians and others stretching back to the early days of human civilization. While time and national liberation have changed the players and rules, the geostrategic game being played today in South Arabia has not altered all that much: super-powers and regional actors alike show special consideration for the PDRY, not necessarily because of what, but because of where, it is.

Such a strategic location can be a major burden for a small weak country seeking to defend its sovereignty, security and national independence. In South Yemen's case 'difficult and dangerous possibilities' are seen to stem from the country's location in a 'strategic and sensitive geographic region' (ʿAli Nasser Muhammed in *Granma Weekly Review*, 14 December 1980, p. 9). At the same time, however, the Republic's geostrategic location has undoubtedly helped Aden to coax economic and other assistance both from socialist allies anxious to secure influence in the area and from conservative Arab neighbours equally anxious to limit the bounds of such influence—a juggling act to be sure, but one at which the regime has proved increasingly adept since the mid-1970s.

Indeed, geostrategic location may well be the sole foreign policy asset bestowed on the Republic by geography. Its land is barren and rugged, inhibiting both national integration and economic development. The country suffers from an almost total absence of exploitable natural resources.

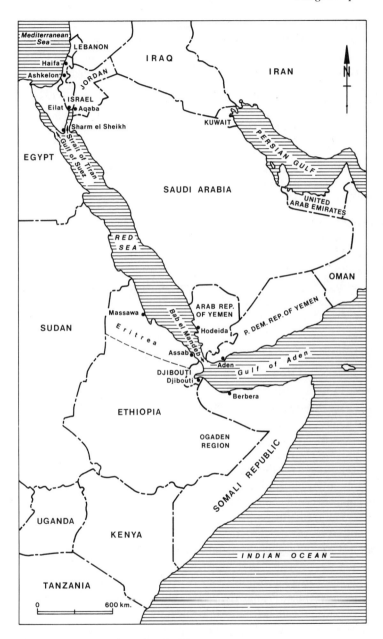

Map 6.1 Geostrategic setting, PDRY

Source: Ethiopia: Politics, Economics and Society, Frances Pinter, 1985.

It also lacks natural frontiers, or (in most places) even a demarcated border. This has made the PDRY vulnerable to subversion and military incursions by hostile neighbours and counter-revolutionary forces. In the early 1970s 'Ali Nasser Muhammed outlined South Yemen's tenuous regional position:

We are besieged from all sides. In the west, the Ethiopians and their Israeli allies scheme and fortify the islands near the Bab el-Mandeb; in the east, the British Air Force bombs our frontier communities under the pretext of pursuing guerrillas from Dhofar; in the north, the counterrevolutionaries in our country, led by revolutionary officers we dismissed, have taken refuge with our North Yemeni brothers at Ta'iz, Hodeida, and San'a, and take part in the assaults which the tribes in the pay of Saudi Arabia unceasingly launch across the northern frontiers, where King Faysal has massed his own troops [Le Monde, 31 May 1972, p. 3].

Similarly, Salem Rubayi 'Ali characterized his country at this time as a 'peninsula surrounded by hostile forces' (Rose al-Yusuf, 15 November 1971, p. 14). This hostile ring has weakened considerably in recent years as a consequence of the Ethiopian revolution and growing *détente* between Aden and its Arab neighbours. Nevertheless, geographic vulnerability continues to be a potential source of concern for South Yemeni decision-makers.

Historical and Ideological Development

Two interrelated themes dominate South Yemen's history, and through that history its foreign policy: colonialism/imperialism and social exploitation. It was in opposition to the former, of course, that the National Front was formed in 1963 and launched its armed struggle against Britain the following year. Because British colonial control of the South Yemeni hinterland rested so firmly on the existing tribal and semi-feudal social order, however, the nationalist agenda of the nascent NF soon grew to embrace the goal of social revolution. As detailed in Chapter 2, local conditions and ideological developments in the broader Arab world progressively radicalized NF cadres in the South, welding indivisibly together their anti-colonialism and their commitment to socialist revolution. Moreover, the crystallization of National Front ideology at a time when the Arab left was beginning to question the petit-bourgeois orientation and nationalist chauvinism that underpinned existing formulations of Arab socialist thought (Nasserism, Ba'athism, etc.) lent the emerging NF a unique political character. Its anti-imperialism and nationalism were highly internationalist in content, and for the most part eschewed any special priority for Arabism. Similarly, its socialism was quasi-Marxist in tone. The organic view of society posited by both Arab and Islamic socialists was rejected in favour of militant struggle by the working classes against those who sought to exploit them.

Economic Capability

While the PDRY's historically-generated commitment to anti-colonialism and social transformation has tended to direct it towards revolutionary goals in both the foreign and domestic spheres, the economic resources available to the State to achieve such goals have been severely limited. As noted in Chapter 4, the South Yemeni economy remains weak, despite considerable economic growth in most sectors since independence.

One implication of this has been a severe limitation of the foreign policy choices open to the government at any one time. Aden is simply unable to match the financial power of most other Arab regimes, or the extensive sophisticated foreign policy apparatus which petrodollars have funded. Another effect of poverty has been to render development a foreign policy imperative in its own right: the PDRY must pursue measures which advance its economic situation both for the domestic benefits of this advancement (improved standard of living, increased regime legitimacy), and because economic growth makes it possible to pursue a more active policy in the international arena.

As noted in Chapter 4, foreign aid has been a very important element in South Yemen's development strategy. Aid has allowed the Republic to embark on impressive capital investment projects. It has also financed an otherwise severe current account deficit in the country's balance of payments. With aid, however, there has also come not only accelerated development but also the risk of dependency. The PDRY's external indebtedness has soared in past years, from a mere $1 million in 1970 to a very considerable $1,263 million in 1983 (World Bank, 1985, p. 204). Thus far the 'soft' nature of most of these loans—an average of only 2.5 per cent interest, twenty-two years maturity, and average grace period of five years—has prevented the PDRY from being caught in the repayment/debt squeeze which afflicts many other developing nations. At the same time, Aden will undoubtedly have to consider the sensibilities of its benefactors when constructing its foreign policy agenda.

This narrowing of options, however, is not the same as external control. Foreign aid has not given either the socialist bloc or conservative Arab donors final say over the outcomes of the South Yemeni foreign policy process. Indeed, the PDRY can and does play the aid game rather well, using the competition for influence between the Soviet Union and its conservative neighbours to its own advantage. Consequently, 'socialist' and 'petrodollar' aid have become positively rather than negatively correlated as each competes with the other. While aid donors on both sides could eventually become annoyed at the failure of foreign aid to alter South Yemen's chosen foreign policy agenda, the strategic importance of South Yemen makes it unlikely that any would abandon the field altogether.

Military Capability

For a small, poor country of only 2.1 million people, the PDRY has sizeable armed forces, consisting of some 27,500 regulars (eighteen thousand of them conscripts), supported by forty-five thousand reservists and a People's Militia of fifteen thousand (Table 6.1). The Popular Defence Forces are relatively well trained, equipped and motivated. Approximately YD55.1 million ($159.4 million) was spent by the State on defence in 1982, representing about 18.4 per cent of central government spending. In the early days of the Republic as much as 48.8 per cent of public funds were expended on the military—a vast burden for a country of such limited means (World Bank, 1979, p. 15; International Institute of Strategic Studies 1985, pp. 88, 171).

Given the prevailing level of regional militarization and the Republic's often conflicting relations with its neighbours, South Yemen's military

Table 6.1 PDRY Armed Forces, 1985

Army:	24,000
	1 armoured brigade, 1 mechanized brigade, 10 infantry 'brigades' (regiments), 1 artillery brigade, 10 artillery battalions, 1 surface-to-surface missile brigade, 2 surface-to-air missile batteries. Total of 450 tanks (T-54/55/62), 400 other armoured fighting vehicles.
Navy:	1,000
	10 fast-attack craft, 4 patrol craft, 7 landing craft.
Air Force:	2,500
	103 combat aircraft, 15 armed helicopters: 4 fighter/ground-attack squadrons (Mig-17/21; Su-20/22), 1 interceptor squadron (Mig-21), 1 transport, 1 helicopter, 1 training squadron; 1 SAM regiment.
Reserves:	(45,000)
Paramilitary:	(15,000 People's Militia)

Source: Heller, 1983; IISS 1985.

preparations can hardly be seen as excessive. The country has twice been at war with North Yemen (1972 and 1979). It has suffered both subversion and military incursion across all three of its borders on numerous occasions since independence. Finally, since 1979 South Yemeni leaders have seen what they perceive as a 'growing concentration of US imperialist forces in the Middle East, Arabian Gulf, and Indian Ocean area', manifest in the formation of a US Rapid Deployment Force, increased naval activity, and the acquisition of United States' military facilities or rights in Oman, Somalia and Egypt (Ali Nasser Muhammed in *Granma Weekly Review*, 14 December 1980, p. 9). Yet, despite all this, the PDRY's defence spending and armed forces are on the whole considerably smaller than those of its neighbours (Table 6.2). As evident from the figures given earlier, the country has consistently reduced defence expenditure as relations with its neighbours have normalized. It must also be kept in mind that (as shown in Chapter 3) the Popular Defence Forces and People's Militias are as much elements of revolutionary socialization as they are agents of national security. Through the armed forces and conscription the party has been given an important mechanism for instilling revolutionary values and ideals in each successive generation of South Yemenis.

Most of South Yemen's arms purchases—$702 million of $738 million by 1982 (constant 1972 dollars)—come from the Soviet Union, often on concessionary terms. An estimated thirteen hundred Soviet and East European military advisers support the Popular Defence Forces (Bennet, 1985, pp. 752-4). Despite *émigré* and Western reports, there is little evidence of Soviet military bases in the country; instead, the Soviet Union's own military

Table 6.2 Regional Defence Spending

	Defence spending (1982)			
	Total ($ m.)	Per capita ($)	Govt. spending (%)	Armed Forces (1985)
Oman	$ 1,682	$ 1,558	42.6%	21,500
Saudi Arabia	27,062	2,706	28.0	62,500
YAR	527	87	27.6	36,600
PDRY	159	76	18.4%	27,500

Source: IISS, 1985, p. 171.

presence in the country would appear to be limited to the use of air and sea port facilities in Aden and Socotra.

Revolutionary Politics and Foreign Policy

Since the Corrective Step questions of foreign policy have been intimately tied to the structure and process of South Yemen's new political order. On a structural level this has meant that foreign policy decision-making has passed into the hands of a state structure dominated by the party and by party considerations. On an ideological level the goals of South Yemen's socialist revolution have, through the party, become the touchstones of foreign policy. In practical terms, foreign policy issues have become an important arena for intra-party conflict, a fact evidenced by their prominence in all of the political crises explored in Chapter 3.

Foreign policy has also become an important component of what Michael Hudson has called the 'legitimacy formula' of the NF/YSP. Within the party the close relations forged by the YSP and PDRY with the socialist community are held up as evidence of the party's correct path. Among the populace at large the intrigues of imperialism and the need for constant vigilance to defend the gains of the revolution are emphasized in order to build an atmosphere of support, loyalty and commitment to party and State (Hudson, 1977, p. 369).

Foreign Policy Orientation

Just as colonialism and social exploitation dominated the emergence of both party and State in South Yemen, the twin themes of anti-imperialism and social revolution dominate the foreign policy of the contemporary PDRY. Their primacy is proclaimed in article 13 of the State Constitution, which sets forth the guiding principles of foreign policy:

The State confirms the application of the principles of the United Nations, the International Declaration of Human Rights, the rules of international law generally recognized.

It supports national liberation movements against colonialism and imperialism.

It shall strengthen its relations with progressive Arab states, Arab peoples, socialist, progressive, and peace-loving states.

The People's Democratic Republic of Yemen shall develop relations of cooperation with [other] states on the basis of equality and mutual respect.

The People's Democratic Republic of Yemen shall not use its armed forces against the freedom of another nation.

Similarly, the *Program of the Yemeni Socialist Party* adopted by the party's first congress in October 1978 declares:

The aim of the foreign policy of the party and state is to create favourable foreign policy conditions for successfully implementing the Party Program, in particular in the sphere of completing the fulfillment of the tasks of the stage of national democratic revolution by the working people of Democratic Yemen and strengthening [militant] solidarity with the revolutionary movement of Arab peoples in the struggle against imperialism, Zionism, and reaction, for national liberation and social progress, for the expansion and intensification of relations of cooperation with the socialist community headed by the Soviet Union, the consolidation of international relations with the international workers movement under the leadership of its vanguard parties, and the strengthening of unity with people's revolutionary struggle for national liberation, social progress, and the defence of peace. Its aim is also energetic activity to implement and observe the principle of peaceful coexistence between states with different social systems and to develop normal relations with all states in the region on the basis of noninterference in international affairs and respect for national sovereignty [Muhammed, 1985, pp. 110–16].

The YSP programme and other public documents and speeches of South Yemeni leaders thus reveal a view of the world expressed in terms of imperialism and opposition to it. The imperialist camp, led by the United States, consists of the imperialist countries of the West and their reactionary allies in the Third World. Zionist Israel ranks among the latter. The world revolutionary movement consists of the socialist community (led by the Soviet Union), national liberation movements, and the communist parties in capitalist countries. The PDRY considers itself (and other progressive Arab regimes) as part of this alliance, in the ranks of an Arab national liberation movement seeking to displace imperialism, Zionism and local reaction from the Middle East.

Two major foreign policy objectives flow from this world view and orientation. First, the South Yemeni decision-makers must protect their revolution and foster its growth as an integral part of the world revolutionary movement. Second, they must lend moral, political and practical assistance to national liberation movements, both as a function of their 'internationalist duty' (Muhammed 1981) and to tip the global correlation of forces further against imperialism. Together these two elements are intended to foster 'suitable international circumstances for the development of the revolutionary process' inside the PDRY (Muhammed in *al-Hurriyah*, 7 July 1980, pp. 8–13). In practice, however, they have often appeared contradictory. Domestic security and development necessitate a conservation of resources, and hence a 'conservative' foreign policy which avoids unnecessary external commitments. Active support for national liberation movements, on the other hand, attracts the opprobrium and hostility of neighbouring regimes and fuels external attempts to isolate or destabilize the revolutionary regime.

However, despite the dangers, it was support for revolutionary movements in the Gulf and elsewhere that was the dominant theme of South Yemeni foreign policy in the early 1970s. In exchange, the PDRY suffered constant infiltration and military incursion from Oman, Saudi Arabia and North Yemen. Aden saw little room for accommodation with these reactionary regimes, the Soviet Union's lack of enthusiasm for the (Peking-orientated) Dhofar rebellion in Oman and the existence of friendly ties between Moscow and the YAR notwithstanding. Further afield, the PDRY demonstrated reservations about the growth of Soviet-American *détente* and its implications for Third World revolutionary struggles (Halliday, 1975, p. 266).

Eventually, however, the horizon of further socialist revolution in South Arabia faded. At the same time vast sums of Arab aid (generated by growing Gulf petroleum earnings) were now being made available to poorer Arab countries. These two developments led South Yemeni decision-makers to conclude that the interests of the revolution and of regional anti-imperialism could best be served by moderation of the Republic's basic foreign policy approach: further militancy would only push neighbouring countries further into the arms of imperialism, and would also inhibit the flow of Arab aid to the PDRY. A relaxation of tensions, on the other hand, would lead to increased aid and increased physical security, thus providing conditions under which the PDRY's own domestic agenda could be better and more safety pursued. It might also allow the PDRY to build some degree of common agreement among states in the region in opposing imperialist and Zionist pressure, the political, ideological and social differences among them notwithstanding.

The first concrete outcome of this revised foreign policy approach came in 1975–6 when an admittedly uneasy rapprochement with the Gulf States and Saudi Arabia was achieved by Salem Rubayi 'Ali. Although retrospectively criticized for his collusion with reactionary forces after his overthrow in 1978, 'Ali's basic policy remained partially intact under 'Abd al-Fattah Ismail and was renewed by 'Ali Nasser Muhammed on his rise to power in 1980. To the north, relations with the YAR sharply improved after a brief border war in 1979. To the east, the PDRY and Oman reached agreement on full diplomatic normalization in 1982. Border tensions declined and ever larger volumes of development assistance flowed from the Gulf to Aden.

The above should not be taken as an indication that the PDRY's commitment to actively support national liberation has fallen by the wayside, however. South Yemen continues to extend training facilities to a number of revolutionary movements from Asia, Africa and Europe, providing 'aid to national liberation movements . . . in proportion to our means . . . [as] . . . a small country with modest resources' (Muhammed in *El-Dieich*, July 1980, p. 29–32). In Ethiopia, South Yemeni troops have fought in support of the socialist government against Eritrean separatists. Moreover, South Yemen has continued to play another role within the world revolutionary movement— that of unifier and alliance-builder in the face of imperialist schemes to sow discord among those fighting for national liberation. In the Middle East, for example, imperialism, Zionism and local reaction are seen as having attempted to 'undercut and bring down patriotic regimes in Arab countries', 'aggravate discord between Arab countries and between progressive patriotic contingents active in the Arab world', and 'drive a wedge in the strategic alliance of the Arab fighters for freedom and independence and the revolutionary forces of the world, primarily the socialist-community countries headed by the mighty Soviet Union' (Muhammed, 1981, p. 23). The PDRY has taken stands against this. It is a member of the Arab Front for Steadfastness and Confrontation, and has urged greater co-operation between its members. It has attempted to foster some degree of unity within the fragmented ranks of the Palestine Liberation Organization. In the Gulf the PDRY has decried the Iran–Iraq War as a useless conflict which only diverts two otherwise anti-imperialist countries from the struggle.

Finally, no discussion of the foreign policy orientation of the People's Democratic Republic of Yemen would be complete without addressing a third, and distinct, theme of that orientation: Yemeni unity. According to the preamble to the PDRY Constitution, North and South Yemen constitute a single cultural and geographic territory, and Yemenis a single nationality. The Yemeni homeland, however, has been divided through the historic impact of imperialism and local reactionary feudalism. In order to reunite the divided homeland, and to consolidate its national liberation, unity is held to be an important long-range objective of both the party and the State. Commitment to unity thus flows both from romantic nationalism, and more fundamentally from a belief that, through unity, anti-imperialism and socialism can best be fostered in the region (Stork, 1973, p. 25). As detailed later in this chapter, the means by which this objective has been pursued have ranged from support for North Yemeni revolutionary movements to formal unity agreements and the establishment of institutions for greater inter-governmental co-operation between Aden and San'a.

Foreign Policy Decision-Making

Although information on decison-making in the PDRY is sparse at best, past experience suggests that three major centres for this exist within the regime: the Presidency, the Council of Ministers, and the party Politburo and Central Committee.

Since independence it has generally been the President who has held sway over regular foreign policy-making, and as a result the international behaviour of the PDRY has always borne something of the personal stamp of the President of the day. Under Salem Rubayi 'Ali, for example, the Republic proved wary of an over-tight Soviet embrace and gradually improved its relations with neighbouring states. This process slowed down with 'Abd al-Fattah Ismail while relations with the Soviet Union improved to the point where a twenty-year Treaty of Friendship and Co-operation was signed with Mosow in 1979, reportedly on presidential initiative. Ismail was also more committed to a militant policy in the North, and it was during his period in office that tensions arose with San'a, culminating in a brief war in 1979. For his part 'Ali Nasser Muhammed, while not lessening ties with Moscow, did moderate foreign policy beyond previous levels, overseeing rapprochement with both the North and Oman.

The resources which have allowed South Yemeni presidents to exert this degree of influence over foreign policy decision-making are numerous. Legally, the President (Presidency Council) is responsible for representing the Republic abroad and for appointing diplomatic and military officials under Chapter 2 of the state Constitution. Through this patronage the President is able to mould much of the foreign policy apparatus of the foreign policy establishment in his own image. There is considerable symbolic power attached to the presidency, lending weight to the President's foreign policy pronouncements at home and abroad. Finally, achieving the position of president in the first place requires considerable skill and influence within the State/party structure—attributes of power that can often also be brought to bear on policy concerns.

The second centre of foreign policy decision-making within the PDRY is the Council of Ministers. Although the foreign minister is nominated by the president and may represent an executive extension of presidential policy, strong political figures in the office do enjoy significant influence over policy formation and implementation. Moreover, other Cabinet ministers may also exert influence over foreign policy decisions, either because of the foreign policy implications of their portfolios or because of their personal political power. Collectively, the Council of Ministers is responsible, under article 103 of the State Constitution, for external security and for approving treaties before their submission to the People's Supreme Council, and collectively it is powerful enough to block or amend presidential foreign policy decisions. With the abolition of the Presidency Council in 1978 the foreign (and domestic) power of the Council of Ministers has grown further.

The final centre of foreign policy decision-making in the PDRY is the YSP, and particularly its Central Committee. All major questions regarding foreign policy orientation and major foreign policy initiatives must be approved by the Politburo, Central Committee, or even a party congress, depending on their import. It is the party—not the State—which determines the broad outlines of the Republic's international actions, and monitors the President, Council of Ministers, and Ministry of Foreign Affairs to ensure compliance. Foreign policy disputes among foreign affairs decision-makers are referred to the Central Committee or Politburo for final arbitration. In some cases (such as party-to-party relations with fraternal socialist and Arab countries) the YSP may even take the lead, managing such relations through the Secretariat of the party Central Committee.

At the risk of over-generalization, the presence of these three centres within the South Yemeni foreign policy process has led to a decision-making process characterized by a practical but individualistic president, an incremental and technocratic Council of Ministers, and an ideological Central Committee—as much a function of the positions themselves as of the persons who have occupied them (Chapter 3). The President has dominated immediate decision-making and external relations, generally supported by the Council of Ministers. The Central Committee, however, has remained the dominant force in terms of defining and operationalizing South Yemen's basic foreign policy orientation. While recent events (the overthrow of 'Ali Nasser Muhammed) will not affect the party's ultimately predominant role, they may lead to a shift in the balance of power between President Attas (not known for his leadership skills) and the Council of Ministers (a body of collective decision-making more likely to win full party confidence).

Foreign Policy Behaviour: Regional and Global Relations

Yemen Arab Republic

Although the people, territory and government of the YAR had played a significant role in South Yemen's liberation struggle, and despite formal support for the ideal of Yemeni unity by both parties, the gap between Aden and San'a widened in the years immediately following South Yemeni independence. The reasons for this trend were many. The Yemen Arab Republic harboured the remnants of FLOSY and other defeated groups, a perennial irritant to Aden. It also furnished a haven for the many splinters of the NF opposed to the ruling caucus. For its part, Aden supported what remained of the left in the North, as well as pro-Southern Shafi tribes along the border. There were also disputes over the demarcation of the frontier itself, and over control of Kamaran Island, historically administered from Aden but occupied by the YAR. Conflict intensified after the Corrective Step in the South and Saudi-sponsored national reconciliation in the North set the two Yemens on very different political and socio-economic courses. In September 1972 conflict in turn became war when Saudi-backed exiles and tribesmen launched an unsuccessful attempt to invade the PDRY and topple the regime.

Following Kuwaiti and Arab League mediation, the North and South agreed to a ceasefire later in September. This was followed by further mediation between the two by Algeria and Libya, culminating in a final ceasefire and unity agreement announced on 28 October 1972. President 'Ali of the PDRY and President 'Abd al-Rahman al-Iryani of the YAR subsequently met in Tripoli, Libya in November to finalize the accord. Joint North–South committees were established to work out the details of union between the two countries.

As might be expected from any attempt to unite two such very different regimes, the joint committees soon got dragged down in a morass of political, social and constitutional difficulties. Aden apparently stepped up its support for dissident nationalist and leftist elements in the North, where reactionary army officers seized upon this as a pretext for purging leftist officers. Amid these problems and rising tensions the PDRY and YAR agreed in September 1973 to postpone unity indefinitely.

With Iryani's resignation and the rise to power of Col. Ibrahim al-Hamdi in the North in June 1974 hopes of further North–South co-operation reappeared. The new North Yemeni President was committed to a policy of weakening ties with Saudi Arabia and improving them with Aden. While this policy was of course welcomed (and reciprocated) by the PDRY, it was much less popular in Riyadh and among the northern Zaydi tribes that Saudi Arabia supported. On 10 October 1977 the depth of their displeasure was made evident: Ibrahim al-Hamdi was assassinated on the eve of his departure for Aden where he was to hold further unity discussions and sign a mutual defence pact. The assassins were never caught, but the motive was clear to all.

Under al-Hamdi's successor, President Ahmad Hussein al-Gashemi, the YAR renewed its pro-Saudi orientation. Rapprochement with the South ground to a halt; Abdullah Asnaj (formerly of FLOSY) was reappointed Foreign Minister. In the YAR's southern regions of Ta'iz and Turba these policies provoked the local military commander and his troops to rebel, ultimately defecting to the PDRY in May 1978.

At this point another unseen assassin intervened. On 24 June 1978 a bomb exploded in the briefcase of a personal envoy from President 'Ali of the PDRY to President al-Gashemi. Both the envoy and al-Gashemi were killed. A number of groups might have planned this action: the President's domestic opponents; Saudi Arabia (attempting to poison inter-Yemeni relations); Salem Rubayi 'Ali; or 'Ali's opponents within the National Front. Whatever the truth of the matter, it was Aden that was blamed for the incident both by al-Gashemi's interim successor al-Qadi 'Abd al-Karim al-Arashi and by the new YAR President, 'Ali Abdallah Salih. The PDRY's denials and condemnation of the act were ignored amid North Yemeni calls for the elimination of the revolutionary regime (*al-Riyadh*, 1 July 1978, p. 1, 13) and a rising number of incidents along the frontier. On 1 July the Arab League, under North Yemeni and Saudi urging, called upon its members to freeze all political and economic ties with the PDRY. (Syria, Libya, Algeria, Iraq and the PLO were absent from the meeting, and ignored the resolution; Djibouti abstained.) South Yemen's membership in the regional organization was temporarily suspended.

It was at this point that the PDRY revised its policies concerning the YAR, returning to the militant approach which had been characteristic of relations in the early 1970s. Salem Rubayi 'Ali's successor as President, 'Abd al-Fattah Ismail, was known to be a strong proponent of this approach, as were other party members from a North Yemeni background. Moreover, in view of the barely restrained hostility now being directed at the South there seemed little reason not to respond in kind. Hence, the PDRY stepped up its support for the National Democratic Front (NDF), a coalition of a half a dozen or so nationalist and leftist groups in the North formed in February 1976. In addition to the radio and administrative facilities offered the NDF in the past, weapons and military training were now supplied. NDF guerrillas began infiltrating the YAR in substantial numbers.

On 24 February 1979 the continuing hostilities between North and South finally escalated into full-scale war. NDF guerrillas, backed by South Yemeni troops, advanced into North Yemen. The border towns of al-Bayda, Harib and Qa'atabah were occupied. Almost immediately the YAR's external supporters came to its assistance. On 28 February Saudi Arabian troops were put on alert. That same day the United States unveiled an emergency $390 million aid allocation to the YAR, funded by Riyadh. Fighting continued until mid-March, when a Syrian and Iraqi-mediated ceasefire went into effect. Military disengagement was completed by 23 March. A few days later President Ismail of the PDRY and President Salih of the YAR opened negotiations in Kuwait. These culminated in the announcement of a new unity agreement on 30 March.

The shift from war to unity was, as it had been in 1972, an abrupt one. In terms of South Yemeni foreign policy a number of factors are likely to have influenced yet another change of approach. First, the PDRY was unwilling to sustain the heavy long-term costs that unity through violence with the YAR would entail. A change in San'a by force of arms seemed particularly unlikely in view of the external support the YAR had now received from Saudi Arabia and the United States; even the Soviet Union was unwilling to break its good relations with the North. Further confrontation it appeared, would only push the North further into the imperialist orbit. Finally, there were signs from San'a of its willingness to reach an accommodation with both the South and the domestic opposition. Asnaj was removed as Foreign Minister, and Salih opened discussions with the NDF. Reflecting its own willingness to participate in the political process in the North (and hence strengthen ties between it and the South), the NDF regrouped into the Popular Unity Party (PUP) early in 1981.

Agreement on these points within the South Yemeni party/State leadership was not absolute, however. Despite the removal of Ismail (the leading supporter of militant unity) in April 1980, others—notably Salih Muslih Qasim—continued to press for support for the NDF and for revolution in the North. The NDF they argued, was, pursuing a continuation of the revolutionary struggle that the leftist wing of the National Front had fought in the South in 1967-9. Many of the NDF leaders, including its President Sultan Umar, had been prominent members of the NF during the liberation struggle. (This overlap led the YAR to charge that the NDF was nothing more than a Marxist front, controlled by the YSP Central Committee. Such accusations were demonstrably false.) Thus to a large degree proponents of a moderate approach vis-à-vis the YAR (including President Muhammed) were ideologically outflanked. When, in the latter half of 1981, negotiations in the North broke down (in part because of Saudi interference), a clear majority in support of the NDF was consolidated. In response to a YAR military offensive against the rebels, South Yemeni support for the NDF was again stepped up. Aden was unable to sustain the Front, however, and by the spring of 1982 some 2,000 NDF fighters and their families had been forced to seek refuge across the border in the PDRY (*Le Monde Diplomatique*, October 1982, pp. 22-3; Halliday, 1984b, p. 361).

Concurrently with support for the NDF, Muhammed continued (albeit unsteadily) with his preference for North-South rapprochement. Meetings between the South Yemeni President and Salih in late 1981 resulted in new agreements on unity measures on 2 December. These included the formation of a Yemen Council, Joint Ministerial Council, and Secretariat to oversee future integration negotiations. By 30 December a 136-article draft constitution was ready for discussion. Under it a Yemeni Republic would eventually be established with San'a as its capital. The Joint Ministerial Council later met over this and other matters in November-December 1982 and August 1984; the Yemeni Council in August 1983 and February 1984. The result was a series of joint agreements regarding movement between the two countries, tariffs and customs, and co-operation in the political, economic and technical fields. Joint corporations were established for tourism, oil exploration, shipping and in other areas. While real unity seems unlikely in view of the fundamental political, ideological and social differences between the PDRY and YAR—not to mention severe Saudi opposition to any such move—it is clear that political co-operation and a degree of economic integration would hold out significant benefits for both sides.

Oman

Relations between the People's Democratic Republic of Yemen and the Sultanate of Oman were, until very recently, unremittingly poor. The primary reason for this was the PDRY's strong support for the Popular Front for the Liberation of Oman in Dhofar Province, abutting on the Sixth Governate. The insurgency there was initiated in June 1965 by the then Dhofar Liberation Front (see Halliday 1975 for a detailed account). In 1968 this organization assumed the title 'Popular Front for the Liberation of the Occupied Arab Gulf' (PFLOAG, later the Popular Front for the Liberation of Oman or PFLO), reflecting its commitment to broaden the revolutionary process in the region. It was resolutely backed by the left wing of the National Front, who saw in the organization an Omani counterpart to their own struggle against the British and local feudalism.

Following the 1969 Corrective Step, South Yemeni support for the PFLO grew to include material as well as political and propaganda assistance. The PDRY also co-operated in passing on Chinese military aid to the Dhofari guerrillas. As a result of this, the period 1970-5 saw British-backed Omani troops and aircraft repeatedly crossing into the PDRY, destroying South

Yemeni property and killing South Yemeni citizens in the process. When its position deteriorated in 1973, the government of Oman invited Iranian troops and advisers to help contain what was seen as an Aden-sponsored Marxist threat to the security of the Gulf. Saudi Arabia and Jordan also assisted, providing financial and military aid respectively. This intervention, and subsequent intensification of the fighting, merely strengthened the PDRY's commitment to the beleaguered PFLO:

the Unified Political Organization and the revolutionary government of Popular Democratic Yemen will continue to pursue a principled position of no compromise, which is a stand of support and aid for our people in Oman toward the withdrawal of the aggressive Iranian forces, the liquidation of foreign military bases, and the establishment of a liberated democratic regime working for the resurgence of the economic and social life of the people ['Abd al-Fattah Ismail, in *al-Thawri*, 12 June 1976, p. 3].

In an attempt to bring about reconciliation, President Numeiry of the Sudan brought the PDRY and Oman together in Ta'iz, Yemen, in February 1976. Aden, however, refused to recognize any agreement with Oman until Iranian troops were withdrawn and Muscat agreed to recognize the PFLO.

Despite South Yemen's support, the PFLO rapidly lost ground in the face of renewed Omani military action. By the end of 1976 the Dhofari revolution had been essentially crushed under the weight of Iranian, British, Jordanian and Omani forces. The collapse of the PLFO did not, however, lead to an immediate improvement in relations between the PDRY and Oman. In 1977 the PDRY Foreign Minister reiterated his country's stand in support of the revolutionaries in a scathing attack on Oman before the United Nations. Aden continued to support the few sporadic actions mounted by the PFLO guerrillas, and border clashes between South Yemeni and Omani forces were reported in 1978, 1980, 1981 and 1982. Nevertheless, the eventual withdrawal of Iranian troops, Arab mediation, and a low-level dialogue with Muscat begun in 1978 did gradually pave the way for a relaxation of tensions between the two countries. Oman's support for the Camp David Accords between Egypt and Israel, coupled with its granting of military facilities to the United States in April 1980, posed serious obstacles to rapprochement, but eventually even these were overcome. In the summer of 1982 mediation by Kuwait and the Gulf Co-operation Council finally resulted in ambassadorial-level discussion between the two sides in Kuwait. This in turn led to a meeting of the South Yemeni and Omani Foreign Ministers in October, and to a four-point agreement outlining the future development of relations. This called for:

1. a commitment by both parties to normalize relations, and to establish a joint technical committee to resolve border disputes;
2. mutual undertakings to deny the use of national territory to any foreign power engaged in aggression against the other;
3. agreement to cease all hostile propaganda;
4. the promise of future diplomatic relations.

Despite continuing tensions over United States bases in Oman and PFLO facilities in the PDRY, the two countries duly established diplomatic relations in 1983. In 1985 the PDRY also agreed to an Omani proposal to formally exchange ambassadors.

Saudi Arabia

Saudi Arabia has long posed particular foreign policy problems for the South Yemeni revolution. The kingdom has always been opposed to the establishment or growth of revolutionary socialism on the Arabian peninsula, recognizing the danger that any such trend poses for its own autocratic and oppressive socio-political system. Consequently, it has always assumed the leading counter-revolutionary role in the area, supporting the Royalists against the Republicans in the YAR, the South Arabian League against the NF in South Yemen, and the Sultanate against the PFLO in Oman. Following South Yemeni independence in 1967 (and even more so after the Corrective Step in 1969), Riyadh threw its weight behind émigre groups and hostile propaganda campaigns aimed against Aden. It has also actively campaigned against Yemeni unity, fearing that a united (and demographically larger) Yemen would pose a serious national security threat to the kingdom. The leaders of the PDRY have always recognized Saudi Arabia's generally opposing interests in the region; indeed, the kingdom's socio-political system and strong ties with the United States rendered it the epitome of local reactionary client regimes of imperialism which the National Front so decried. Yet at the same time Saudi Arabia is too close, too big and too powerful to make direct confrontation easy.

Nevertheless, confrontation was rife during South Yemen's first decade of independent existence. Some of this was direct—notably periodic attacks by Saudi-based counter-revolutionary groups (and sometimes Saudi regular forces) along the two countries' common undemarcated border. Most, however, was indirect. The war between the Saudi-backed Sultanate and Aden-backed PFLO in Oman provided one arena for competition. The unity issue in the YAR provided another. However, even indirect conflict with the Arabian Peninsula's most powerful country involved significant costs for the

PDRY, and in 1975 Salem Rubayi 'Ali set down a series of conditions under which he would be prepared to normalize relations. These were subsequently formalized at the National Front Sixth Congress in March 1975, which accepted the principle of normalization with Saudi Arabia provided it 'respect our sovereignty and our national independence, that it not interfere in the internal affairs of our country, that it stop its repeated attacks upon us, that it terminate the mercenary camps on the borders and that it stop the propaganda campaigns' (*al-Safir*, 28 March 1975, p. 7).

A breakthrough in this regard took place on 10 March 1976 when, after protracted negotiations and Arab League mediation, the PDRY and Saudi Arabia finally agreed to establish diplomatic relations. Though denied by Aden, some suggested that there were a number of secret conditions attached. Aden would receive $400 million from Saudi Arabia, of which $100 million was reportedly transferred almost before the ink on the agreement was dry (*Arab Report and Record*, 1–15 April 1976, p. 351). The PDRY was expected to drop its support for the PFLO forthwith, though in compensation Iranian troops would be withdrawn from Oman and the PDRY could expect further aid from the Gulf states. The Saudis exhorted South Yemen to lessen its reliance on Soviet aid and advisers. For its part, Riyadh was expected to cease hostile activity against the Republic.

Whatever the specific conditions of the agreement, ambassadors were duly exchanged and the South Yemeni Foreign Minister paid visits to various Gulf capitals and Riyadh in search of foreign aid funds in March and July 1976. Other points were not so well observed. The PDRY continued it support for the PFLO and close ties with the Soviet Union. Saudi Arabia continued to sponsor South Yemeni counter-revolutionaries along the border and anti-unity forces in the YAR. Relations between the two thus deteriorated, and on 14 November 1977 Saudi Arabia recalled its ambassador from Aden. By January 1978 sporadic fighting along the frontier was being reported. Later that same year Saudi Arabia played a leading role in attempting to isolate the PDRY after the assassination of President al-Gashemi in the YAR, and was that country's major supporter when war between North and South broke out in 1979. Meanwhile, in Aden, Salem Rubayi 'Ali, the chief architect of rapprochement, was toppled from power. Ismail, 'Ali's successor as President, was largely unreceptive to a renewal of improved ties between Aden and Riyadh.

The situation began to change once more in 1980, however, when Ismail was in turn replaced by 'Ali Nasser Muhammed. Muhammed visited Saudi Arabia in June 1981, at which time mutual comments were heard about the desire of each country to improve relations. South Yemeni normalization with Oman also speeded up rapprochement. In July 1983 Riyadh and Aden agreed to exchange ambassadors again for the first time since 1977. According to Muhammed, the object of such normalization was to 'build bridges of fraternity, peace, security and stability in the area in general and also to keep our area free of the imperialist bases that threaten the region's peoples' (*al-Hawadith*, 4 February 1983, pp. 30-2).

Ethiopia

Whereas South Yemen's normalization of relations with North Yemen, Oman and Saudi Arabia have primarily been the consequence of a conscious decision by Aden to revise its foreign policy priorities in favour of domestic development and regional security, the transformation of its relations with Ethiopia was stimulated by external developments, specifically the latter's 1974 revolution and the subsequent adoption by Addis Ababa of a revolutionary socialist domestic and foreign policy. Aden's close ties with its fellow socialist regime across the Red Sea are in strong contrast to the policies adopted by most other Arab countries, who have tended to support Somalia (a Muslim nation and fellow member of the Arab League) and secessionist guerrillas in Eritrea. It thus provides perhaps the clearest evidence available of the degree to which anti-imperialism and socialist internationalism—rather than the Arabism, Islamic solidarity (or counter-revolution) of other Arab states—guides South Yemen's actions in the regional and international spheres.

Much of Aden's current enthusiasm for the Ethiopian revolution is based on what preceded it. Until 1974 Ethiopia was seen as a major threat by South Yemeni decision-makers. The regime of Emperor Haile Selassie was not only feudal and reactionary, it also had close ties with the United States. Worse, it had a warm relationship with Israel. The Israelis supplied arms and advisers to Ethiopia and reportedly established commando units on Ethiopian islands near the PDRY at the mouth of the Red Sea (Halliday, 1975, p. 267). It was in this context that South Yemen, like other Arab countries, threw its support behind Selassie's major opponents in Somalia and Eritrea.

Matters began to change with the Ethiopian revolution of 1974. Relations between Addis Ababa and its erstwhile Israeli and American supporters deteriorated sharply (Schwab, 1978). The new ruling Dergue and its eventual leader, Mengistu Haile Mariam, set the country on a path of socialist development. In response, South Yemeni support for Somalia and the Eritrean Liberation movement was stopped and Salem Rubayi 'Ali declared his country's willingness to struggle alongside the Ethiopian revolution

(Bidwell, 1983, p. 290). The Eritrean's Aden offices were closed down in June 1976. When war broke out with Somalia and Somali-backed insurgents in 1977, Mengistu jettisoned what remained of his relationship with the United States and consolidated close relations between Ethiopia and the socialist states (Schwab, 1985, pp. 95–110). The PDRY also moved to back Ethiopia. Military advisers were immediately committed to help Ethiopia stop the Somali assault. Later, several hundred South Yemeni troops (including helicopter, armoured and artillery units) were to assist Ethiopian offensives in Eritrea. These actions were condemned in many Arab quarters, who accused South Yemen of acting as 'Arab Cubans', intervening in African affairs at Moscow's behest.

The rationale behind South Yemen's change of policy towards Ethiopia was later provided by 'Ali Nasser Muhammed, who defended it in terms of the regional correlation of anti-imperialist forces:

We are not concealing our relations with Ethiopia which . . . are strategic relations. We have stood with Ethiopia against imperialism and against the counterrevolutionary forces. We consider the victory of the Ethiopian revolution a victory for our Arab causes and the Palestinian people's cause. Ethiopia was previously a US and an Israeli base. Is it not in the interest of the Arab peoples and the Palestinian cause to have this new regime that is hostile to the United States and Israel? I believe that it is indeed in the interest of the Arab peoples and our interest in the PDRY for such a regime to emerge, stand fast and triumph against all internal and external conspiratorial forces [*al-Hawadith*, 4 February 1983, pp. 30–2].

Subsequent to South Yemen's initial gestures of support, further steps were taken to consolidate relations between the two revolutions. On 2 December 1979 Ethiopia and the PDRY signed a trade agreement, a six-year programme of action and a fifteen-year treaty of Friendship and Co-operation. An additional protocol covering political, economic and military co-operation was signed the following month. In August 1981 a tripartite treaty of alliance was concluded in Aden between South Yemen, Ethiopia and Libya. It called for common struggle against the conspiracies of imperialism, Zionism and reactionary forces, support for national liberation movements, and political, military and economic co-operation and mutual defence.

Other Regional Relations

Further afield, in the Middle East, the 'progressive' regimes of the area—Algeria, Libya, Syria, Iraq and Iran, together with the PLO, Arab communist parties and 'Saharwi Arab Democratic Republic' (Polisario)—represent another important focus of the PDRY's regional foreign policy. With all these actors the PDRY has sought to build close political ties based on common opposition to imperialism, Zionism and local reaction. It has also sought to promote greater unity within progressive ranks, and to foster better and better ties between the progressive countries of the Middle East and the World socialist community.

The Palestine Question—the single most important international issue in the Arab world—exemplifies the PDRY's policies in this area. Since independence the Republic has strongly upheld 'the Palestinian people's right to armed struggle against those who usurped their lands' (Foreign Minister Muhammed Salih Muti², in *14 Uktubar*, 9 September 1975, p. 8). As evidence of this it has provided significant material, diplomatic and moral support to the Palestine Liberation Organization. It has particularly close ties with the two main leftist organizations within the PLO—the Popular Front for the Liberation of Palestine (PFLP) and the Democratic Front for the Liberation of Palestine (DFLP), both of which share common roots with the NF/YSP in the Arab Nationalists' Movement of the 1950s and 1960s (Ismael, 1976, pp. 98–100). Like these groups, the PDRY has been bitterly critical of what it sees as imperialist-sponsored capitulationist 'solutions' to the Palestine Question. It was among the founding members of the Arab Front for Steadfastness and Confrontation, originally formed in 1977–8 in response to President Sadat's initiatives *vis-à-vis* Israel. It has condemned the Camp David Accords and subsequent Egyptian–Israeli peace treaty, the European Community's 1980 Venice Declaration, and the 1982 Reagan inititive as having all failed to meet the legitimate national aspirations of the Palestinian people. It has also expressed reservations about the 1985 Amman Accords between PLO leader Yasser Arafat and King Hussein of Jordan. At present South Yemeni leaders advance the 1982 resolutions of the Arab League summit conference held at Fez, and Soviet proposals for international negotiations leading to an independent Palestinian state, as offering the best hope for a settlement of the conflict (Muhammed, 1985).

The PDRY has also been strongly supportive of the Arab confrontation states, especially Syria. A token South Yemeni military force has been stationed in Syria in recent years as a concrete gesture of this support. Unlike Syria and Libya, however, the PDRY has not thrown its weight behind attempts since 1983 by some groups within the PLO to split the organization and topple Arafat's leadership. Instead it has stressed the need for unity within PLO ranks, and together with Algeria has played a leading role in trying to reconcile the various Palestinian factions.

While the PDRY has endeavoured to maintain good relations with all progressive regimes in the Middle East, both as a means and an end to its foreign policy, this has not always been possible. Syria, for example, has been annoyed by Aden's refusal to support a frontal challenge to Arafat's leadership of the PLO. Relations with Libya have also suffered for this reason, and because of Aden's refusal to endorse Libyan involvement in Chad. In early 1984 Libyan aid to the PDRY was suspended, the 1981 tripartite treaty notwithstanding (Halliday, 1984b, p. 363). Nevertheless, the PDRY has continued to back Libya in the face of United States diplomatic and economic pressure and military attacks.

With regard to Iraq, a far more serious breach opened between Aden and Baghdad in 1979. In June of that year an Iraqi communist professor teaching at Aden university was assassinated. The Iraqi Embassay was implicated in the affair, and after several days of stand-off South Yemeni security forces stormed the embassy and seized three suspects. (Two of the three were later released on the grounds of diplomatic immunity.) In response, Iraq recalled its ambassador and the South Yemeni embassy in Baghdad was attacked. Relations deteriorated still further the following year: in April the PDRY arrested a number of people as Iraqi spies, and Iraq expelled a number of South Yemeni students in retaliation. While the official press on both sides reflected the new hostility between Baghdad and Aden, the latter generally avoided direct attacks on the Iraqi regime. Instead, *14 Uktubar* (11 April 1980, p. 6) repeated the condemnation of others (notably the Iraqi Communist Party) of the Iraqi Ba'ath as 'reactionary' and 'dictatorial'.

Following the Iranian revolution, friendly political and economic relations were soon established between the PDRY and the once-hostile Iran. This, coupled with the outbreak of the Iran–Iraq War in 1980, angered Baghdad to the point that it threw its active support behind South Yemeni counter-revolutionary groups in June 1981. 'Ali Nasser Muhammed nevertheless upheld his country's position:

It is well known that during the shah's reign Iran was hostile to our country. It used to have relations with Israel and did not recognize the Palestinian people's rights. . . . Ever since the victory of the Islamic revolution the Islamic Republic of Iran has been pursuing an anti-imperialist and anti-Zionist policy. . . . Iran extended the hand of friendship to the PDRY. . . . At present relations between our two countries are normal and serve the interests of our two peoples and the interests of the Arab peoples [*al-Siyasah*, 30 December 1982, p. 23].

Despite its hostility to Baghdad and its ties with Tehran, however, the PDRY was careful not to favour either side in the Gulf War. Instead, its primary concern was a resolution of the dispute (and of the dispute between it and

Iraq) in the interests of regional anti-imperialism: the continuation of discord between anti-imperialist regimes, it argued, could only benefit the imperialists. Aden thus called for an immediate ceasefire between Baghdad and Tehran, a position in fact closer to that of Iraq than Iran (Halliday, 1984b, p. 362). Baghdad gradually recognized this, Iraqi–South Yemeni relations normalized in the latter half of 1981, and on 4 January 1982 the two sides agreed to once more exchange ambassadors.

Besides the progressive regimes, the conservative Arab Gulf states have been another important focus of Aden's regional policies—albeit for very different reasons. In the early 1970s the PDRY supported the revolutionary activities of the PFLOAG against the British-dominated sheikdoms in the area, seeing such activities as a natural continuation of the National Front's own struggle. When the British withdrew in 1971 the PDRY refused to recognize the independence of Bahrain, Qatar, or the United Arab Emirates, seeing them as nothing more than reactionary puppets. It thus opposed their entry into both the Arab League and the United Nations. Only with Kuwait, independent since 1961 and generally more neutralist in international affairs, were diplomatic relations established.

As noted earlier, however, Aden's foreign policy approach began to moderate in the mid-1970s. Its attitude towards the Gulf states was an early manifestation of this. Relations with Bahrain, Qatar and the United Arab Emirates normalized in 1975 (Stookey, 1982, p. 103). Several factors lay behind this. First, Aden sought to find some common anti-imperialist ground with these countries, particularly in response to the Arab–Israeli conflict and growing Western concern for the 'security' of energy supplies in the wake of the 1973 Arab oil embargo. More importantly, however, Aden saw in the Gulf States a potential source of economic aid and diplomatic entrée. Normalization was soon rewarded. Kuwait and the UAE have become among the single most important sources of foreign aid for the PDRY in the last decade (Chapter 4). The UAE (26.8 per cent of exports, 24.7 per cent of imports) and Kuwait (12.5 per cent of imports) have become the Republic's largest trading partners. On the diplomatic front, Kuwait in particular has played a fundamental role in mediating relations between Aden and the YAR, Saudi Arabia, and Oman. It is also notable that Kuwait refused, despite Saudi blandishments, to co-operate in the isolation of the PDRY in 1978.

Although not actually constituting 'regional relations', South Yemeni policy towards Third World countries outside the Middle East follows a broadly similar pattern to that outlined above but at a lower level of interaction. As shown below, the PDRY has closest ties with Third World socialist states (Cuba, Vietnam, North Korea, etc). Leading non-aligned and anti-imperialist states also warrant South Yemeni foreign policy attention. Of these, India has been the most important, both for political reasons and because of historical attachment between South Yemen and the Indian subcontinent through Yemeni *émigrès*. India has an embassy in Aden. Indian contractors are at work on a number of South Yemeni development projects, and India has become the PDRY's third largest export market (7.7 per cent of total in 1982). There is significant interaction with Somalia and Djibouti, largely for economic and historical reasons. As for other Third World States, the PDRY has neither the resources nor the interests to maintain significant contact other than through the United Nations and the Non-Aligned Movement.

The Socialist States

Diplomatic relations between the Soviet Union and the then People's Republic of South Yemen were established almost immediately at independence, on 1 December 1967. Under President Sha'abi these relations did not progress much beyond mutual cordiality. A Soviet Embassy in Aden was established in February 1968, and economic and military aid agreements were announced later that year. By June 1969, however, little or none of this had yet been delivered.

After the 22 June 1969 Corrective Step the situation changed. The new socialist leadership in Aden embarked on a radical transformation of South Yemeni policy, not only domestically but also on the international front where close ties with the socialist community were quickly forged. In response, Soviet and other socialist aid to the PDRY grew steadily, soon representing the largest source of aid for the struggling Republic. The Soviet Union helped to finance or build dams, wells, irrigation systems, geological surveys and oil exploration, power plants, transport and communications facilities, and a host of other projects. Civilian advisers helped to train personnel and organize government services. The Soviet Union also became the overwhelmingly largest supplier of military arms and advisers to the PDRY. A similar expansion took place in the relations between Aden and the Soviet Union's chief allies. The German Democratic Republic, recognized by the PDRY in July 1969, supplied light arms and specialists to train the police and intelligence services. It also helped build bridges and, together with Czechoslovakia, undertook a number of mineralogical surveys. Hungary has financed agricultural aid projects throughout the country, as has Bulgaria. Cuba has provided medical and agricultural experts, and played a major role in the establishment of the PDRY's People's Militia. Bulgaria, Cuba,

Czechoslovakia, East Germany, Hungary, North Korea, Romania, Vietnam and the Soviet Union all have embassies in Aden.

Parallel with such economic co-operation, close co-operation and exchange in political and foreign policy issues has grown up. As Stookey (1982, p. 104) observes, this was manifest in an intense pattern of official visits: 'during the decade of 1971–1980 the South Yemeni president or premier travelled to Moscow several times, East Germany twice, and at least once each to Hungary, Poland, Czechoslovakia, Romania, Bulgaria, China, North Korea, and Vietnam.' Furthermore, Soviet Premier Kosygin, Cuban leader Fidel Castro, and the Hungarian and East German chiefs of state all visited Aden during this time.

Confirmation of the scope and depth of these relations came in October 1979 when President Ismail and Soviet President Brezhnev signed a twenty-year Treaty of Friendship and Co-operation between the PDRY and the Soviet Union. Its sixteen articles called for even closer consultation and co-operation in the political, economic and military fields. Similar treaties were later signed with East Germany (November), Czechoslovakia (September 1981), Hungary and Bulgaria (November) and North Korea (October 1984). 1979 also saw the PDRY gain observer status within the Council for Mutual Economic Assistance (CMEA), the Soviet-led economic organization. Direct links between the YSP and ruling communist parties were established or strengthened (Anthony, 1982, 1984b). The pace of foreign policy interaction also quickened. Muhammed made state visits to Eastern Europe in 1981 (Soviet Union, German Democratic Republic, Bulgaria, Hungary, Czechoslovakia), 1982 (Soviet Union), and 1984 (Soviet Union, German Democratic Republic, Poland, Bulgaria). (Abu Bakr al-Attas flew from India to Moscow in January 1986 when fighting first broke out in Aden in that month, and it was while he was there that he was appointed interim President by the YSP.) Moreover, the PDRY has echoed the Soviet foreign policy position on numerous issues, ranging from Afghanistan (with which Aden established diplomatic relations in 1984) to the boycott of the Los Angeles Summer Olympics (Cigar, 1985, p. 782).

It is thus evident that since 1969, and particularly since the late 1970s, fundamentally closer ties between the PDRY and socialist states have been established. It is also clear that Soviet counsel has gained strong influence in Aden. It is one thing to recognize this, however, and quite another to assert (as many analysts do) that 'Moscow can apparently generate sufficient leverage to get its way' on all important matters of South Yemeni domestic and foreign policy (Cigar, 1985, p. 792). While it is true that Moscow and Aden commonly agree, there are several explanations for this. First, such agreement is often precisely that—i.e. concurrence based on a broadly similar world view and interests—rather than evidence of Soviet domination. In other cases it is likely that Aden echoes Moscow's position because the issue itself is relatively unimportant to the PDRY, and because greater benefit can be gained from supporting an ally than not. By contrast, there is absolutely no evidence that the PDRY has ever been forced to adopt a foreign policy position contrary to its own perceived national interest. Indeed, in a number of cases significant variations betwen the South Yemeni and Soviet positions has been evident:

1. *Regional Foreign Policy.* Soviet–South Yemeni divergence has long been evident with regard to relations with the countries of the Arabian Peninsula. In the North the Soviet Union has long cultivated friendly ties with San'a, ties which it has maintained even at times of significant hostility between North and South. Whereas the PDRY has thrown various degrees of support behind the NDF, Moscow has never done so. Indeed, it was ultimately the Soviets—not the Saudis or Americans—who re-equipped the North Yemeni armed forces in the aftermath of the 1979 war and hence allowed San'a to launch its subsequent assault against leftist forces at a time when they enjoyed strong support from the South. In Oman a similar situation has existed with regard to the PFLO. Anxious not to set back its relations in the Gulf and viewing the Chinese-supported Dhofari revolutionaries with not a little suspicion, the Soviet Union was never really very enthusiastic about the revolutionary struggle in Oman (Halliday, 1984a, p. 227). The PDRY, on the other hand, has always been strongly supportive of their brother revolutionaries to the East. In the end it was the defeat of the insurgents—not Soviet reservations—that led South Yemen to de-emphasize the PFLO and to normalize relations with Muscat.

2. *Relations with China.* While recognizing the Soviet Union as the leading socialist state, the PDRY has never allowed Sino–Soviet hostility to interfere with its friendly relations with the People's Republic of China. Relations between the PROSY and the PRC were in fact established soon after independence (China provided South Yemen with some of its earliest aid), and a Chinese embassy in Aden was set up within a month of the Corrective Step. Chinese economic assistance to the PDRY, while less than that provided by the Soviet Union, has been substantial and continuous. China supplied some $84 million in development assistance to the PDRY as of 1980 (Halliday, 1984a, p. 222). It also represents South Yemen's single most important socialist trading partner, accounting for 3.6 per cent of imports in 1982. It can safely be assumed that, given China's modest resources and the

level of hostility between Moscow and Beijing, the Chinese would hardly extend such assistance if they considered South Yemen to be a Soviet satellite. For its part, the PDRY although critical of some aspects of Chinese foreign policy (*détente* with the United States, support for President Numeiry of the Sudan and the Shah of Iran in the 1970s; conflict with Vietnam), has largely portrayed its relations with China in a positive light (Halliday, 1975, p. 266). This was particularly the case with Salem Rubayi ʾAli, who was fairly sympathetic to the Maoist model. Although ʾAbd al-Fattah Ismail was less enthusiastic about Beijing, ʾAli Nasser Muhammed made a significant attempt to improve bilateral relations. In recognition of this China unilaterally rescheduled South Yemen's debt to it in 1983 (Halliday, 1984b, p. 361).

3. *Development Strategies*. Development in the PDRY owes much to the Soviet Union in terms of inspiration and financial and technical assistance. This should not obscure the fact, however, that the PDRY's development strategy has been and continues to be formulated according to domestic priorities. In the early 1970s much was imported from the Maoist model in the rural sector, in large part because of the influence of Salem Rubayi ʾAli (Chapters 3 and 4). Under Ismail the PDRY did adhere more closely to Soviet advice and assistance. In many respects this proved deficient, however, and within the government and party criticisms of the quantity of aid disbursed, the slowness and inefficiency of Soviet development projects (notably dam and powerplant construction), and reported Soviet overfishing of South Yemeni waters were heard. YSP and state officials made their disquiet known to the Soviets (Halliday, 1984a, pp. 223-4). Indeed, as Chapter 3 showed, excessive adherence to the Soviet model was a major factor in Ismail's downfall. Under ʾAli Nasser Muhammed the PDRY cautiously established improved economic ties with the Gulf and the West, effectively reducing the relative importance of Soviet assistance. The Soviet Union has never accepted the PDRY as a 'socialist' state—its economy is too underdeveloped and its 'scientific socialism' too eclectic and indigenous to meet Moscow's rather doctrinaire standards. Instead, the PDRY is considered to be a state of 'socialist orientation', when it is considered at all.

These three areas are not the only points of difference; South Yemen–Soviet divergence is also evident on the Palestine Question, the Polisario's struggle against Morocco in the Western Sahara, and other issues (Halliday, 1984a). What they indicate is that although South Yemen's foreign policy options are limited by its size, resources, and close ties with the socialist community, they have not been eliminated. In other words, the PDRY's 'strategic alliance' with the Soviet Union is not maintained by Soviet control of South Yemeni decision-making, by South Yemen's dependence, or by a threat of Soviet intervention, but rather by a conscious foreign policy decision by Aden, founded on the PDRY's basic principles of foreign policy and a sober appraisal of its regional and international position.

The West

In contrast to the important political relations with regional and socialist states outlined above, this final area of South Yemen foreign policy is extremely circumscribed. Only five Western countries—Britain, France, West Germany, Italy and Japan—maintain embassies in Aden. Relations with the United States, severed in 1969, have not been re-established; projected discussions between an American envoy and the South Yemen leadership on this point in 1979 were scuttled by the outbreak of war with the YAR, and have not been publicly resumed. The PDRY has, however, expressed a willingness to normalize relations with Washington provided that the United States respect South Yemen's sovereignty and not interfere in its internal affairs.

Economic interaction with the West has been far more significant. Although Aden's economic (re)opening to the West was initiated in December 1976 when PDRY Foreign Minister Muti' made an official visit to Paris where he called for closer relations between the European Community and South Yemen, it was not until the 1980s that substantial developments in this area became evident. 'Ali Nasser Muhammed pursued a deliberate policy of improving commercial relations with the capitalist countries, and within weeks of his assuming the presidency rumours of South Yemeni approaches to West Germany, France, Italy and other Western countries were being reported (*New York Times*, 15 June 1980). As noted in Chapter 3, the South Yemeni offshore and hinterland were opened to oil and mineral exploration by Italian, British, Canadian, French and other firms. Companies from West Germany, France, Italy, Greece, New Zealand, Britain, Denmark and Japan received construction contracts as part of the Second Five Year Plan. Japan and the PDRY have long operated a joint company in the fisheries sector, and late in 1985 Japan agreed to provide the PDRY with a $4.4 million grant to establish a fisheries research center. In the area of foreign aid Denmark has been a significant contributor since the early 1970s, as has Japan. Western countries played an important role in providing emergency food aid in the aftermath of the 1982 floods. Of the 9,200 metric tons of cereals provided, 8,500 tons came from Sweden, 300 tons from the European Community, and 200 tons from Japan (FAO, 1985a). A similar pattern of significant economic relations with the West exists with regard to South Yemen's foreign trade. In 1982 the largest share of exports went to France (31.3 per cent), with Britain (7.3 per cent) and Italy (3.5 per cent) also playing their part. That same year Japan and the United Kingdom were the third and fourth largest sources of South Yemeni imports, accounting for 8.2 and 5.7 per cent respectively.

Retrospect and Prospect: Foreign Policy and Socialist Transformation

In recent years the PDRY, while continuing a course of commitment to anti-imperialism and revolutionary ideals, has moderated its foreign policy approach to the point of rapprochement with its conservative Arab neighbours. This policy has paid considerable dividends: it has increased the country's security, reduced the burden on it necessitated by national defence, and provided the conditions under which substantial capital aid could be secured, to fuel economic growth. The result has been a consolidation of the South Yemeni revolution and progress towards socialist transformation amid the otherwise economically and politically inhospitable climate of the Arabian Peninsula.

But what of the future? 'Ali Nasser Muhammed, the chief architect of South Yemen's post-1980 foreign policy, has been displaced from power. Criticisms of the former president as a 'mere stooge of imperialism' have been voiced from within the new leadership, reflecting some dissatisfaction with the foreign policy directions implemented by Muhammed. Does this suggest a more militant foreign policy, a return to the active espousal of Gulf and Arabian revolution that exemplified South Yemen's international behaviour in the 1970s?

While prediction is always difficult, such a return does not seem likely—unless regional conditions change dramatically. The PDRY's moderation in the mid-1970s, it must be remembered, was not based on a particular leader or on a restructuring of the Republic's basic foreign policy orientation, but rather on an appraisal that regional socialist revolution seemed unlikely in the near future. In the absence of marked revolutionary potential, Aden decided that both its immediate interests as a state and the broader interests of regional anti-imperialism could best be served by improving ties with its conservative neighbours and hence providing more auspicious conditions for the PDRY's own internal revolutionary development. Thus, given the absence of political turmoil in North Yemen or the Gulf, this policy seems likely to continue. Moreover, the majority of the new party/state leadership are, for all their routine condemnations of former President Muhammed, equally associated with past international policies. Attas, for example, previously served as Minister of Construction and was instrumental in opening up the PDRY to foreign (Western) contractors. The new leadership has gone out of its way to reassure neighbours that, in the words of the YSP, the PDRY 'will continue to march with the trend on which its peaceful foreign policy is based' and hence 'will continue to consolidate its ties of unity ... with the northern part of the homeland ... and strengthen its fraternal ties with all fraternal Arab countries' as well as the socialist community.

To reinforce this point state and party officials made important visits to the Gulf States as well as the PDRY's close allies as soon as the domestic situation had stabilized. Foreign Minister 'Abd al-Aziz al-Dhali visited the United Arab Emirates, Qatar, Bahrain, Kuwait and Saudi Arabia in March 1986, while Prime Minister Yaseen Said Numan travelled to Kuwait, Syria, Algeria and Libya. In Oman South Yemen Deputy Prime Minister Salih Abu-Bakr Bin Hussainoun declared that the PDRY would 'adhere to the agreement of principles' concluded with Muscat in 1982 (*MEED*, 15 February 1986, p. 34). President al-Attas has appealed to Western companies to restart work interrupted by the January fighting (*MEED*, 8 February 1986, p. 49). YSP Secretary-General 'Ali Salem al-Bidh attended the 27th Soviet Communist Party Congress in March. Hence, it seems that foreign policy will continue to be moderated by the PDRY's efforts to consolidate and advance the socialist revolution at home.

7 Conclusion: The Politics of Socialist Transformation

South Yemen's transition from a tribal colony to a socialist state reflects a process of revolutionary development that makes the PDRY the only Arab state with an institutionalized socialist structure. This process was initiated by the transformation of the struggle for political independence into a social revolution. It was institutionalized by the transformation of the social revolution into formal political institutions. The foundation of the state, then, rests on these critical transformations. Three stages in the process of transformation can be distinguished: the transformation of the struggle for independence into a social revolution; the transformation of the social revolution into formal state structures; and the transformation of the institutions of the state into a viable socialist structure.

A number of objective conditions in South Yemen at the initiation of the struggle for independence can be identified from this study as having contributed to the transformation of the struggle for independence into social revolution: the historical phase of European imperialism in the Arab world; the ideological phase of development of Arab nationalism; South Yemen's social, political and economic geography. Each of these factors played a part in turning what began as an anti-colonial movement into a revolutionary socialist one.

South Yemen's struggle for independence was initiated in the early 1960s in the final phase of the dismantling of Britain's colonial empire. Aden, indeed, was the last vestige of empire in the Arab world. The geopolitical and strategic importance of Aden placed South Yemen at the fulcrum of existing international and regional power struggles, delaying the process of independence to the point where armed struggle became a viable alternative for anti-colonial forces. The sustained failure of Britain to forge a successful alliance of comprador forces in Yemen to assume post-colonial political power rendered the more militant factions of the nationalist movement all the more powerful.

The transition to a strategy of armed struggle by anti-colonialist forces was also conditioned by the ideological stage of development of Arab national-ism. This development was (and is) complex, and its full details—covered elsewhere (Kazziha, 1975; Ismael, 1976)—are far beyond the scope of this book. In essence, however, the point demonstrated in this study is that polarization of Arab nationalist forces in the region around ideological issues—reflected in the fragmentation of the Arab Nationalist Movement—impacted directly on the anti-colonial struggle in Yemen. The increasing attention within the Arab world focused this debate on class issues and the role of armed struggle. With the break-up of the United Arab Republic in 1961 and the radicalization of Nasserism around social reform issues (a radicalization evident in the UAR nationalization laws and the issuing of the National Charter in 1961), Arab nationalist forces began to split along clear class lines. Bourgeois elements advocated traditional programmes of political development and popular factions advanced revolutionary programmes of social transformation. Furthermore, Egyptian and Saudi involvement in the civil war in North Yemen manifestly crystallized this split in the Yemeni area, advancing the case and cause for armed struggle against the British and their local class allies.

Both historical and ideological developments at this time occurred against the backdrop of South Yemen's social, political and economic geography. As the poorest country in the region, and one that had experienced the longest period of imperialism in its most overt form (colonialism), the vast majority of South Yemen's population had little to gain by a mere transfer of power from colonial administrators to an independent government controlled by a class of traditional elites. It was this class, after all, and not the British colonial administrators, who directly oppressed the hinterland. The British were really only visible in Aden; the sultans and sheikhs were their visible counterpart outside the capital. They owned the land and exploited its resources to maintain lifestyles lavish in comparison with the mass of poor peasants who worked it. Furthermore, the fragmentation and isolation of the rural population, the difficulty of the terrain and the lack of all but the most primitive transport and communication networks rendered modern methods of military counter-insurgency impotent. While these same factors also hindered the pace of rural guerrilla warfare, they did not obviate it. The population were ready to revolt against clearly identified oppressors and were accustomed to operating within the rugged environment. The sultans and sheikhs who controlled the countryside could neither co-operate with each other nor muster sufficient support individually to stem the tide of rebellion once it had started.

All these factors came together, each reinforcing the other to propel the transformation of the struggle for independence into a social revolution. As more peasants were recruited into the fighting cadres, the social basis of their struggle became more significant. As the social dimension of the struggle became more significant, more peasants were recruited. Those who did not enter combatant ranks directly were nevertheless sympathetic to the struggle and provided aid and comfort to the growing guerrilla army as it moved across South Yemen and took its struggle into the streets of Aden. As shown in Chapter 2, by the time of independence this stage of the transformation was complete.

With independence, the second stage of the transformation was initiated—the transformation of the social revolution into formal state structures. This stage was played out in the struggle within the National Front, between those active cadres radicalized by the anti-colonial struggle and external cadres who represented the revolutionary elite. The latter, not exposed to the close relationship between colonial rule and the domestic social order laid bare by the guerrilla war, rejected the radical transformation of South Yemeni society. In contrast, the former saw socialist transformation, and the National Front's vanguard role in that transformation, as a natural continuation of the liberation struggle. While the reins of state control passed initially into the hands of the external elite at the time of independence, the 1969 Corrective Step represented the ascendancy to power of the fighting vanguard of the party.

The process of transformation of the social revolution into state structure immediately ensued. The socialization of the economy (discussed in Chapter 4) and the primacy placed on the eradication of rural–urban inequalities (discussed in Chapter 5) reflected the institutionalization of the social revolution as the primary objective of the state. A clear commitment to scientific socialism—however eclectically that might be understood in the South Yemen context—has provided the ideological blueprint for state intervention in the economic and social spheres, thus resolving conflicts within the state over its role such as occurred before the Corrective Step.

The final stage of transformation—the transformation of the institutions of the state into a socialist structure—represents the transcendence of socialism over statism in the evolution of the PDRY. The first dimension of this twofold transformation was manifested in the power struggles between leaders and the factions they represented. The successive efforts of Qahtan al-Sha'abi, Salem Rubayi 'Ali, 'Abd al-Fattah Ismail, and 'Ali Nasser Muhammed to consolidate power in their hands were each defeated by the formation of coalitions in the party that opposed the concentration of power in the hands of one individual. Each time, full-scale civil war was barely averted. But the success of the coalitions in effect further diminished the role of tribal politics in the PDRY, checked the rise of the cult of personality, and further institutionalized the praxis of collective leadership.

The second dimension of this phase—the transcendence of socialism over statism—has been manifested in an implicit struggle between the party and the state for political domination. This struggle was part of, and reinforced, the efforts of individuals to consolidate power in their hands. Nevertheless, it is distinguished from the aspect of tribalism by the fact that power consolidation was primarily a process within the state structure, while coalition formation was primarily a party process. The success of the party over the state is reflected in its full integration and supervision of the state structure at all levels.

The PDRY is the only state in the Arab world where the government structure is not delimited by the personality in power. In other words, the structure of government is sufficiently institutionalized to have survived four different transitions of leadership. While the leadership transitions have been violent, the institutions of the socialist state have none the less survived and been strengthened. The transcendence of the institutions of the state over the individual leader is reflected by the relative anonymity of the new leaders of the PDRY since the January 1986 transition of power.

The socialist transformation of South Yemen has progressed through government policy as evidenced by the socio-economic transformation initiated in the aftermath of the Corrective Step. Throughout all the struggles which have accompanied the PDRY's development, the ideology and goals of socialist transformation have remained central to state policy.

There remains, however, the precarious balance between domestic and foreign policy that results from the potential tensions of revolutionary commitment versus internal development, as discussed in Chapter 6. The need for internal and external security and economic assistance, coupled with the absence of significant revolutionary potential in the region at present, has led the PDRY to seek accommodation with hostile conservative neighbours. But this accommodation always poses a threat to social revolution. There are dangers of dependency, ideological corruption through co-option, and subversion that can arise from policy pragmatism and attempts to acquire aid. The January 1986 conflict within the Aden government in part reflected an internal debate over the long-term implications of the Republic's foreign policy course. The direction taken by the new government on this issue remains to be seen.

Finally, it is important to note the government and the party's attitude towards Islam. Before independence and the revolution Islam served as the primary ideology legitimating the social order of Yemen. Following the revolution, the regime was faced with the difficult question of how best to deal with a belief system that was deeply woven into the socio-cultural fabric of the country, yet which at the same time posed a potential challenge to the new ideology and the social reality it sought to establish.

Although the PDRY is often accused of being an 'athiest' state by its hostile neighbours, it has in fact adopted a cautious and accommodating attitude towards Islam. It has done so both by stressing the 'socialist' aspects (egalitarianism, commitment to community and social justice) of Islam and by avoiding actions which might unnecessarily antagonize the faithful. According to 'Abd al-Fattah Ismail, the problem lies not with any inherent contradiction between socialist ideology and Islamic belief, but rather in the distorted interpretations of the latter espoused through the ages by the rich and powerful:

Islam was exposed to extreme distortion and falsification, especially after the Rightly Guided Caliphs. In the Abbasid and Ummayid eras, the aristocratic forces were able to divert Islam to goals and concepts other than that for which it had come. They did that to serve their interests and to serve the thrones, the kingdoms, and the hereditary caliphate which had nothing at all to do with Islam. . . . Islam, which came essentially as a revolution, was transformed by feudal and aristocratic forces, devoiding Islam of its revolutionary essence and diverting it to serve other goals [*Nida ʿal-Watan*, June 1978, pp. 22–3].

Evidence of the regime's attempt to reach accommodation with a revolutionary version of Islamic belief is evidenced in the 1970 Constitution and in day-to-day state policy. Islam is officially recognized as the religion of the PDRY, and it is guaranteed protection in so far as it is consonant with other constitutional principles (article 31, 46). Local mosques are maintained by the state, in comparison for income lost when *waqf* (religious endowment) lands were expropriated under the 1970 land reform law. Islam is part of the public primary school curriculum in the country, with two hours per week of Islamic instruction being given in the classroom. Islamic holidays are official, and are publicly observed by leading state and party officials (Hudson, 1977, p. 357; Halliday, 1983, pp. 53–4).

Bibliography

Ahmad, Makram Muhammed, 1968. 'Four Questions Raised by Independence'. *al-Tali'ah* (Cairo) **4**, 1 (January), pp. 122–31 (in Arabic).

Aitchison, C. U., 1983. *A Collection of Treaties, Engagements and Sanads Relating to India and Neighbouring Countries*, Delhi, Manager of Publications, Government of India, **11**.

'Ali, Hussein, & Whittingham, Ken, 1974. 'Notes Towards an Understanding of the Revolution in South Yemen'. *Race and Class* **16**, 1 (July), pp. 83–100.

Amnesty International, 1976. *Annual Report*. London, Amnesty International Publications.

——, 1977. *Annual Report*. London, Amnesty International Publications.

——, 1985. *Annual Report*. London, Amnesty International Publications.

Anthony, John Duke, 1982. 'Yemen: People's Democratic Republic of Yemen', Richard F. Staar (ed.), *1982 Yearbook on International Communist Affairs*. Stanford, Hoover Institution Press.

——, 1984a. 'The Communist Party of the People's Democratic Republic of Yemen: An Analysis of its Strengths and Weaknesses', in B. R. Pridham (ed.), *Contemporary Yemen: Politics and Historical Background*. London, Croom Helm.

——, 1984b. 'Yemen: People's Democratic Republic of Yemen', Richard F. Staar (ed.), *1984 Yearbook on International Communist Affairs*. Stanford, Hoover Institution Press.

Arif, Muhammed, 1983. 'People's Democratic Republic of Yemen Seeks to Develop Productive Capacity of Economy'. *IMF Survey* **12**, 8 (18 April 1983), pp. 119–22.

al-Ashtal, Abdalla, 1976. 'PDRY: Politics in Command'. *Race and Class* **17**, 3 (1973), pp. 275–80.

Banking System Law for the People's Democratic Republic of Yemen, 1972. Text in *Dirasat 'Arabiyya* **8**, 6 (April 1972), pp. 124–53 (in Arabic).

Bennett, Alexander, J., 1985. 'Arms Transfers as an Instrument of Soviet Policy in the Middle East'. *Middle East Journal* **39**, 4 (Autumn), pp. 745–74.

Bidwell, Robin L., 1983. *The Two Yemens*. Boulder, Col., Westview Press.

Braun, Ursula, 1984. 'Prospects for Yemeni Unity', in B. R. Pridham (ed.), *Contemporary Yemen: Politics and Historical Background*. London, Croom Helm.

Brinton, J. Y., 1964. *Aden and the Federation of South Arabia*. Washington, DC, American Society of International Law.

Bujra, Abdalla S., 1970. 'Urban Elites and Colonialism: The Nationalist Elites of Aden and South Arabia'. *Middle East Studies* **6**, 2 (May), pp. 189–211.

——, 1971. *The Politics of Stratification: A Study of Political Change in a South Arabian Town*. Oxford, Clarendon Press.

Bukair, Salem Omar, 1984. 'The PDRY: Three Designs for Independence', in B. R.

Pridham (ed.), *Contemporary Yemen: Politics and Historical Background*. London, Croom Helm.

Cigar, Norman, 1985. 'South Yemen and the USSR: Prospects for the Relationship'. *Middle East Journal* **39**, 4 (Autumn), pp. 775–95.

Constitution of the People's Democratic Republic of Yemen, 1970. Balustein Flanz (ed.), *Constitutions of the World*. vol. 15. Dobbs Ferry, NY, Oceana Publications, 1976. The Arabic original is reproduced in *Dirasat ʾArabiyya* **7**, 2 (December 1970), pp. 142–53.

Countryman, John R., 1986. 'South Yemen: The Socialist Façade Crumbles'. *Middle East International* (7 February), pp. 12–13.

Doe, Brian, 1971. *Southern Arabia*. New York, McGraw Hill.

Efrat, Moshe, 1982. 'The People's Democratic Republic of Yemen: Scientific Socialism on Trial in an Arab Country', in Peter Wiles (ed.), *The New Communist Third World*. London, Croom Helm.

al-Fattah, Fathi Abd, 1974. *Tairubat al-Thawrah fi al-Yaman al-Demuqratiyah* (The Revolutionary Experience in Democratic Yemen). Beirut, Dar Ibn Khaldun.

Fisher, W. B. & Unwin, T., 1986. 'The People's Democratic Republic of Yemen', *Middle East and North Africa 1986*. London, Europa Publications.

Food and Agriculture Organization (FAO), 1983. *FAO Production Yearbook 1982*. Rome, Food and Agriculture Organization.

——, 1984a. *FAO Production Yearbook 1983*. Rome, Food and Agriculture Organization.

——, 1984b. *Yearbook of Fishery Statistics: 1983 Catches and Landings*. Rome, Food and Agriculture Organization.

——, 1985a. *Food Aid in Figures 1984*. Rome, Food and Agriculture Organization.

——, 1985b. *Monthly Bulletin of Statistics* **8**, 11 (November).

——, 1985c. *The State of Food and Agriculture 1984*. Rome, Food and Agriculture Organization.

Foreign Area Studies (FAS), 1971. *Area Handbook for the Peripheral States of The Arabian Peninsula*. Washington, DC, US Government Printing Office.

——, 1977. *Area Handbook for the Yemens*. Richard F. Nyrop (ed.), Washington DC, US Government Printing Office.

Gavin, R. J., 1975. *Aden Under British Rule 1839–67*. London, C. Hurst & Co.

Great Britain, 1966. *Statement on Defence Estimates 1966 I: The Defence Review*. Cmd. 2901. London, HMSO.

Habash, George, 1985. *Hakimu al-Thawrah: Qisat Hayat al-Duktor George Habash* (Philosopher of the Revolution: A Narrative on the Life of Dr George Habash). With Fuad Matar, London, Highlight.

al-Habashi, Muhammed ʾOmar, 1968. *al-Yaman al-Janubi* (South Yemen). Beirut, Dar al Taliʾah.

Harper, Stephen, 1978. *Last Sunset*. London, Collins.

Heller, Mark (ed.), 1983. *The Middle East Military Balance 1983*. Tel Aviv, Jaffee Center for Strategic Studies.

Halliday, Fred, 1975. *Arabia Without Sultans: A Political Survey of Instability in the Arab World*. New York, Vintage Books.

—, 1979. 'Yemen's Unfinished Revolution: Socialism in the South'. *MERIP Reports* **81** (October), pp. 3–20.

—, 1982. *Threat From the East? Soviet Policy From Afghanistan and Iran to the Horn of Africa*. Harmondsworth, Penguin.

—, 1983. 'The People's Democratic Republic of Yemen: The "Cuban Path" in Arabia', Gordon White, Robin Murray and Christine White (eds), *Revolutionary Socialist Development in the Third World*. Brighton, Wheatsheaf Books.

—, 1984a. 'Soviet Relations with South Yemen', in B. R. Pridham (ed.), *Contemporary Yemen: Politics and Historical Background*. London, Croom Helm.

—, 1984b. 'The Yemens: Conflict and Coexistence', *The World Today* **40**, 8–9 (August–September), pp. 335–62.

Hasan, 'Abd al-Razeq, 1974. 'The Experience of Democratic Yemen in Six Years'. *Dirasat 'Arabiyya* **7**, 10 (May), pp. 12–46 (in Arabic).

Hassan, Muhammed Salman, 1969. 'General Outline of the Industrial Plan and Policy of the People's Republic of South Yemen'. *Dirasat 'Arabiyya* **5**, 10 (August), pp. 114–49 (in Arabic).

—, 1972. 'The Role of People in Economic Development'. *Dirasat 'Arabiyya* **8**, 5 (March), pp. 65–81 (in Arabic).

—, 1974. 'What is New in the National Democratic Revolution of Yemen: A Dialogue Around the Class Element, the Political Organization, and the Socialist Horizon in Democratic Yemen'. *Dirasat 'Arabiyya* **10**, 12 (October), pp. 3–17 (in Arabic).

Hawatmeh, Naif, 1968. *Azmat al-Tawrah fi al-Janub al-Yamani* (The Crisis of the Revolution in South Yemen). Beirut, Dar al-Tali'ah.

Hickinbotham, Tom, 1958. *Aden*. London, Constable.

Hudson, Michael, 1977. *Arab Politics: The Search for Legitimacy*. New Haven, Yale University Press.

Hutchinson, C. U., (ed.), 1933. *Treaties, Engagements and Sanads*. vol. xi, 5th edn., Delhi, Government of India.

Ingrams, Harold, 1966. *Arabia and Isles*. 3rd edn. London, John Murray.

International Institute of Strategic Studies (IISS), 1985. *The Military Balance 1986–1986*. London, International Institute of Strategic Studies.

International Labour Office (ILO), 1977. *Labour Force Estimates and Projections 1950–2000*. vol. I: Asia, Geneva, International Labour Organization.

International Monetary Fund (IMF), 1984. *Supplement to Output Statistics*. Washington, DC, International Monetary Fund.

—, 1985. *International Financial Statistics Yearbook*. Washington, DC, International Monetary Fund.

Ismael, Tareq Y., 1976. *The Arab Left*. Syracuse, NY, Syracuse University Press.

—, 1981. 'The People's Democratic Republic of Yemen', in Bogdan Szajkowski (ed.), *Marxist Governments: A World Survey*, vol. 3. London, Macmillan.

Ismail, 'Abd al-Fattah, 1977. *The Present and Future of the People's Democratic Republic of Yemen*. London, Embassy of the PDRY.

—, 1979. 'A New Vanguard Party'. *World Marxist Review* **22** , 1 (January), pp. 14–21.

Johnston, Sir Charles H., 1964. *The View from Steamer Point*. London, Collins.

Kazziha, Walid, 1975. *Revolutionary Transformation in the Arab World*. New York, St. Martin's.

Korany, Bahgat & Dessouki, Ali E. Hillal, 1985. *The Foreign Policies of Arab States*. Boulder, Col., Westview Press.

Kostiner, Joseph, 1981. 'Arab Radical Politics: Al-Qawmiyyun al-Arab and the Marxists in the Turmoil of South Yemen, 1963-1967'. *Middle Eastern Studies* **17** , 4 (October), pp. 454–76.

—, 1984. *The Struggle for South Yemen*. London, Croom Helm.

Lackner, Helen, 1984. 'The Rise of the National Front as a Political Organization', in B. R. Pridham (ed.), *Contemporary Yemen: Politics and Historical Background*. London, Croom Helm.

Little, Tom, 1968. *South Arabia: Arena of Conflict*. New York, Praeger.

Makkawi, 'Abd al-Qawi, 1979. *Shahadati lil Tarikh* (My Testimony to History), Cairo, 'Asimah Press.

Mansfield, Peter, 1973. *The Middle East and North Africa: A Political and Economic Survey*. London, Chaucer Press.

Mashahdi, Kamil, 1963. *Haqayiq 'an al-Janub al-'Arabi wa Nidhal 'Aden* (Facts on the Situation in the Arab South and the Struggle in Aden), Beirut, n.p.

Molyneux, Maxine, 1982. *State Policies and the Position of Women Workers in the People's Democratic Republic of Yemen, 1976-77*. Women, Work and Development Series 3, Geneva, International Labour Office.

Mondesir, Simone Luchia (ed.), 1977. *A Select Bibliography of the Yemen Arab Republic and People's Democratic Republic of Yemen*. Durham, University of Durham Centre for Middle Eastern and Islamic Studies.

Muhammed, 'Ali Nasser, 1976. *Government Programmes for 1976 and 1977*. Nottingham, Russell Press, 1977.

—, 1981. 'Fidelity to the Revolution'. *World Marxist Review* **24** , 3 (March), p. 23–6.

—, 1983. 'Development of the Revolutionary Process and the Leading Role of the Party in Democratic Yemen'. *Partiynaya Zhizn* **12** (June), pp. 70–5.

—, 1985. 'Foreign Policy of Democratic Yemen and the Struggle Against Imperialism'. *Kommunist* **10** (July), pp. 110–16.

Murshed, Abdullah 'Ali, 1981. *Nishu' wa Tatawor al-Harakah al-Naqabiyah wa al-'Umaliyah fi al-Yaman* (The Evolution and Development of the Labour and Union Movement in Yemen), Aden, Ministry of Culture.

Mwafi, 'Abd al-Hamid, 1980. 'Latest Changes in Aden and Coexistence in the Arab Peninsula'. *al-Mawqef al-'Arabi* **35** (April–May), pp. 31–7 (in Arabic).

Mylroie, Laurie, 1983. *Politics and the Soviet Presence in the People's Democratic Republic of Yemen: Internal Vulnerabilities and Regional Challenges*. Rand Corporation Report N-2052-AF.

Nagi, Sultan (ed.), 1973. *Biblioghrafia Mukhtarah wa Tafsiliyah 'an al-Yaman*. (Selected and Annotated Bibliography on Yemen), Kuwait, University of Kuwait.

—, 1984. 'The Genesis of the Call for Yemeni Unity', in B. R. Pridham *Contemporary Yemen: Politics and Historical Background*. London, Croom Helm.

National Front, 1972. *al-Thawrah al-Wataniyah al-Demuqratiyah fi al-Yaman*. (The National Democratic Revolution in Yemen), Introduction by 'Abd al-Fattah Ismail, Beirut, Dar Ibn Khaldun.

—, Organizational Committee ('Ali 'Abd al-Alim, Khaled 'Abd al-Aziz, 'Abd al-Fattah Ismail, Faysal 'Abd al-Latif). 1969. *Kayfa Nafhamu Tajrubat al-Yaman al-Janubiyah al-Sh'abiyah* (How Do We Understand the Experience of Popular South Yemen): A Report Written by the Organization Committee of the National Front, 24 August 1968, Beirut, Dar-al-Tali'ah, 1969.

Naumkin, V., 1978. 'Southern Yemen: The Road to Progress'. *World Marxist Review* **21**, 1 (January), pp. 64–9.

al-Nolan, Saeed Abdul Khair, 1984. 'Education for Nation-Building: The Experience of the People's Democratic Republic of Yemen', in B. R. Pridham (ed.), *Contemporary Yemen: Politics and Historical Background*. London, Croom Helm.

Omar, Sultan Ahmad, 1970. *Nadhrah fi Tatawor al-Mujtama' al-Yamani* (A Perspective on the Development of Yemeni Society), Beirut, Dar al-Tali'ah.

Paget, Julian, 1969. *Last Post: Aden 1964-67*. London, Faber.

People's Democratic Republic of Yemen, Central Planning Commission, 1974. *Quinquennial Plan for Economic and Social Development 1974/75-1978/79*. Aden, Central Planning Commission.

—, 1977a. *The Achievements of Social Development in Democratic Yemen*. Nottingham, Russell Press.

—, 1977b. *Economic Achievements of Democratic Yemen*. Nottingham, Russell Press.

—, Ministry of Information. 1977c. *Government Programme for 1977*. Aden, 14 October Corporation.

—, Embassy of the PDRY in Britain. 1978. *The Agrarian Law; the Housing Law; the Family Law; the Fundamental Labour Law*. Nottingham, Russell Press.

Peterson, John, 1984. 'Nation-building and Political Development in the Two Yemens', in B. R. Pridham (ed.), *Contemporary Yemen: Politics and Historical Background*. London, Croom Helm.

—, 1985. 'The Two Yemens and the International Impact of Inter-Yemeni Relations', in William L. Dowdy & Russell B. Trood (eds), *The Indian Ocean: Perspectives on a Strategic Arena*. Durham, NC, Duke University Press.

Pridham, B. R. (ed.), 1984a. *Contemporary Yemen: Politics and Historical Background*. London, Croom Helm.

— (ed.), 1984b. *Economy, Society, and Culture in Contemporary Yemen*. London, Croom Helm.

Rybakov, Vsevold, 1982. 'Process of Growth'. *World Marxist Review* **25** 8 (August), pp. 42–50.

Schwab, Peter, 1978. 'Israel's Weakened Position on the Horn of Africa', *New Outlook* **20**, 10 (April), pp. 21-5, 27.

——, 1985. *Ethiopia: Politics, Economics and Society*. London, Frances Pinter.

Shahari, Muhammed 'Ali, 1972. *al-Yaman: Thawrah fi al-Janub wa al-Intikasah fi al-Shamal* (Yemen: Revolution in the South and Relapse in the North). Beirut, Dar Ibn Khaldun.

Sh'aibi, Muhammed 'Ali, 1972. *Jumhuriyat al-Yaman al-Demuqratiyah al-Shaabiyah* (The People's Democratic Republic of Yemen), 2nd edn., Beirut, Dar al-Umam.

Shamiry, Naguib A. R., 1984. 'The Judicial System in Democratic Yemen', in B. R. Pridham (ed.), *Contemporary Yemen: Politics and Historical Background*. London, Croom Helm.

Smith, Rex G. (ed.), 1984. *The Yemens*. World Bibliographical Series 50, Santa Barbara, Clio Press.

Stork, Joe, 1973. 'Socialist Revolution in Arabia: Report from the People's Democratic Republic of Yemen'. *MERIP Reports* **15** (March), pp. 1–25.

Stookey, Robert W., 1982. *South Yemen: A Marxist Republic in Arabia*. Boulder, Col., Westview Press.

Sultan, 'Abd al-Rahman, 1979. *al-Thawrah al-Yamaniyah wa Qadhayah al-Mustaqbal* (The Yemeni Revolution and the Issues of the Future). Cairo, Madbouli.

Trevaskis, Sir Kennedy, 1967. *Shades of Amber*. London, Hutchinson.

Unified Political Organization–National Front, 1975a. *al-Mutamar al-Tawhidi* (The Unification Congress, October 1975). Introduction by 'Abd al-Fattah Ismail, Beirut, Dar Ibn Khaldun, 1976.

——, 1975b. *The Constitution of the Unified Political Organization, The National Front*. Nottingham, Russell Press, 1977.

——, 1975c. *Programme of the Unified Political Organization, The National Front*. Nottingham, Russell Press, 1977.

United Nations, 1978. *People's Democratic Republic of Yemen: Report of a Mission on Needs Assessment for Population Assistance*. United Nations Fund for Population Activities, Report No. 7, New York, United Nations.

——, 1981. *Yearbook on Human Rights for 1975-1976*. New York, United Nations.

——, Department of International Economic and Social Affairs, 1985a. *World Population Prospects*. Population studies No. 86, New York, United Nations.

——, 1985b. *World Population Trends, Population and Development Interrelations, and Population Policies*. vol. I, Population Studies No. 93, New York, United Nations.

Vasileva, Tsveta, 1980. 'Vanguard of the Yemeni Revolution'. *Politicheska Agitatsiya* **2**, pp. 61–8.

Waterfield, Gordon, 1968. *Sultans of Aden*. London, John Murray.

Wenner, Manfred W., 1970. 'The People's Republic of South Yemen', in Tareq Y. Ismael (ed.), *Government and Politics of the Contemporary Middle East*. Homewood, Ill., Dorsey Press.

——, 1984. 'South Yemen Since Independence: An Arab Political Maverick', in B. R. Pridham (ed.), *Contemporary Yemen: Politics and Historical Background*. London, Croom Helm.

World Bank, 1979. *People's Democratic Republic of Yemen: A Review of Economic and Social Development*. Washington, DC, World Bank.

—, 1983a. *World Tables*. vol. I: Economic Data, Baltimore, Johns Hopkins University Press.

—, 1983b. *World Tables*. vol. II: Social Data, Baltimore, Johns Hopkins University Press.

—, 1985. *World Development Report 1985*. New York, Oxford University Press.

—, 1986. *World Bank Atlas 1986*. Washington, DC, World Bank.

Wrase, Michael, 1979. 'South Yemen: A Soviet Outpost'. *Swiss Review of World Affairs* **29**, 4 (July), pp. 25–7.

Periodicals cited

al-Adhwa ʿ (Manama)
Arab Report and Record (London)
el-Dieich (Algiers)
Dirasat ʾArabiyya (Beirut)
al-Dustur (London)
Facts on File
Foreign Broadcast Information Service
Globe and Mail (Toronto)
Granma (Havana)
Gamma Weekly Review (Havana)
The Guardian (Manchester)
al-Hadaf (Beirut)
al-Hawadith (London and Beirut)
al-Hurriyah (Beirut)
al-Jumhurriyyah (Baghdad)
al-Jundi (Aden)
Keesings Contemporary Archives
al-Madinah (Jiddah)
al-Masar (Aden)
Middle East International (London)
Middle East Economic Digest (MEED) (London)
Middle East Economic Survey (Nicosia)
Le Monde (Paris)
Le Monde Diplomatique (Paris)
New York Times
Nida ʿal-Watan (Aden)
The Observer (London)
al-Ra ʿy al-ʾAmm (Kuwait)
Rose al-Yusuf (Cairo)

al-Safir (Beirut)
al-Sharara (Aden)
al-Siyasah (Kuwait)
al-Riyadh (Riyadh)
14 Uktubar (Aden)
al-Tali'ah (Cairo)
al-Tali'ah (Kuwait)
al-Thawri (Aden)
al-Wahdah (Cairo)
World Marxist Review (Prague)

Index

al-'Aulaqi, Muhammed Salih 34, 65
'Aulaqi mutiny 34
Awadh, Ja'afar 'Ali 27
'Ayyad, 'Ali Salih 28

Ba'ath Party 24, 132, 152
Ba-Dhib, Abdullah 37
Bahrain and PDRY 153
Bakish, Hassan Ismail Khadah 23
balance of payments 105-7, 108, 133
Bali'id, Muhammad Ahmad 32
banking and insurance 82
Ba-Salem, Salem 48
bedouin population 127-8
al-Bidh, 'Ali-Salem 28
  as Minister of Defence 32, 35
  as YSP Secretary 38, 75, 160
  ideology 30
al-Bishi, Muhammed Ahmad 28
Braspetro 101
Brazil and PDRY 101
British Petroleum 82
Bulgaria and PDRY 154, 155
bureaucracy *see* civil service

caste system 8
Central Planning Commission 88
Chad 152
Charity Association 15
children *see* young people
China 30
  and PDRY 63, 100, 103, 107, 156-7
  military aid 145
Civil Aviation Administration 104
civil rights 43, 50
civil service 47-9
civil wars 19, 28-9, 32-5, 74
Clandestine Organization of Free Officers
  and Soldiers 24
climatic conditions 2-3
CMEA xvi, 155
collective leadership 36, 70, 75-6
College for Economic and Management
  Studies 48
colonial period 5, 9-10, 12-19, 20-8, 161
Comecon *see* CMEA
Committee for the Unification of the Hadhramawt 15

communications *see* transport and communi-
  cations
Confederation of Trade Unions 124
construction industry 99
co-operative farming 86, 96, 98
Corrective Step, 1967 29, 35, 42
Council of Ministers 45-6, 140-1
Council for Mutual Economic Assistance *see*
  CMEA
Cuba and PDRY 63, 77, 153
Czechoslovakia and PDRY 100, 101, 155

dams *see* irrigation
defence 134-6
  Committees 60-1
  People's Militias 62-3, 67, 134, 135
  Popular Defence Forces 61-2, 67, 134, 135
  supplies 135-6
  see also armed forces; internal security
Democratic Front for the Liberation of
  Palestine *see* DFLP
Democratic Yemen Airlines Company
  (Alyemda) 104
Democratic Yemen Peasants' Union 56-7
Democratic Yemen Youth Union 40, 57,
  58-9
detention camps 67
Development Fund 90
Development of Northern Areas Project 128
development plans 89-92, 115, 117-18,
  121-2
DFLP 151
al-Dhali, 'Abd al-Aziz 48, 150
al-Dhali'i, Saif 27
Dhib, Ali Ba 73
Dhofar Liberation Front 145
diplomatic relations with xvi-xviii, 141-59
  China 63, 100, 103, 107, 156-7
  Ethiopia 149-50
  Gulf States 153
  North Yemen 141-5
  Oman 145-7
  Saudi Arabia 147-9
  Socialist countries 154-5
  Third World countries 153-4
  USA 135, 137, 152, 158
  USSR 77, 99, 101, 102, 107, 129, 135-6,
    138, 140, 148, 154-8